On 20 August 2003 Chief Justice Roy Moore of the Alabama Supreme Court defied a federal district court order to remove a 5,280 pound Ten Commandments monument he erected in the courthouse rotunda (see p. 32). The preceding Saturday, according to Associated Press, "as many as 10,000" people, coming in "buses and vans from as far away as California," rallied in his support at the state capitol. Evangelist Jerry Falwell spoke to the crowd and said that "Civil disobedience is the right of all men when we believe breaking man's law is needed to preserve God's law."

On 1 July 2003 the 11th U. S. Circuit Court of Appeals had upheld the district court's order. The appellate court said that "Any notion of high government officials being above the law . . . will not save this chief justice from having to comply with the court order in this case. . . . The chief justice of a state supreme court, of all people, should be expected to abide by that principle." The court agreed to stay its order for a month but lifted that stay on 5 August, giving Moore until midnight of 20 August to comply.

On 19 August Moore twice asked the Court for another stay. Both requests were rejected. The next morning Moore asked the U.S. Supreme Court to stay the order. The Supreme Court immediately declined. Moore still refused to meet the deadline, so his eight associate justices met the next day and voted unanimously to overrule him. The following day the Alabama Judiciary Inquiry Committee suspended Justice Moore from his position, pending a full trial on his possible removal from office; and on Wednesday, 27 August, the monument was moved to a less public location in the building.

Rhetoric and Public Affairs Series

Eisenhower's War of Words: Rhetoric and Leadership
Martin J. Medhurst, Editor

The Nuclear Freeze Campaign: Rhetoric and Foreign Policy in the Telepolitical Age
J. Michael Hogan

Mansfield and Vietnam: A Study in Rhetorical Adaptation
Gregory A. Olson

Truman and the Hiroshima Cult
Robert P. Newman

Post-Realism: The Rhetorical Turn in International Relations
F. A. Beer and R. Hariman, Editors

Rhetoric and Political Culture in Nineteenth-Century America
Thomas W. Benson, Editor

Frederick Douglass: Freedom's Voice, 1818–1845
Gregory P. Lampe

Angelina Grimké: Rhetoric, Identity, and the Radical Imagination
Stephen Howard Browne

Strategic Deception: Rhetoric, Science, and Politics in Missile Defense Advocacy
Gordon R. Mitchell

Rostow, Kennedy, and the Rhetoric of Foreign Aid
Kimber Charles Pearce

Visions of Poverty: Welfare Policy and Political Imagination
Robert Asen

General Eisenhower: Ideology and Discourse
Ira Chernus

The Reconstruction Desegregation Debate: The Politics of Equality and the Rhetoric of Place, 1870–1875
Kirt H. Wilson

Shared Land/Conflicting Identity: Trajectories of Israeli and Palestinian Symbol Use
Robert C. Rowland and David A. Frank

Darwinism, Design, and Public Education
John Angus Campbell and Stephen C. Meyer, Editors

Christianity and the Mass Media in America: Toward a Democratic Accommodation
Quentin J. Schultze

Religious Expression and the American Constitution

❖❖❖❖❖❖❖

Franklyn S. Haiman

Michigan State University Press
East Lansing

+/05

Copyright © 2003 by Franklyn S. Haiman

∞ The paper used in this publication meets the minimum requirements of
ANSI/NISO Z39.48-1992 (R 1997) (Permanence of Paper).

Michigan State University Press
East Lansing, Michigan 48823-5245

Printed and bound in the United States of America.

09 08 07 06 05 04 03 1 2 3 4 5 6 7 8 9 10

LIBRARY OF CONGRESS CATALOGING-IN-PUBLICATION DATA

Haiman, Franklyn Saul.
   Religious expression and the American Constitution / Franklyn S. Haiman.
      p. cm.—(Rhetoric and public affairs series)
   Includes bibliographical references and index.
      ISBN 0-87013-690-9 (case bind : alk. paper)—ISBN 0-87013-691-7
      (paper : alk. paper)
   1. Freedom of religion—United States. 2. Freedom of speech—United States. 3.
   Church and state—United States. I. Title. II. Series.
      KF4783.II345 2003
      342.7308'53—dc22

                                                          2003018527

Cover design by Julia Herzog
Book design by Sans Serif, Inc.

Visit Michigan State University Press on the World Wide Web at:
www.msupress.msu.edu

Congress shall make no law respecting an establishment of religion, or prohibiting the free exercise thereof . . .

First Amendment to the United States Constitution

. . . no religious test shall ever be required as a qualification to any office or public trust under the United States.

Article VI, United States Constitution

. . . it is time enough for the rightful purposes of civil government, for its officers to interfere when principles break out into overt acts against peace and good order. . . .

Thomas Jefferson's Virginia Act for Establishing Religious Freedom

. . . ecclesiastical establishments, instead of maintaining the purity and efficacy of religion, have had a contrary operation. During almost fifteen centuries . . . what have been its fruits? More or less, in all places, pride and indolence in the clergy; ignorance and servility in the laity; in both, superstition, bigotry, and persecution. . . .

James Madison's Memorial and Remonstrance against
Religious Assessments

Contents

Preface

I am an agnostic. To me that means I simply do not know who or what, if anything, is outside our skins that human beings for centuries have called God or gods.

I do marvel at the complexity of the human mind and body and of the other forms of life on earth, and at the order that exists in the orbiting of planets around our sun. So I am tempted by the notion that there is some kind of intelligent design behind it all. Yet, again, I have no idea what the cause of that might be, or even if the notion of a "cause" for it makes any sense. I am sure, at least, that I cannot agree with any advocates of a theory of "intelligent design" who reject clear evidence that humans have evolved over many millennia from so-called lower species of animal life. Gaps though there may be in the theory of evolution, its essential validity makes sense to me.

I believe that there have been great religious prophets who have enunciated ideal moral standards for human behavior (e.g., Buddha, Confucius, Moses, Jesus, and Mohammed). Yet, like some of the Founding Fathers of our country, I find that organized religion is not for me. The mixed feelings I had about it prior to the terrorist acts of 11 September 2001 are now stronger than ever. I have always recognized and am now more acutely aware of the important place organized religion plays in the lives of so many people, perhaps most significantly in the comfort it provides in times of emotional crises and in confrontations with death. It serves to give social support to offset the isolation and loneliness that many people may otherwise feel. It has been a rallying point for struggles against slavery and for civil rights and, when true to the faith of its prophets, gives life-sustaining help to the poor and downtrodden.

Yet I am also now reminded of its historic evils. It is not only the perversions of a faith such as those of a terrorist like Osama Bin Laden or of a cross displayed by the Ku Klux Klan that repel me. The authoritarian structure of most religious institutions, the creed of many of them that theirs is the only true faith, and the dogmatic self-righteousness that cannot tolerate the existence of other beliefs, are among the features that have led to the "holy wars" and massacres of millions of people throughout the centuries. Christians have mounted Crusades against Muslims in the Middle East and an Inquisition against Jews in Spain. Catholics and Protestants have killed each other on the European Continent in the sixteenth century and in Northern Ireland in the twentieth century, as have Muslims and Hindus in Kashmir. We have witnessed religious and ethnic cleansing in Bosnia, Kosovo, and Macedonia, and now a war by Islamic fanatics against civilization itself.

However, this book is motivated neither by hostility to organized religion nor by endorsement of it. Rather, it grows out of a concern I have, that for me is akin to a religion, for the preservation of a pluralistic, democratic, and secular society in the United States of America. I am, in short, a First Amendment junkie.

1

Historical Background

❖❖❖❖❖

Insofar as we know anything about the history of humankind, it appears that the need to engage in religious expression has always been present. African and Native American tribes, the Egyptians, Greeks, and Romans all had their pantheons of gods. In the sixth century B.C. a mystic in India called Buddha (born Siddhartha Gautama) and Chinese philosophers named Confucius and Lao-Tzu gave birth to religions that persist to this day throughout Asia, as has Shintoism in Japan. What is most striking, however, at least to this author, is not so much the universality of the religious impulse but the vast variety of the kinds and names of gods that have been worshipped. This diversity of religious expression has continued into the centuries since the birth of Christ and despite the appearance on the world stage of monotheistic beliefs such as those adhered to by the Jews, Christians, and Mohammedans.

In order to appreciate the complexity of the relationship between religious expression and government in the United States today we must understand something of the background out of which it has grown. It is particularly important to know the essentials of what transpired in the Middle East and Europe long before the Spaniards, English, French, and Dutch set sail for the New World, and to be aware that in many parts of the

globe a secular society, where church and state are separate, has never existed or even been sought. Yet since this book is intended to be concerned
primarily with issues that engage contemporary Americans, our explo-
ration of history and of lands beyond our borders will be relatively brief.

The most relevant story really begins with the crucifixion of Jesus and
the development thereafter of the Christian religion. The books of the New
Testament, written by the disciples of Jesus, planted seeds for the centuries
of anti-Semitism that followed, for they blamed the Jewish authorities
even more than the Roman governor, Pontius Pilate, for the killing of their
Messiah. The Christians were themselves, of course, the victims of repression in the Roman Empire until the fourth century, when the emperor
Constantine converted, and succeeding emperors made Christianity the
empire's official religion. Here we had the beginnings in the Western world
not only of divergent religious beliefs but also of often deadly conflict
among them.

The books of both Mark (12:17) and Luke (20:25) admonished Christians to "render unto Caesar the things that are Caesar's, and to God the
things that are God's," an early version of the concept of the separation of
church and state. Yet it was also a central tenet of Christian doctrine that
the spiritual realm was of more importance than the worldly or "carnal"
realm and thus had primacy. Jews who did not accept Jesus as their savior,
and who were seen as more concerned with the here-and-now than the
hereafter, were thus relegated to a subservient status.

Another early tenet of Christianity was that theirs was the only "true religion." Therefore Jews were a logical target for conversion or for ostracism
from the mainstream of community life. It was not until Mohammed came
upon the scene at the beginning of the seventh century that there was another target for Christian animosity. By that time the old Roman Empire
had disintegrated and the Byzantium Empire, based in Constantinople, had
taken its place. The bishop of Rome, who had not taken on the title of pope
until that century, lost his primacy as the spiritual leader of the Catholic
world and thenceforth had competitors in Constantinople, which became
the birthplace of the present-day Eastern Orthodox Church. We need not
go into the details of internecine warfare and the ups and downs of the relationship between emperors and popes that occurred during those centuries in the Byzantium Empire, but simply note that Christianity
remained the dominant religious force, although sometimes under the
governance of the emperor and sometimes of the pope. Meanwhile,

Mohammedanism was growing rapidly in numbers and strength as it conquered lands in Asia Minor.

Mohammed had founded the Islamic or Muslim faith during the A.D. 620s in Medina on the Arabian peninsula and had expanded its reach by defeating the Meccans in battle. Thus Medina and Mecca are today the most sacred sites of the Islamic world. Inevitably the Mohammedans came into military conflict with the Byzantines; then later with the Frankish, Catholic empire of Charlemagne; and ultimately with the Normans of France and England, plus the Roman Catholics of Spain. During the seventh century the Muslims conquered Persia, Syria, and Jerusalem, but failed in their effort to capture Constantinople. In the eighth and ninth centuries they occupied southern Spain and Sicily. Starting in 1096 and stretching into the thirteenth century Christian forces responded with a series of bloody Crusades, battling the Muslims in Asia Minor and reconquering Jerusalem in 1187. In Spain, Catholics and Mohammedans fought for and divided control of the Iberian Peninsula until the final expulsion of the Muslims at the end of the fifteenth century. The Jews, many of whom had settled in Spain after the Diaspora out of Palestine, were better off (ironically, in view of the present day) in the Muslim than in the Christian territories, where they were subjected to an Inquisition that gave them the choice of converting to Christianity, fleeing, or perishing.

Beginning in 1517, when Martin Luther posted his ninety-five Theses on a church door in Germany, the Protestant Reformation posed a new challenge to the dominance of Roman Catholicism. Still further schisms occurred in the 1530s when King Henry VIII of England broke with the pope, establishing the Anglican Church, and John Calvin, in Geneva, Switzerland, founded Calvinism, the forerunner of the Presbyterian Church in America. Yet one branch or another of Christianity was still dominant in most European countries—Anglicanism in England, Lutheranism in the North German states and Scandinavia, and Roman Catholicism in the southern states of Germany, in France, and on the Iberian and Italian Peninsulas. Thus any separation of church and state was still far in the future, although one might expect that the increasing diversity of faiths would create pressures for such separation, as in fact it ultimately did. In the meanwhile, however, subordination or outright persecution of religious dissenters remained the norm. One of the saddest chapters in the history of state-sponsored religion occurred in the New World in the sixteenth century when Spanish Conquistadors swept through Peru, Central America, Mexico, and what is now the southwestern United States, destroying

entire Native American cultures with their military might and superimpos-
ing the Catholic faith upon those that remained.

Unlike Catholicism, the Protestant belief in freedom of conscience and
individual choice, appended to the traditional Catholic dichotomy between
the spiritual and the carnal, did provide a soil in which the concept of separation might grow. Furthermore, Protestants, in contrast to the Catholics
of the Spanish Inquisition, believed that Jews and other nonadherents to
Christ should be converted by persuasion rather than coercion. Thus dissenters were allowed to survive, albeit as separate members of the community who were commonly despised and degraded. Disraeli, born and raised
as a child in the Jewish faith, succeeded in becoming British prime minister in 1868 and 1874 despite the established Church of England, but his
family had converted to Christianity when Benjamin was thirteen years
old.

The Calvinist Puritans experienced so much discrimination in England,
as did their Huguenot counterparts in France, that they sought out the
New World as a refuge and founded the Massachusetts Bay Colony. Free as
these Pilgrims then were to practice their religion unhindered, they mim-
icked their European brethren by making their own faiths into established
colonial religions with little or no tolerance for those with dissenting views.
These Congregationalists, as they were called, were dominant in Massachusetts, New Hampshire, and Connecticut, and banished Roger Williams
from Massachusetts because of his "Separatist" brand of Congregational-
ism. At least Williams, in developing Rhode Island, refrained from making
his own Baptist faith into an established church in that colony. Indeed,
Rhode Island, Pennsylvania, New Jersey, and Delaware were the only
colonies among the original thirteen that never had an established church.
Anglicanism was the established church in the colonies of New York, Virginia, North Carolina, South Carolina, and Georgia. Maryland was founded
by Lord Baltimore as a haven for Roman Catholics, and passed into the
hands of Puritans in 1654, but was restored to the control of Lord Baltimore in 1660.

In an essay entitled "The Bloudy Tenent of Persecution," Roger Williams
deplored the fact that "the blood of so many hundred thousands of Protestants and Papists [had been] spilt in the wars of present and former ages for
their respect consciences."[1] He went on to write that "an enforced uniformity of religion throughout a nation or civil state, confounds the civil and
religious, [and] denies the principles of Christianity and civility." Furthermore, in a letter to John Cotton in 1643, he spoke of "a wall of separation

between the garden of the church and the wilderness of the world." Although the metaphor of a "wall of separation between Church and State" is most commonly credited by the U.S. Supreme Court and others to Thomas Jefferson, who used it in a frequently quoted letter to the Baptist Association of Danbury, Connecticut, in 1802, Jefferson may well have borrowed the idea from Roger Williams.[2]

William Penn, a Quaker and the founder of Pennsylvania, likewise believed that there should be no coercion of religious thought. His Great Law of 1682 provided that no persons who acknowledged one God were to be prevented from practicing the religion of their choice. However, only Christians could hold public office in that colony, as was the case in the colonies that had established churches, and, ironically, in Roger Williams's Rhode Island as well.

Massachusetts and Virginia, where the first Europeans settled, were examples, until the time of the American Revolution, of colonies with the least tolerant establishments of religion.[3] The first charter of Virginia called for the "propagating of Christian religion," and in 1624, when King James I made it a royal colony, the Church of England was established as the official religion and people were taxed to support it. Yet soon after the American Revolution, in 1779, Thomas Jefferson proposed a disestablishment bill to the Virginia legislature, which was not adopted. However, the tax to support the Anglican Church was repealed. It is surely not a mere coincidence that by that time there had been a large increase in the number of Baptists in the colony. In 1785 James Madison addressed "A Memorial and Remonstrance against Religious Assessments" to the Virginia General Assembly,[4] and the following year that legislature finally enacted Jefferson's famous "Act for Establishing Religious Freedom,"[5] writing the separation of church and state into law. It declared in words now emblazoned on the wall of the Jefferson Memorial in Washington, D.C., that, "it is time enough for the rightful purposes of civil government, for its officers to interfere when principles break out into overt acts against peace and good order." In his "Notes on the State of Virginia," written in 1781, Jefferson had also said: "The legitimate powers of government extend to such acts only as are injurious to others. But it does me no injury for my neighbor to say there are twenty gods or no god. It neither picks my pocket nor breaks my leg."[6]

On the other hand, in South Carolina, where the Anglican Church had been established at the beginning, as it had been in Virginia, North Carolina, and Georgia, a constitution adopted in 1778 eliminated the Anglican establishment but substituted a Protestant one in its place. "The Christian Protestant religion shall be . . . the established religion of this state," it read.

The colony of Maryland, in what was ironically titled its "Toleration Act" of 1649, protected the "free exercise" of religion, but only for those "professing to believe in Jesus Christ."[7] It further provided that anyone who denied Christ "shall be punished by death." The following year a man who is believed to have been the only Jew in the colony was indicted for blasphemy, but he escaped execution, possibly because he converted or because of a general amnesty that had been issued by the British government of Oliver Cromwell.

Massachusetts, where alleged witches had been burned and Roger Williams had been banished, became one of the several colonies during the Revolutionary period to adopt what have been labeled "multiple establishments." This system allowed people to choose which denomination they wished to support with their taxes, but it still had to be within the framework of Protestantism or of Christianity. Article III of the Massachusetts Constitution of 1780 authorized each town within the state to decide on the Protestant sect that would be tax-supported, and many communities where Baptists predominated went that route. The colony of New York had done the same thing in 1664, long before the American Revolution, but also limited the choice to Protestant denominations.

North Carolina was one of the first states after the revolution to disestablish its Anglican church (Virginia, South Carolina, and Georgia following suit in the ensuing two decades) but, like most of the other states, it retained a prohibition against anyone holding public office who denied "the being of God or the truth of the Protestant religion." Despite that barrier, however, the state legislature voted in 1809 to seat a Jew by the name of Jacob Henry who had been duly elected.[8]

In 1833, Massachusetts, by a ten to one margin of the voters to amend their constitution, became the last state in the Union to abolish entirely any establishment of religion, sole or multiple. Maryland had done so in 1810, Connecticut in 1818, and New Hampshire in 1819.

It is undisputed that the creators of our federal government were believers in God and that a majority of them were, to one degree or another, adherents to either a specific Protestant denomination or to Christianity in general. It is also true, as we have already seen, that they had no hesitancy about creating sole or multiple establishments of religion in their respective colonies despite their theological belief in some sort of separation between the spiritual and material worlds and thus between church and state. Yet when it came to the federal government, whose powers were to be limited vis-à-vis the states and the people, their attitude about the role of religion was very different. Although the Declaration of Independence in 1776 began deistically by invoking the name of God, asserting that "men . . . are endowed by their Creator with certain unalienable rights," there is no mention of God, let alone of Christianity, in the Constitution that was adopted seven years later. Indeed, there is only one reference to religion in that entire original document, and that is the provision of Article VI that "no religious test shall ever be required as a qualification to any office or public trust under the United States"—a provision in direct contrast to a practice that was taken for granted in most of the colonies. This, like many other parts of the Constitution, may be a reflection of the influence on the founders of the political philosophy of John Locke, whose views were so forcefully articulated in a 1689 "Letter Concerning Toleration."[9] That philosophy is clearly seen in the First Amendment's religion clauses, ratified in 1791, which provide that "Congress shall make no law respecting an establishment of religion, or prohibiting the free exercise thereof . . ."[10]

The extent to which the United States today should be legally bound by the Constitution and by what its authors intended, or should take into account what their practices actually were regarding religious expression, is a matter of considerable dispute, as we shall see in the next chapter. Part of that debate arises from the circumstance that no one can know with certainty what their intentions were and that, indeed, there were surely different intentions in the minds of the various founders. There are, however, some things that are entirely clear. It is a fact, for example, that despite the prohibition against federal government actions "respecting an establishment of religion," our first presidents (Washington, Adams, and Madison—Jefferson excepted) proclaimed days of prayer and thanksgiving. Furthermore, the same Congress that gave final approval to the phrasing of the First Amendment in 1789 had voted just three days earlier to establish chaplaincies for the House and Senate.[11] President Madison, reflecting on these matters in his retirement, expressed the view that the establishment of the chaplaincies in both Congress and the military, as well as presidential proclamations recommending thanksgivings, had constituted forbidden establishments of religion.[12] He also rationalized his own proclamations for fasting and thanksgiving by claiming that he had "found it necessary" to deviate from "strict principle" because it was a time of war.[13]

It is true as well that at one point during the Constitutional Convention, after an unusually tense meeting that almost broke up the group, Benjamin

Franklin proposed opening the sessions with a prayer—a motion that was not passed, although some of the delegates got together for their own prayer gathering. According to historian Leonard Levy, the failure of Franklin's motion was due to "practical considerations—an unwillingness to let the public think the convention was in trouble, lack of money to pay a minister, and deference to Philadelphia's Quakers."[14] It is likewise of interest in this connection that Franklin, generally regarded as a deist like Jefferson, wrote a letter to President Ezra Stiles of Yale University in 1790 in which he had this to say about Christianity: "As to Jesus of Nazareth . . . I think the System of Morals and his Religion . . . the best the world ever saw or is likely to see; but I apprehend it has received various corrupt changes, and I have, with most of the present dissenters in England, some doubts as to his Divinity. . . ."[15]

It is also a fact that during the congressional debate on adoption of the First Amendment in 1789, Madison proposed an amendment that would have prohibited the states as well as the federal government from establishing any religion. Although his motion was passed by the House of Representatives, it failed in the Senate. We will return to this issue in more detail in the next chapter.

There are other undisputed historical facts, but they have been interpreted with radically different implications by those who argue for or against the idea that the United States was, is, and should be considered a "Christian America."

One of the basic premises of the "Christian America" advocates is that the Europeans who colonized our shores were religious people, and that most of them were Christians. No one disputes that premise or the further fact, as we have already seen, that the Protestant faith became the established church in a majority of the *colonies.* When it comes to the creation of the *United States,* however, the evidence they adduce to support their cause is flimsy and out of context.

God, to be sure, is invoked in the Declaration of Independence, but not Jesus, and God, as just noted, is nowhere mentioned in the Constitution. A paragraph the "Christian America" adherents often quote from George Washington's Farewell Address of 1796 is, admittedly, a strong endorsement of religion, and it does suggest a possible link between religion and government, though rather ambiguously and with no mention of Jesus or Christianity. Yet, to provide a larger context for the views of Washington, who for the most part kept his religious beliefs and activities to himself, it is useful to read another of his comments on the subject:

If I could now conceive that the general government might be so administered as to render the liberty of conscience insecure, I beg you will be persuaded, that no one would be more zealous than myself to establish effectual barriers against the horrors of spiritual tyranny, and every species of religious persecution . . . every man, conducting himself as a good citizen, and being accountable to God alone for his religious opinions, ought to be protected in worshipping the Deity according to the dictates of his own conscience.[16]

The second president of the United States, John Adams, became a Unitarian and believed in neither the Trinity nor the deity of Jesus. During his term of office as president the Senate ratified and he signed a Treaty of Peace with the Mohammedan nation of Tripoli, a treaty that had actually been negotiated during the Washington administration. Article XI of that treaty stated: "As the government of the United States is not in any sense founded on the Christian religion—as it has in itself no character of enmity against the laws, religion or tranquility of Musselmen . . . it is declared by the parties that no pretext arising from religious opinions shall ever produce an interruption of the harmony existing between the two countries."[17]

The strongest evidence offered by adherents to the "Christian America" thesis are a handful of comments, all penned long ago, by justices of the U.S. Supreme Court, that are far out of the mainstream of that Court's strong judicial opinions enforcing the separation of church and state. For example, the first chief justice of the Supreme Court, John Jay, who served in that post for six years before becoming governor of New York, is quoted as saying that the country should "select and prefer" Christians for office. Not only was that view contrary to the explicit provision of the Constitution that forbade any religious test for the holding of federal office, but Jay was a well-known anti-Catholic who, as governor, tried (unsuccessfully) to have Catholics banished from the state of New York.[18]

In 1844, in a case called *Vidal v Girard's Executors*, Justice Joseph Story described Pennsylvania as "Christian country," but that was a reference to a state, not the nation, and curiously to a state where the Quaker majority had never created an establishment of religion.[19] In 1892, the Supreme Court, in a unanimous opinion written by Justice David Brewer in the case of *Church of Holy Trinity v United States*, did refer to the entire country as "a Christian nation."[20] Yet that was only *obiter dicta*, not part of the official holding of a decision. Furthermore, in a 1905 lecture at Haverford College, Brewer made it clear that what he had meant was that the United States was Christian in its roots and culture but that

Christianity should not be an established church or receive any special legal privileges.[21]

Finally, in 1931, archconservative Justice George Sutherland, in *U.S. v Macintosh*, described Americans as a "Christian people."[22] This parochial view of the country was not only a startling demographic overgeneralization in 1931, but was merely a reference to the "people," not the government.

All of this is in stark contrast to the Court's opinion in *Everson v Board of Education* in 1947, reaffirmed many times thereafter.[23] Justice Hugo Black, writing for the majority, said:

> The "establishment of religion" clause of the First Amendment means at least this: Neither a state nor the Federal Government can set up a church. Neither can pass laws which aid one religion, aid all religions, or prefer one religion over another. . . . No person can be punished for entertaining or professing religious beliefs or disbeliefs, for church attendance or nonattendance. No tax in any amount, large or small, can be levied to support any religious activities or institutions, whatever they may be called, or whatever form they may adopt to teach or practice religion.

The dissenters in Everson wholeheartedly agreed with this meaning of the establishment clause. In fact, they felt that the wall of separation had been breached in this particular instance by the use of taxpayer-supported buses to transport children to parochial schools, which the majority did not believe to be the case. Since the Everson decision in 1947, the separation of church and state in the United States has been firmly established as Supreme Court doctrine as well as having thoroughly permeated our culture as a generally accepted concept.

2

Understanding the First Amendment

❖ ❖ ❖ ❖ ❖

People who know about the First Amendment are most likely to think
of freedom of speech in connection with it. They may be unaware either of its provisions with respect to religion or that those provisions actually *precede* the ones regarding speech and press. In its entirety the
amendment reads: "Congress shall make no law respecting an establishment of religion, or prohibiting the free exercise thereof; or abridging the
freedom of speech or of the press, or of the right of people peaceably to as-
semble, and to petition the government for a redress of grievances."

The order in which the phrases of the amendment appear is most probably not accidental. The founders of our country came to these shores primarily to escape the discriminatory hand of the established Church of
England, and that would have been uppermost in the minds of the authors
of the First Amendment. Yet a second reason for the ordering of the
phrases is that the freedom to speak or to commit one's thoughts to print
presumes that one first has ideas to express. That requires a freedom of *conscience* that underlies *all* parts of the amendment but is most commonly associated with religious belief.

Another observation about the various phrases of the First Amendment
that is too little appreciated is that its prohibition against any establishment

of religion and its prohibition against interference with the free exercise thereof are mutually dependent concepts—two sides of the same coin. If a state or nation has a preferred, established religion then those who are not of that faith or who have no religious faith at all are disadvantaged second-class citizens whose exercise of *their* freedom is inhibited. This is not to say that the two concepts are never in conflict, and the tensions between them that may occasionally occur will be discussed later in this book. Yet those instances are exceptions to the larger generality that the nonestablishment of religion and the free exercise thereof are basically supportive of one another. Author Derek Davis put it well when he wrote that "it may be said that the framers' central purpose in both clauses was to protect religious liberty."[1]

On a much broader canvas, a fundamental disagreement that has engaged, and continues to engage, constitutional scholars is whether the Supreme Court, in interpreting the meaning of the First Amendment or any other provisions of the Constitution, should attempt to discern and follow the "original meaning" or "original intent" of the authors or should regard the Constitution as a "living document" that changes with the times. Clearly the adoption of amendments many years after the first ten that were enacted as a Bill of Rights immediately after ratification of the Constitution indicates that going beyond the Founding Fathers, at least by the formal process of amendment provided for in the Constitution, was expected and is permissible. Thus, while slavery was accepted by the original Constitution in counting slaves as three-fifths of a person, and women were not allowed the right to vote, both of those anachronistic provisions were eliminated by constitutional amendments when the values of society progressed.

What is really at issue, then, is whether *in the absence of formal amendments* the Supreme Court may invoke contemporary societal values in interpreting the meaning of the Constitution and the Bill of Rights. The "original intent" school of thought, whose foremost champion on the Supreme Court is Justice Antonin Scalia, holds that the Court should always adhere to the plain language of the Constitution or, if that language is unclear, should attempt to discover what the words meant or were intended to mean by those who wrote them. Even if one accepts that view, there are at least three problems with it.

The first is that even the plainest of words often do not mean the same thing to different people who are reading them, and perhaps not even to those who voted to adopt them. Does the "press," for example, mean only books and newspapers or does it include handbills and posters? Deciding what such a seemingly simple word means allows significant latitude to the Supreme Court in making its decisions. The phrases in the Constitution about which there can be no doubt, such as the specification that a president must be at least thirty-five years old, are few and far between.

A second problem is that those who wrote the words of the First Amendment or any other constitutional provision could not know about the technological advances that would occur after their time. Thus with the advent of radio, television, and film the Court had to decide if those media were intended to be encompassed by the words "speech" or "press." Justice Scalia and other proponents of the original intent school of thought seem to think it is obvious that the writers of those words would have included these new media had they known about them. Yet in an interview I had in 1969 with a lawyer who was then the chief executive of Denmark's public broadcasting system I was told that radio and television had never, up until that time, been considered to be "speech" or "press" under *that* country's constitution. Here again the Supreme Court has considerable latitude in interpreting the intent of the constitutional language that has been used. Justice Hugo Black, for instance, never accepted the idea of the majority of his colleagues that wiretaps would have been included by the authors of the Fourth Amendment under the rubric of "searches and seizures" had that technology been in existence at the time the amendment was written.

The third and greatest dilemma that confronts the proponents of original intent is that many of the phrases of the Constitution, including the First Amendment, are so rubbery that many different meanings can be derived from them. With respect to the Fourth Amendment's prohibition against "unreasonable searches and seizures," for instance, what constitutes unreasonableness? Or with respect to the Eighth Amendment's prohibition against "cruel and unusual punishments," what kinds of punishments are cruel and unusual? In the nineteenth century the Supreme Court ruled that the "equal protection of the laws" provision of the Fourteenth Amendment was satisfied by "separate but equal" public schools,[2] but in the twentieth century the Court decided that separate schools were "inherently unequal."[3]

Conversely, those who believe the Constitution was meant to be a "living document" ask what the words mean, or should mean, in contemporary society. Thus, for example, many, including former justices William J. Brennan Jr. and Thurgood Marshall, have argued that, given contemporary values and practices, capital punishment is cruel and unusual punishment, despite the fact that it was clearly not so considered by the authors of the Constitution. Indeed, Justice Brennan once said, "I approach my responsibility as a justice as a 20th century American not confined to [the] framer's vision in 1787. The ultimate question must be, I think, what do the words of the Constitution and Bill of Rights mean to us in our time."[4] Long before, Justice Oliver Wendell Holmes had written: "The case before us must be considered in the light of our whole experience and not merely in that of what was said a hundred years ago."[5]

Most relevant to our concern in this book is the language of the First Amendment and the question of what constitutes "an establishment" of religion. Those who adhere to the original intent school of thought attempt to divine what the authors had in mind by looking at the historical context in which the words were written—their actual practices and such evidence as letters, papers, and notes they wrote or read. We have already seen in the previous chapter that at the same time the adopters of the amendment were placing limits on the powers of the new federal government, "establishment" meant a single institution in some states and multiple beliefs in others. Today, as we shall now see, a debate rages within the Supreme Court and among legal scholars as to whether an establishment of religion means an explicit endorsement of a particular religion, an endorsement of all religion as against irreligion, or more passive and implicit forms of support to one or more religions. On this subject those who adhere to original intent have little more to go on than those who feel freer to depart from what the founding fathers may have meant or intended.

It was indicated in the last chapter that the opinion written by Justice Black for a majority of the Supreme Court in *Everson v Board of Education* has been "reaffirmed many times thereafter." It was also reported that even the dissenters agreed at that time on the meaning of the establishment clause described by Black, and disagreed only as to its application to the use of publicly supported buses for transporting students to parochial and private schools. Finally, the chapter concluded with the assertion that "the separation of church and state has been firmly established as Supreme Court doctrine as well as having thoroughly permeated our culture as a generally accepted concept."

Although those statements are all true, they mask an underlying complexity to which we now turn. The *Everson* opinion has been characterized as an "absolutist" interpretation of the establishment clause, since it says that the government is not only prohibited from aiding or preferring one religion over another, but that it also may not aid or prefer religion over nonreligion. Furthermore, it states in unqualified terms that "no tax in any amount, large or small, can be levied to support any religious activities or institutions, whatever they may be called, or whatever form they may adopt to teach or practice religion."

Yet there are alternative schools of thought to which some of the current Supreme Court justices adhere that take a less absolutist view of the establishment clause. The most sharply divergent alternative, known as "nonpreferentialism," springs from the premise that the absolutist position is actually one of hostility to religion, a premise that the proponents of absolutism deny. Nonpreferentialism holds that the establishment clause does not forbid support by the government to religion so long as it is done neutrally for all religious institutions and prefers none of them. That position is taken by Chief Justice William Rehnquist in his dissenting opinion in *Wallace v Jaffree*,[6] and was most vehemently advocated prior to that in a 1982 volume by Robert Cord.[7] Vigorous rebuttals followed in a 1986 book by Leonard Levy[8] and a law review article published that same year by Douglas Laycock.[9]

Professor Cord asserts boldly in the preface to his book that "with the use of primary historical documents, I show conclusively that the Supreme Court has erred in its interpretation of the First Amendment."[10] He argues that there is "no historical evidence that the First Amendment was intended to preclude Federal government aid to religion when it was provided on a nondiscriminatory basis."[11] In a chapter entitled "Resurrecting Madison and Jefferson," Cord reminds us that Madison proclaimed days of prayer and thanksgiving and that Jefferson gave his support to a treaty with the Kaskaskia Indians in 1803 that provided for money to be paid for a Catholic priest and for the building of a church.[12] He also points out that there have been many Supreme Court decisions in the years since *Everson* that have departed from an absolutist position, and contends that even *Everson* itself was internally inconsistent. He writes that "when I first read *Everson v. Board of Education* as an undergraduate student, until I reached the seventeenth page of the eighteen page opinion of the Court, I was certain the Court intended to strike down the School Board Resolution and the New Jersey Statute as unconstitutional."[13] Yet then, Cord continues, comes the last paragraph, where, after Justice Black has proclaimed that "the wall of separation between church and state . . . must be kept high and impregnable" and that "we could not approve the slightest breach," he announces for the Court that "New Jersey has not breached it here."[14]

As Cord notes, the *Everson* majority relied on what is known as a "Child Benefit Theory" to uphold the New Jersey program.[15] That theory holds that in approving an activity like school busing the state is not intending to foster or aid religion but simply to help children to get to school. Any indirect support to religion is incidental. The theory, it is sometimes argued, is analogous to providing police and fire protection to church buildings. In Cord's view, however, the child benefit theory has simply been used as a rationalization for a Supreme Court that has been unwilling or unable to abide by an absolutist interpretation of the establishment clause.

Professor Levy, who is widely recognized as perhaps the foremost American scholar on the history of the First Amendment, maintains that Jefferson and Madison clearly intended that amendment to forbid giving any preference to religion over nonreligion. In his view the Black opinion in *Everson* is right on the mark. He notes that at the time of the American Revolution and thereafter all of the states that had had preferential establishments as colonies had switched to multiple establishments (although none for Jews, Muslims, or Buddhists), and that it was this kind of multiple arrangement that Jefferson and Madison wanted to forbid to the federal government.[16]

Yet Levy's most convincing refutation of the Cord thesis, reaffirmed by Professor Laycock, is that in debating the First Amendment the Congress in 1789 specifically rejected nonpreferentialist language.[17] Laycock sums up the argument as follows:

> The prominence and longevity of the nonpreferential aid theory is remarkable in light of the weak evidence supporting it and quite strong evidence against it. . . . The fact is that the First Congress . . . considered and rejected at least four drafts of the establishment clause that explicitly stated the "no preference" view. . . . The establishment clause actually adopted is one of the broadest versions considered by either House. . . . It forbids any law respecting an establishment of "religion." It does not say "*a* religion," "a national religion," "one sect or society," or "any particular denomination of religion." It is religion generically that may not be established.[18]

Another school of thought that is close to nonpreferentialism but is a softer version of it is what some refer to as accommodation.[19] Accommodationists would abstain from the kind of nonpreferential financial aid that the Supreme Court has, as we shall see in ensuing chapters, sometimes approved. Yet they would not hesitate to allow governmental accommodations for religious practices when they do not involve the use of taxpayer funds. This view was forcefully stated in a 1952 opinion by Supreme Court Justice William O. Douglas when the Court approved a program in the public schools that gave students "released time" to leave the school building for the purpose of going to religious centers for "religious instruction or devotional exercises."[20]

Justice Douglas wrote:

> The First Amendment . . . does not say that in every and all respects there shall be a separation of Church and State. Rather, it studiously defines the manner, the specific ways, in which there shall be no concert or union or dependency one on the other. That is the common sense of the matter. Otherwise the state and religion would be aliens to each other—hostile, suspicious, and even unfriendly. . . . Prayers in our legislative halls; the appeals to the Almighty in the messages of the Chief Executive; the proclamations making Thanksgiving a holiday; "so help me God" in our courtroom oaths—these and all other references to the Almighty that run through our laws, our public rituals, our ceremonies would be flouting the First Amendment. . . .
>
> We are a religious people whose institutions presuppose a Supreme Being. We guarantee the freedom to worship as one chooses. We make room for a wide variety of beliefs and creeds as the spiritual needs of man deem necessary. We sponsor an attitude on the part of the government that shows no partiality to any one group and that lets each flourish according to the zeal of its adherents and the appeal of its dogma. When the state encourages religious instruction or cooperates with religious authorities by adjusting the schedule of public events to sectarian needs, it follows the best of our traditions. . . . To hold that it may not would be to find in the Constitution a requirement that the government show a callous indifference to religious groups. That would be preferring those who believe in no religion over those who do believe. Government may not finance religious groups nor undertake religious instruction nor blend secular and sectarian education. . . . But we find no constitutional requirement which makes it necessary for government to be hostile to religion.[21]

The last school of thought we will consider is one that has received little approval among legal scholars and virtually no support from the Supreme Court. It is of interest, however, because of the plausible, albeit problematic, alternative it offers to the more generally accepted points of view. It is called "equal separation" or "strict neutrality" by its leading advocate, Paul J. Weber. He describes it as follows:

> *Equal separation* rejects all political or economic privilege, coercion, or disability based on religious affiliation, belief, or practice, or lack thereof, but guarantees to religiously motivated or affiliated individuals and organizations the

same rights and privileges extended to other similarly situated individuals and organizations. It provides protection to religion without providing privilege. It treats the right to religious belief and practice as a human right to be protected along with other human rights in an even-handed manner. It protects the right of religiously motivated groups and individuals to participate in the political process and the economic system in the same manner and to the same extent as it protects the rights of similar groups and individuals to participate.[22]

Professor Laurence Tribe, the country's most prominent constitutional scholar, has dismissed this point of view in two succinct and powerful sentences: "The Framers, whatever specific application they may have intended, clearly envisioned religion as something special; they enacted that vision into law by guaranteeing the free exercise of *religion*, but not, say, of philosophy or science. The strict neutrality approach all but erases this distinction."[23]

There is one notable Supreme Court decision that straddles the fence between an "equal separation" point of view and the more traditional separationist tests for determining if a law or government practice violates the establishment clause. At the same time it illustrates the virtual impossibility of "strict neutrality." The case was *Walz v Tax Commission of the City of New York,* and involved the question of exempting churches and their noncommercial real estate from taxation.[24] Chief Justice Warren Burger delivered the opinion of the Court:

> The legislative purpose of a property tax exemption is neither the advancement nor the prohibition of religion; it is neither sponsorship nor hostility. New York, in common with other States . . . has not singled out one particular church or religious group or even churches as such; rather, it has granted exemption to all houses of religious worship within a broad class of property owned by non-profit, quasi-public corporations which include hospitals, libraries, playgrounds, scientific, professional, historical and patriotic groups. . . .
>
> Determining that the legislative purpose of tax exemption is not aimed at establishing, sponsoring, or supporting religion does not end the inquiry, however. We must also be sure that the end result—the effect—is not an excessive government entanglement with religion. The test is inescapably one of degree. *Either course, taxation of churches or exemption, occasions some degree of involvement with religion* [emphasis mine]. Elimination of exemption would tend to expand the involvement of government by giving rise to tax evaluation of church property. . . .
>
> Granting tax exemption to churches necessarily operates to afford an indirect economic benefit and also gives rise to some, but yet a lesser, involvement than taxing them. . . . . The grant of a tax exemption is not

sponsorship since the government does not transfer part of its revenue to churches but simply abstains from demanding that the church support the state. . . .

Separation in this context cannot mean absence of all contact. . . . Few concepts are more deeply embedded in the fabric of our national life, beginning with pre-Revolutionary colonial times, than for the government to exercise at the very least this kind of benevolent neutrality towards churches and religious exercise generally so long as none was favored over others and none suffered interference.

Just as those who attempt to discern the original intent of the authors of the Constitution have their divergent schools of thought, proponents of the "living document" point of view also have their difficulties and differences. If one is to depart from whatever we think the intention of the founders may have been, how far may that departure go? Most would agree that we should begin the task of constitutional interpretation with the plain language before us and adhere to at least the spirit of those words, insofar as that can be discerned. Beyond that there arises the question of the source from which we derive the values to be used in making interpretations. No one believes, or would admit to the belief, that judges may use their personal prejudices for that purpose. Yet what are the alternatives that have been offered?

One is a resort to so-called natural law, which the Declaration of Independence invokes when it asserts that "all men are created equal . . . [and] are endowed by their creator with certain unalienable Rights, that among these are Life, Liberty, and the pursuit of Happiness." Justice Clarence Thomas, in his Senate confirmation hearings, avowed his belief in natural law. As a supporter of original intent on the Supreme Court bench he appears to think that the provisions of the Constitution, as written, are derived from natural law even though there is no reference whatsoever to natural law in the Constitution. Natural law, it should also be noted, is itself subject to different interpretations. It used to be argued by some respectable people, like the famous Senator John Calhoun, for example, that natural law proved the inferiority of blacks, whereas only racial bigots would maintain that position today.[25]

Another possibility, and one that can be used in conjunction with others, is to look to the general themes of the Constitution as a whole—within its "four corners," as legal scholars often put it—to help give meaning to particular provisions. The Supreme Court also sometimes relies on tradition, although that, too, can be problematic because the outcome depends on whose or which traditions one chooses to select.

The most widely accepted and utilized alternative for going beyond original intent is to rely on some version of contemporary social values. The most conservative of these approaches is to invoke what are termed the "fundamental values" of a democratic society or, as Justice Benjamin Cardozo put it, those that are "implicit in the concept of ordered liberty."[26] Another version is to refer to the "ethos" of the society or the societal norms about which there is a general consensus.[27] Looser still is the idea that the Supreme Court should make reasoned moral decisions,[28] or that they should rely on contemporary standards of human rights.[29]

All of these versions of the living document school of thought depend, of course, upon *choices* by Supreme Court justices that hopefully transcend their personal beliefs. Yet, as we have seen, that is just as much a problem for those who claim to be following original intent. Thus it is my contention that commentators who describe the Court as engaging in interpretivism versus noninterpretivism, exercising judicial restraint versus judicial activism, or being conservative versus liberal ignore the reality that various justices sometimes lean one way and sometimes the other and that sometimes, despite their best intentions or disavowals, they allow their personal prejudices or political ideologies to influence their choices. Many people felt that this was true of the Court's 5-4 decision that effectively made George W. Bush the president of the United States.[30]

There are other issues that are unique to interpreting the First Amendment. One is whether the use of the word "Congress" limits the application of that amendment to the federal legislature or whether it also applies to the executive branch of the federal government. Another is whether the states as well as the federal government are bound by its provisions.

As to the first of those questions, the Supreme Court has always assumed that officers of the executive branch of the federal government are implicitly included under the rubric of "Congress." No one has seriously questioned that interpretation, even though the plain language of the amendment does not make it explicit.

The second question is a much more complicated matter, for it is obvious that when originally adopted the First Amendment did *not* apply to the states. Indeed, as we noted in the preceding chapter, a proposal by James Madison, the father of the Constitution, to make the First Amendment applicable to the states was voted down by the Congress in 1789.

Again in 1876, *after* the adoption of the Fourteenth Amendment, shortly to be discussed, Congress debated and failed to adopt a proposal to make the religion clauses binding on the states.[31] What is more, it has been persuasively argued by a prominent legal scholar, Akhil Reed Amar, that those who wrote the opening words of the amendment, "Congress shall make no law respecting an establishment of religion," did not have as their purpose the protection of individuals from the dominance of government-supported religion at all.[32] Their motivation, he asserts, was to prevent the new federal government from interfering in any way with the right of the states to maintain the established churches most of them had at that time. Yet, despite the intent of the majority of those who voted for the First Amendment that it not be applicable to the states, the U.S. Supreme Court, beginning in 1925 with the case of *Gitlow v New York*, began making it so.[33]

The authority they relied on for doing so is referred to in the legal community as the doctrine of "incorporation"—that is, applying many of the provisions of the Bill of Rights to the states via the Fourteenth Amendment. That amendment, adopted in 1868, provided that "No State shall make or enforce any law which shall abridge the privileges or immunities of citizens of the United States; nor shall any State deprive any person of life, liberty, or property without due process of law; nor deny to any person within its jurisdiction the equal protection of the laws." It was one of three adopted in the wake of the Civil War, the preceding one (the Thirteenth Amendment) abolishing slavery, and the ensuing one (the Fifteenth Amendment) providing that no one was to be denied the vote, "on account of race, color, or previous condition of servitude." Although there are some who have claimed that it is an unwarranted stretch to use the Fourteenth Amendment for purposes other than the protection of former slaves from discrimination by the states, the Supreme Court has not hesitated to use it more broadly, operating on the premise that "the decision to use general language, not tied to race, was a conscious one."[34] That premise is well supported by a vast body of historical evidence.[35]

It should also be noted that the Supreme Court did not apply the entirety of the First Amendment to the states in one fell swoop. The *Gitlow* decision incorporated only the free speech and press clause. Two years later, in *DeJonge v Oregon*, it incorporated the peaceable-assembly clause.[36] In 1940, in *Cantwell v Connecticut*, it applied the free-exercise-of-religion clause to the states, and it added the no-establishment-of-religion clause seven years later in *Everson*.[37] Since those decisions there has been no doubt whatever that the Court regards the states and all of their subordinate governing bodies, such as city councils and school boards, as being just as bound by the strictures of the First Amendment as is the federal government.

Furthermore, it is not only legislative bodies of the state governments that are so bound. As it has done at the federal level, the Supreme Court has always interpreted the First Amendment as being just as applicable to the executive branches of state government as to their legislatures. Thus, governors, mayors, school superintendents, policemen, and even public school teachers, acting in their official capacities, must respect the principles of that amendment.

It should be noted here that although the doctrine of incorporation has been accepted and used with full force by the Supreme Court whenever a provision of the original Bill of Rights has been applied to the states, there have been dissenting voices about that process. One is that of no less a personage than Chief Justice Rehnquist, who, although learning to live with it, has argued that it should play a much more modest role in the Court's decisions.

Writing in 1976, the chief justice said:

> I am of the opinion that not all of the strictures which the First Amendment imposes upon Congress are carried over against the States by the Fourteenth Amendment, but rather that it is only the "general principle" of free speech that the latter incorporates.
>
> Given this view, cases which deal with state restrictions on First Amendment freedoms are not fungible with those which deal with restrictions imposed by the Federal Government.[38]

There is a final point that needs to be made about understanding the First Amendment. One who is not familiar with how the Supreme Court works might assume that because the amendment says that "Congress shall make *no* law . . ." the Court would strike down as unconstitutional *any* legislation respecting an establishment of religion (however defined), prohibiting the free exercise thereof, or abridging the freedom of speech and press. Yet even Justice Black, who repeatedly described himself as a First Amendment absolutist, did not take those words literally. He and all other members of the Court have always held that what they have called "compelling interests" of society may justify making exceptions to those general principles. Were that not the case, this book would have to end here because there would be no cases in controversy or difficult questions to be resolved. It is only because the Supreme Court has decided, on a case by case and issue by issue basis, that there are compelling social interests that may excuse restrictions on freedom of religion or speech, and government actions that might or might not be considered an establishment of religion, that we can and must proceed to examine those matters in detail in the chapters that follow.

3

Religious Expression in Public Places

❖❖❖❖❖

There is one aspect of religious expression that is, atypically, entirely noncontroversial. It is that individuals and groups are entirely free to display their religious symbols on their own property and to speak out orally in public places about their beliefs. What becomes problematic, and a potential violation of the establishment clause of the First Amendment, is when people attempt to display their religious symbols on *public property* or when taxpayer money is used in part or in whole to support the expression of their religious beliefs or displays.

Religious Displays in Public Buildings and on Public Land

A source of intense debate in this country over many years has been the erection during the Christmas season of crèches—the Christian nativity scene—in the lobbies or in front of city halls and county or federal buildings, or in public parks. In all of these places except for the public parks it is clear that the government is giving its implicit if not explicit imprimatur to the Christian religion, regardless of who is paying the bill for the display or its erection. In a public park, however, assuming it has been an acceptable forum for other kinds of displays, religious or not, it is relevant to know if the taxpayer's money is involved. If not, the display arguably enjoys the same rights of free speech as any symbols financed by private groups. A closely related matter that has also stirred great emotion is the placement atop high hills on public lands, or on public buildings, of the Christian cross. The presence of these symbols has led to many lawsuits and a multitude of court decisions, a number of which have gone all the way to the U.S. Supreme Court. There have also been cases involving displays of the Ten Commandments on the walls of public schools or at other public buildings, and involving crosses used as shoulder patches on the uniforms of police and fire department personnel. For the issues to be discussed throughout this book on which the Supreme Court has spoken, we will generally not address the multitude of lower court cases that preceded them. On those matters not yet addressed by our highest court, we will examine a sampling of significant lower court decisions that stand as precedents within the geographical areas they govern.

The U.S. Supreme Court has dealt with the creche issue in two important decisions five years apart in the 1980s, both by votes of 5-4, and leaning in opposite directions. The first case, decided in 1984, involved a creche that was erected by city workers each year in a downtown park in Pawtucket, Rhode Island, surmounted by a banner that read, "Season's Greetings."[1] In reversing the decision of a lower court, Chief Justice Warren Burger, writing for the Supreme Court's majority, said that although the display "advances religion in a sense," and "is identified with one religious faith," it "engenders a friendly community spirit of goodwill in keeping with the season." He noted that the display of the creche was accompanied by a reindeer and Santa Claus, as well as the greetings of the season, which presumably secularized it enough to make it acceptable to five of the justices. He further expressed for the first time the troublesome view that the historic "wall of separation" phrase, though perhaps a "useful metaphor," need not be "solely determinative" in adjudicating First Amendment establishment cases.

Justice Brennan, speaking for the four dissenters, described the creche as being at "the heart of the Christian faith," and the majority's decision as a serious departure from long-standing precedent. One could add, as I would, that it is just as demeaning to serious believers in Christianity to describe a creche as merely a nonreligious seasonal icon as it is to non-Christians to have public monies used to erect a symbol that, as the chief justice admitted, "advances in a sense" a religious faith they do not share.

Five years later, in a case from Pittsburgh, Pennsylvania, with facts that were only slightly different, a majority of the justices coalesced around a different point of view.[2] Here a Catholic organization had been permitted to erect a creche in the lobby of the county building surmounted with a banner that read, "Gloria in Excelsis Deo." Five of the justices found that to be a violation of the establishment clause. Justice Sandra Day O'Connor, who had voted with the majority in the Pawtucket case, found this display too much for her, describing it in a concurring opinion as "a message to Christians that they are favored members of the political community." The Court's decision was complicated by the fact that it also encompassed a companion case that split the Court in so many ways that that one commentator has described the plethora of majority, concurring, and dissenting opinions written for the combined cases as "like nine Christmas carolers, each singing a different song."[3]

That second case dealt with a display in front of a city building just a block away from the county building that consisted of a Christmas tree and an eighteen-foot Jewish menorah.[4] On this issue a majority of six justices, including those who dissented with respect to the creche in the county building, found it to be a harmless display that did not violate the establishment clause. Justice Brennan, in dissent, was not persuaded that simply adding a Jewish symbol to one associated with Christianity cleansed the case of an establishment violation. He explained that the First Amendment was designed "to require neutrality, not just among religions, but between religion and nonreligion."

The United States Ninth Circuit Court of Appeals, governing California and many of the other western states, has had to deal with several running battles involving crosses. A Latin cross sat on public land at the peak of Mt. Soledad in the city of San Diego; another was atop Mt. Helix just outside the city of La Mesa in San Diego County; La Mesa also had crosses on its letterheads, public buildings, and police shoulder patches; and a cross had long sat atop Mt. Davidson in San Francisco. A federal district court judge, a three-judge panel of the court of appeals, and finally a unanimous *en banc* ruling by twenty-eight judges of the court of appeals, all found the display of the crosses in the city and in the county of San Diego in violation of the no-preference clause of the California Constitution.[5] Article 1, Section 4, of that constitution guarantees "the free exercise and enjoyment of religion without discrimination or preference." In the wake of these court decisions San Diego County decided to transfer the entire Mt. Helix park to a private organization called the Foundation for the Preservation of the Mt.

Helix Nature Theatre and to eliminate La Mesa's uses of the crosses as a symbol. This was agreed to by the American Civil Liberties Union (ACLU), representing the plaintiffs in that case.

Meanwhile, the City of San Diego sold the Mt. Soledad cross and the land underneath it to a private Christian group, the Mt. Soledad Memorial Association, whose announced intention was to "Save the Cross." When the sale was declared invalid because it had been conducted without open bidding, a second, presumably more properly structured, sale was held. The same religious group won out over other bidders. That became the basis for further litigation, pursued for several years by Philip Paulson, the plaintiff and an avowed atheist. He failed to succeed at first when a federal district court found the new sale to be constitutional and a three-judge panel of the Ninth Circuit Court of Appeals affirmed that decision.[6] Yet his request for an *en banc* rehearing of the case was granted by the appellate court, and a year later, by a vote of 7-4, the three-judge panel was reversed and the second sale was held to be as flawed as the first in granting a preference to religion.[7]

As to San Francisco, the appellate court also held that the Mt. Davidson concrete cross, said to be the largest Latin cross in the United States, was in violation of California's no-preference constitutional provision.[8] Following that decision the city sold the cross at auction, plus one-third of an acre parcel of land around it, to the Council of Armenian American Organizations of Northern California. The sale included an agreement that the cross would not be illuminated more than twice a year and that no other religious displays would be erected on the land. Two atheists challenged that sale as invalid, but it was approved by the Ninth Circuit Court of Appeals and the U.S. Supreme Court declined to review the circuit court decision.[9]

The Tenth Circuit Court of Appeals has also been called upon to address two cross cases, one from Bernalillo County, New Mexico, and the other from Edmond, Oklahoma. Bernalillo County, with its historic Hispanic and Catholic background, had been using as a seal of county government a Latin cross with the motto "Con Esta Vencemos," meaning "With This We Conquer." The reference was presumably to the Spanish Conquistadors' vanquishing of the Native American population of the area centuries earlier. The court, in an *en banc* reversal of one of its three-judge panels, found that emblem to be in violation of the establishment clause of the First Amendment.[10] Similarly a city seal with a cross that was being used in Edmond, Oklahoma, was struck down by the court.[11]

A related, but slightly different, issue was raised in cases decided by the Seventh Circuit and the Ninth Circuit. In the latter case the court again resorted to the no-preference clause of the California constitution to strike down displays of statuary depicting the life of Christ from the New Testament scattered throughout a public park in San Bernadino County's Yucca Valley.[12] The Seventh Circuit case, emanating from the small city of Ottowa, Illinois, was more complicated because the sixteen religious paintings that were installed in a public city park had been turned over during the course of the litigation to a private organization, the Ottowa Freedom Association. A district court judge, sustained by a three-judge panel of the Seventh Circuit, had found that the paintings constituted an "endorsement" of religion in violation of the establishment clause of the First Amendment. Yet in a unanimous *en banc* ruling by eleven judges of the circuit court those decisions were reversed as overbroad, inasmuch as they banned private as well as public displays.[13] Since the city was already working on a new ordinance that would limit the duration of these religious displays to the Christmas season, and would require the erection of a sign indicating that they were installed and maintained with private funds, the ACLU, which brought the case, decided to sign a consent decree and not appeal to the U.S. Supreme Court.

In another reversal of a three-judge panel by a federal court of appeals *en banc* ruling, the Sixth Circuit held by a 9-4 vote that the State of Ohio's use on its official stationery and on a bronze plaque in the entryway of the statehouse of the motto "With God All Things Are Possible," did *not* constitute an impermissible endorsement of religion.[14] Writing for the majority, Judge David Nelson said that the motto was permissible so long as it did not attribute the phrase to its New Testament source. He added that "just as the motto does not have as its primary purpose the advancement of religion, it does not have the primary effect of advancing religion, either."

The two criteria referred to by Judge Nelson, purpose and effect, are part of a trilogy of criteria the Supreme Court had enunciated in 1971 in a case involving financial aid to parochial schools that we will be discussing in detail later.[15] The third criterion was that in order to avoid violating the establishment clause there must be no "excessive entanglement" of religion and the state. These criteria, commonly referred to as the *Lemon* tests, became in the years following 1971 the primary tools used by the courts in adjudicating establishment clause cases, and we will be encountering them again and again throughout this volume.

Displays of the Ten Commandments on public property have been at issue in various places around the country. They have met a very different judicial fate when they have been posted in public school classrooms than when they have appeared in, or in front of, courthouses or other public buildings. The strongest decision against them came in a 5-4 decision of the U.S. Supreme Court in 1980 when the majority found that posting them in a classroom had no secular purpose and served no educational function. The Kentucky statute that required their posting was therefore held to be a violation of the establishment clause.[16] The fact that they had been paid for and donated by private contributions was regarded as irrelevant, but the fact that public school children were their intended viewers was presumably of considerable concern. "The pre-eminent purpose for posting the Ten Commandments on schoolroom walls is plainly religious in nature," declared the Court. Chief Justice William Rehnquist, in dissent, complained that "The Court's summary rejection of a secular purpose articulated by the legislature and confirmed by the state court is without precedent in Establishment Clause jurisdiction."

As for displays of the Ten Commandments beyond the public schools there have been at least four U.S. Circuit Court of Appeals decisions on that matter, all involving large granite structures with the Ten Commandments embossed upon them standing in or in front of public buildings. In three of the instances, at the county courthouse in Salt Lake City, the city hall in Elkhart, Indiana, and the state capitol of Kentucky, the monoliths had been donated by the Fraternal Order of Eagles. The Tenth Circuit upheld the Salt Lake City display in 1973, but the Seventh Circuit in 2000, over a bitter dissent by Judge Clarence Manion, ruled 2-1 against the Ten Commandment display on the lawn in front of the Elkhart municipal building, as did the Sixth Circuit in 2002 in the Kentucky case.[17] The U.S. Supreme Court declined to review the Sixth Circuit's decision in that Kentucky case.[18]

When the Elkhart case was appealed to the Supreme Court, it failed to receive the four votes needed to be accepted for review. Thus it stood as the final word for that circuit. In an unusual revelation of the views of some of the justices in a case that was not going to be heard by them, three members of the Court—Chief Justice William Rehnquist, Justice Scalia, and Justice Thomas—joined together in a dissent from the denial of review that was written by the chief justice. Not only had they wanted to review the lower court decision, but they made it clear that they would have voted to overturn it. Their opinion argued that the Elkhart display "is part of the city's celebration of its cultural and historical roots, not a promotion of religious faith."[19]

In an even more unusual move, Justice John Paul Stevens wrote a rejoinder to their opinion in which he objected to their exceptional use of a dissent from a refusal to review a case to state their views on its merits. Not wanting those views to go unanswered, as they would have if written in a decided case, he pointed out that the first two lines of the monument's text, in a larger font than the remainder, read "THE TEN COMMAND-MENTS—I AM the LORD thy GOD." This is "hard to square," Justice Stevens said, "with the proposition that the monument expresses no particular religious preference." What the five other justices who also voted to deny review felt about the substance of the matter would not be known until some other case on the issue would be accepted for review and decided.

That did not happen, however, when the Supreme Court declined to review a Seventh Circuit Court of Appeals decision in another case emanating from Indiana. The state's governor, Frank O'Bannon, had been prevented from erecting on the statehouse grounds a seven-foot-tall limestone monument embossed with the Ten Commandments. The Indiana Civil Liberties Union had sought and obtained an injunction from a federal district court judge against the erection of the monument, and the court of appeals upheld that ruling.[20]

A prominent controversy about the posting of the Ten Commandments also occurred when Judge Roy Moore, then a circuit court judge in Etowah County, Alabama, posted them on his courtroom wall and began jury selection with prayers by local ministers. In 1996 another circuit court judge ruled that these actions violated the First Amendment and ordered the removal of the Ten Commandments. Judge Moore, with the backing of then-governor Fob James, refused to do so. Governor James was quoted as saying, "I will use all legal means at my disposal, including the National Guard and state troopers, to prevent the removal of the Ten Commandments from Judge Moore's courtroom."[21] In the Republican primary of June 2000, Judge Moore defeated a more moderate Republican in a contest for chief justice of the Alabama Supreme Court and went on in November to defeat the Democratic candidate and become chief justice.

The following August, without consulting the other eight justices, Chief Justice Moore installed a granite monolith in the rotunda of the court building, engraved with various historic documents and with the Ten Commandments surmounted on the top.

A group of black members of the state legislature then attempted to place a copy of Martin Luther King's "I Have a Dream" speech in the same rotunda. The building manager barred their entry to that area and told them they could put it in the basement rotunda, where there already was a civil rights display. "I'll decide when and if and where it will be displayed," he said. An African American state senator commented that this reminded him of the days when blacks were relegated to the back of the bus. Two months later the ACLU and Americans United for Separation of Church and State filed a lawsuit against the display in federal court. In November 2002, district court judge Myron Thompson, in a ninety-three-page opinion, offered by the 11th Circuit Court of Appeals in July 2003, found the monument to be a clear violation of the First Amendment and ordered its removal within thirty days.[22]

The State of Ohio capitol building figured in the last of the cases we will be looking at in this section. It was another difficult one that resulted in a U.S. Supreme Court decision.[23] In an area in front of the capitol building where groups of all sorts had been permitted to put up displays on a temporary basis, the Ku Klux Klan sought to erect one of its crosses. It was refused permission to do so by the Capitol Square Review Board on the grounds that it would constitute a violation of the separation of church and state, the cross being considered a religious symbol. In a 7-2 decision the Supreme Court held that the state could not discriminate against expression on the basis of its religious content, and that since other groups had been allowed to use the area on a temporary basis, the KKK had a free-speech right to do so as well. Furthermore, the justices did not think that allowing this display would constitute a violation of the establishment clause. Indeed, Justice Thomas indicated in a concurring opinion that he did not even regard the display of a cross by the KKK as a religious symbol, but rather a political one.

Although seven of the justices had concurred with most of the majority opinion written by Justice Scalia, there was a part of it (section 4) with which several of them could not agree and hence wrote separately. Justices David Souter, Steven Breyer, and Sandra Day O'Connor expressed the view that since an *unattended* display on the capitol grounds might be perceived by passers-by as a government endorsement of the message, it would be permissible for the state to prohibit all unattended displays so long as they did so on a content-neutral basis. That was obviously not what the state had done in this case. The two dissenters, Justices Stevens and Ruth Bader Ginsburg, had somewhat different reasons from one another for their dissents. Justice Stevens felt that *any* unattended religious display on government property, such as this one, implied endorsement of religion and was thus not permissible. Justice Ginsburg objected to the display because it did not include a disclaimer of government endorsement, and presumably would have voted to allow it if it had.

Government-Sponsored Prayers

It should be noted at the outset of this section that we will not be discussing at this point prayers that are said in public school settings. That is a special circumstance we will come to later. What is at issue here are the practices of Congress and many state legislatures of opening their sessions with prayers by a chaplain; prayers said at public events such as presidential and gubernatorial inaugurations; and the employment of chaplains by the military services.

As we have seen earlier, James Madison, the primary proponent of the First Amendment, wrote a revealing document called "Detached Memoranda" in 1817, after his retirement from the presidency. In it he expressed the view that having chaplains in Congress and the military violated the establishment clause.[24] He also considered proclamations by the president of fasts and Thanksgiving Days to be violations, although he himself had proclaimed several such days. He explained in a letter in 1822 that those proclamations were deviations from "strict principle," which he found necessary when the nation was at war [he was in office during the War of 1812 when the British burned down the White House].[25]

Madison is not alone in having questioned the propriety of the government not only *accepting* chaplains in the military but actually *financing* an entire corps of chaplains who hold officer rank in all the services and are entitled to the benefits that accrue to those ranks. The reason this practice has never been seriously challenged is that there are strong freedom-of-religion considerations that are thought to outweigh the establishment concerns one might have. In order for military personnel who are stationed on navy ships or in distant places to fully practice their religion, whether for counseling, confession, or rites and rituals, they need the availability of clergymen. Of course it is not possible to provide everybody everywhere with chaplains of their own faith, but conscientious chaplains try, insofar as possible, to provide such services as they can to the servicemen and women who are within their reach.

Although the hiring of chaplains, or the use of ministers who volunteer their services, for legislative bodies or official ceremonies does not have justifications like those in the military, the practice has gone almost as universally unchallenged. This may be due in part to the fact that frequently care is taken to rotate the performance of the role among clergy of different faiths, thus reducing the number of people who might take offense at the practice. Furthermore, sometimes those who pronounce the prayers have the sensitivity to make them nondenominational, though that is still not satisfactory from the point of view of members of unrepresented minority faiths or of agnostics and atheists. A blatant example of insensitivity in this matter occurred at the inauguration of George W. Bush as president in January 2001. On that occasion, in contrast to the pattern established at most previous inaugurations, the ministers who delivered both the invocation and benediction invoked the name of Jesus Christ in their prayers. Many non-Christians were deeply offended by that incident.

There has been one significant legal challenge to the saying of prayers in legislative bodies, in a case that was decided by the Supreme Court in 1983.[26] The lawsuit had been brought by a state senator in Nebraska where the same Presbyterian clergyman had been serving as a paid chaplain and offering prayers at the beginning of each session of its state legislature for nearly two decades. Both a U.S. district court and the circuit court of appeals had found the practice to be in violation of the establishment clause, but a six-justice majority of the Supreme Court surprisingly reversed those decisions. Speaking for that majority, Chief Justice Burger justified the outcome by resort to history and tradition. "From colonial times through the founding of the Republic and ever since," he wrote, "the practice of legislative prayer has coexisted with the principle of disestablishment and religious freedom." He went on to point out that just three days before agreeing on the language of the Bill of Rights, the Congress had in 1789 authorized the appointment of paid chaplains for their own two houses. "Clearly," he argued, "the men who wrote the First Amendment Religion Clause did not view paid legislative chaplains and opening prayers as a violation of that Amendment, for the practice of opening sessions with prayer has continued without interruption ever since that early session of Congress."

This reliance on "original intent" did not impress the three dissenters. Justice Brennan, confessing that in an earlier case involving Bible reading in the public schools [to be discussed later in this book], he had come "very close to endorsing essentially the result reached by the Court today," now declared that "after much reflection, I have come to the conclusion that I was wrong then and the Court is wrong today." He reasoned that the three *Lemon* tests the Court had been relying on as binding precedent for the previous dozen years in adjudicating establishment cases should have governed the decision, and said, "I have no doubt that, if any group of law students were asked to apply the principles of *Lemon* to the question of legislative prayer, they would nearly unanimously find the practice to be unconstitutional." Joined in his dissent by Justice Marshall, he pointed out how those tests had been failed. First, he explained "that the 'purpose' of legislative prayer is preeminently religious rather than secular seems to me to be self-evident." Second, "the 'primary effect' of legislative prayer is also clearly religious. . . . invocations in Nebraska's legislative halls explicitly link religious belief and observance to the power and prestige of the state." Third, "there can be no doubt that the practice of legislative prayer leads to excessive 'entanglement' between the State and religion. . . . The process of choosing a 'suitable' chaplain . . . and insuring that the chaplain limits himself or herself to 'suitable' prayers, involves precisely the sort of supervision that agencies of government should if at all possible avoid." Here we have a clear example of how sharply different results can come from the use of "original intent" in interpreting the Constitution versus reliance on new precedents that have developed over time.

Justice Stevens, in a brief two-paragraph opinion, chose to rest his dissent on different grounds, namely that "the designation of a member of one religious faith to serve as the sole official chaplain of a state legislature for a period of sixteen years constitutes the preference of one faith over another in violation of the Establishment Clause of the First Amendment." He opined that while a Catholic priest might be chosen to say prayers in the Massachusetts legislature and a Presbyterian in Nebraska, "I would not expect to find a Jehovah's Witness or a disciple of Mary Baker Eddy [founder of the Christian Science Church] or the Reverend Moon serving as the official chaplain in any state legislature."

Celebrating Religious Holidays

If President Madison had second thoughts about having proclaimed Thanksgiving a national holiday, one can imagine how he would have felt about Good Friday, Easter, and Christmas in that regard. It is undoubtedly because our history and culture as a nation have been so intertwined with Christianity that little thought has been given to this question, particularly since Christmas has become so secularized with gift-giving, Santa Claus and his reindeer, and Easter with its bunnies and eggs. Good Friday is a different matter, however, because it is so clearly and solely a Christian religious holiday. As a result, in very recent years there have been First Amendment challenges to state and local laws that have declared Good Friday to be a holiday.

These cases must be viewed against the backdrop of a much older Supreme Court decision involving Sunday closing laws—so-called blue laws. Those laws, which forbade merchants to do business on Sundays, competitively disadvantaged Jews, Seventh-Day Adventists, and others whose faith required them to close their shops on a second day of the week. They have become anachronisms, not because of any Supreme Court decision but because of the economic pressures of the marketplace. Indeed, the Supreme Court, while admitting "the strongly religious origin of these laws," decided that the government's interests in providing for the "health, safety, recreation and general well-being of our citizens" had converted their purpose and effect into secular ones.[27] With only Justice William O. Douglas dissenting, Chief Justice Earl Warren wrote for the Court that "To say that the States cannot prescribe Sunday as a day of rest for these purposes solely because centuries ago such laws had their genesis in religion would give a constitutional interpretation of hostility to the public welfare rather than one of mere separation of church and State."

That was in 1961, and it is obvious to the millions of Americans who now shop on Sundays that the purposes and effects attributed to the blue laws by the Supreme Court were and are highly questionable. Perhaps wanting to avoid being enmeshed in a similar situation today, the Supreme Court has thus far declined to review any of the several U.S. Circuit Court of Appeals decisions that have recently addressed the Good Friday question, in all of which those courts have used the Supreme Court's Sunday closing precedent to uphold the observance of Good Friday as a holiday.

Thus, in 1991 a three-judge panel of the Ninth Circuit decided by a 2-1 vote that Good Friday was sufficiently secularized that Hawaii's statute making it a state holiday did not violate the establishment clause.[28] Three similar decisions followed in 1999. The Sixth Circuit, also by a 2-1 vote, upheld a policy of Kenton County, Kentucky, to close all its county and state offices on Good Friday.[29] The Seventh Circuit, again voting 2-1 and using the *Lemon* tests as its criteria, sustained an Indiana law that that made Good Friday a paid holiday for state employees.[30] Finally, the Fourth Circuit, by a unanimous 3-0 vote, upheld a Maryland statute that provided for public school holidays on Good Friday, along with Christmas, Memorial Day, and spring vacation centered around Easter.[31] That case originated in Montgomery County, essentially a suburb of Washington, D.C., where the school board had exercised its option to add Rosh Hashanah and Yom Kippur to the list of school holidays.

If this was an attempt to demonstrate that Montgomery County was respecting the spirit of the First Amendment by not giving preference to one religion, it did nothing for adherents to faiths other than Christianity and Judaism. If, on the other hand, the school district was motivated, as have been school boards in many other communities with large Jewish populations, by the secular consideration that there is little point in conducting classes when there will be vast numbers of absentees, one can reasonably argue that such a policy has nothing to do with the First Amendment. The problem with that reasoning as applied to Good Friday, however, is that even in communities that are predominantly or even exclusively Christian it is unlikely that large numbers of parents would believe that their faith required them to keep their children at home on that particular holiday. That is quite different from the great number of Jews who do expect their children to stay out of school on Rosh Hashanah and Yom Kippur.

A Nation under God?

In his campaign for the presidency of the United States in 1988, George Bush Sr. made much of the fact that his opponent, Michael Dukakis, was, as he put it, "a card-carrying member of the American Civil Liberties Union." Bush claimed that the ACLU, among other things he deplored, opposed the use of the phrases "In God We Trust" on our coins and "under God" in the Pledge of Allegiance.

An examination of the Policy Guide of the ACLU demonstrates that there is no reference whatsoever to the phrase "In God We Trust," proclaimed by Congress in 1956 to be the nation's official motto. It is true, however, that after Congress broke the rhythm of the Pledge of Allegiance in 1954 by ordering that the words "under God" be inserted into it, the ACLU board of directors did declare that it considered the amendment a violation in principle of the separation of church and state. The change was made by Congress, in the midst of the Cold War with the Soviet Union, after being lobbied for it by the Knights of Columbus, a Catholic organization, to distinguish the United States from "godless communism." Yet no action was ever taken by the ACLU to do anything about it. Certainly

urging the Congress to undo what it had done would have been unsuccessful. Nor would litigation have been likely to succeed, given the acceptance by the Supreme Court of even larger breaches in the supposed
"wall" of separation, such as legislative chaplaincies and national religious
holidays.

However, forty-eight years later two members of a three-judge panel of
the U. S. Ninth Circuit Court of Appeals shocked the nation by declaring
the amendment to be unconstitutional.[32] The case had been brought by an
atheist, who also happened to be an emergency room physician with a law
degree. He complained that his eight-year-old was being subjected to the
amended pledge as a daily ritual in her second-grade Sacramento, California, classroom. The reaction in Washington, D.C., was one of instanta-
neous outrage. The president condemned it, Congress adopted resolutions
denouncing it, and the attorney general announced that the Justice Department would seek a rehearing *en banc* by the Ninth Circuit.[33] Within
twenty-four hours, the author of the opinion, a moderate Republican who
had been appointed to the bench by President Nixon, issued a stay of the
ruling until the full court could decide whether to hold a rehearing. Eight
months later the same panel amended its opinion, pulling back from its
original ruling that had declared the federal law to be unconstitutional because to do so was now believed to be beyond the court's authority. The
modified opinion, which the full court simultaneously declined to review
en banc, held that conducting the pledge with the "under God" phrase in it
violated the separation of church and state only when performed in public
school settings. Perhaps the panel hoped that this more limited decision
might survive in the U.S. Supreme Court, to which the Justice Department
would almost certainly appeal. The incident was a dramatic example of
how difficult it is to maintain strict adherence to the separation of church
and state in a society as devoted to religion, at least symbolically, as ours.

Fraudulent Ministries

We close this chapter with an exceptionally difficult issue that implicates
the free-exercise-of-religion clause rather than the establishment clause of
the First Amendment. It has to do with ministers or self-appointed ministers who make appeals for money or adherents to their "faith" by employ-
ing dubious claims or outright falsehoods. These may range from claiming
to have performed miracle cures for illnesses to asking for money for the
construction of a church that is then actually diverted to their personal use.

There is nobody who looks with enthusiasm on the government monitoring the speech of religious leaders and passing judgment on its truth or falsity. To engage in such an enterprise is seriously to endanger the free exercise of religion. Yet the state has a legitimate interest in protecting the public from fraud, be it committed by unscrupulous sellers of merchandise or of alleged religion.

The problem in dealing with alleged religious fraud is that most of it cannot objectively be proven to be false, even if most reasonable people believe it to be so. Tempted as we may be to try to prevent mass suicides by gullible people who follow charismatic leaders to their death, as in the Jonestown and Waco events, or to deter them from membership in cults that practice deception in recruiting, like the Moonies, we cannot do so without intruding on their freedom to make their own religious decisions. That would be akin to telling people they may not patronize fortune-tellers or go to Lourdes to seek a cure for a fatal disease. Just as we respect the right of adult Jehovah's Witnesses to refuse blood transfusions to save their lives and of adult Christian Scientists to reject medical treatment, so we must respect the right of people who can ill afford it to give their money to causes in which they choose to believe.

The Supreme Court, in the only decision it has rendered in this area, did draw a line, albeit it an unusually fuzzy one, against one kind of alleged religious expression, although by the narrow margin of 5-4, back in 1944.[34] The case also illustrates the complexities faced by any court that is attempting to be respectful of religious freedom while at the same time protective of legitimate competing interests. What was at issue in this instance was a mailing by Guy and Edna Ballard, leaders of the "I Am" movement, who claimed among other things that they had been designated as "divine messengers" by Saint Germain, "otherwise known as Jesus and George Washington," and had cured hundreds of people afflicted with diseases and ailments. They had been indicted and convicted of using the mails to defraud in a trial at which the district court judge instructed the jury that they were not allowed to judge the truth or falsity of the Ballard statements, but could find them guilty if they concluded that the Ballards did not themselves sincerely believe in what they said. The jury did so conclude. The circuit court of appeals sent the case back for retrial on the grounds that the jury should have been told that they *could and should* judge the truth or falsity of the statements. That decision was in turn reversed by a majority of the Supreme Court, which agreed with the original instructions given to the jury by the trial judge. On that basis the

Supreme Court sent the case back to the circuit court for reconsideration, and this time that court, following the Supreme Court's lead, reaffirmed the district court's original decision.

However that was not to be the end of the story. By the time the earlier trial had occurred, Guy Ballard was dead and his wife, Edna, was the principal defendant. Yet women had been excluded from the jury, a circumstance to which the defense had objected in vain. When that issue was raised anew in a claim that the trial had violated the Sixth Amendment's guarantee of an impartial jury and the Fifth Amendment's due process clause, the Supreme Court, in still another bite of the apple, invalidated the conviction on those procedural grounds.[35]

Nevertheless, something of a precedent had presumably been set by the majority in its first decision in the case, to the effect that religious expression can be punished if and only if it is found that its authors do not believe what they are saying. Justice Douglas, speaking for that five-member majority, declared that "Heresy trials are foreign to our Constitution. Men may believe what they cannot prove. . . . The miracles of the New Testament, the Divinity of Christ, life after death, the power of prayer are deep in the religious convictions of many. If one could be sent to jail because a jury in a hostile environment found those teachings false, little indeed would be left of religious freedom." He made clear, on the other hand, that punishment was permissible where a jury had found the beliefs to be insincere.

Justice Robert Jackson, writing for three of the four dissenters, was eloquent in his rejection of this dichotomy. "If I might agree to their conviction without creating a precedent, I cheerfully would do so. I can see in their teachings nothing but humbug, untainted by any trace of truth. But that does not dispose of the constitutional question. . . . It rather emphasizes the danger of such prosecutions. . . . I do not see how we can separate an issue as to what is believed from consideration as to what is believable. . . . Any inquiry into intellectual honesty in religion raises profound psychological problems. . . . [Religion's] vitality is in the religious experiences of many people. . . . If religious liberty includes, as it must, the right to communicate such experiences to others, it seems to me an impossible task for juries to separate fancied ones from real ones, dreams from happenings, and hallucinations from true clairvoyance."

Chief Justice Harlan Fiske Stone, in a separate dissent, was the only justice who would allow passing judgment on truth itself. "I am not prepared to say," he wrote, " that the constitutional guarantee of freedom of religion

affords immunity from criminal prosecution for the fraudulent procure-
ment of money by false statements as to one's religious experiences, more
than it renders polygamy or libel immune from criminal prosecution. . . . If
it were shown that the defendant in this case had asserted . . . that he had
physically shaken hands with St. Germain in San Francisco on a day
named, or that . . . he 'had in fact . . . cured hundreds of persons afflicted
with diseases and ailments,' I should not doubt that it would be open to
the Government to submit to the jury proof that he had never been in San
Francisco and that no such cures had ever been effected."

4

Religious Expression in Public Schools

❖❖❖❖❖

The most intense struggles over religious expression and the separation of church and state have occurred and continue to occur within the public schools of the nation. That is because so many people perceive, either rightly or wrongly, that the shaping of young minds is at stake. Although the family is probably as important as, and very likely more important than, what goes on in the schools in influencing a young person's religious beliefs, the concern is legitimately widespread that the money of taxpayers should not be used to tip the scales one way or the other. Since the free-exercise-of-religion clause of the First Amendment indisputably protects the right of private and religious grade schools and colleges to do what they wish in propagating their faith, the constitutional battle has been confined to the public schools—most often at the high school level, but occasionally in the lower grades and sometimes at public colleges and universities as well. There it will continue so long as religious believers try to use the public school setting as a place to encourage their faith, and separationists, whether religious or not, fight those efforts. The struggle, as we shall now see, has taken place with respect to a wide variety of activities.

Prayer in Classrooms, at Graduation, and at Sports Events

Ever since 1962 it has been clear to the U.S. Supreme Court, as well as to lawyers who represent and advise public boards of education, that prayers led by teachers in the classroom or by school officials over the school's public address system, whether nondenominational or not, violate the First Amendment. Even most adherents to the nonpreferentialist or accommodationist points of view would concede that when authority figures with influence over youngsters in a compulsory public education setting conduct religious exercises, that constitutes a government endorsement of religion that is forbidden by the establishment clause. Only hard-line opponents of the separation of church and state would argue otherwise.

The precedent established in 1962 by the Supreme Court in *Engel v Vitale* involved the striking down of the daily reading of a prayer in New York schools, endorsed by the State Board of Regents, that said, "Almighty God, we acknowledge our dependence upon thee, and we beg thy blessings upon us, our parents, our teachers, and our country."[1] The following year the Court also invalidated Bible reading by classroom teachers in Pennsylvania and Maryland.[2] Surveys taken in ensuing years indicated that many school districts across the country were ignoring these decisions, primarily in communities where the population was overwhelmingly of one religious faith and where no one was present or willing to challenge the practice.

In more recent times, however, such practices have been abandoned in most places, but sometimes they have been replaced with compulsory moments of silence during which students may pray unheard if they wish to do so. Even that practice was invalidated in one instance by the Supreme Court in 1985 because it was clear to a majority of the justices that the intent of the particular statute adopted by the Alabama state legislature in mandating the observance, as revealed by its legislative history, was to encourage students to pray.[3] Its sponsor even admitted, ungrammatically, to the district court where the case was originally tried that "No, I did not have no other purpose in mind." Since that decision it has been left to the lower courts to examine the motivation of other moment-of-silence practices, and if they are found to have a neutral purpose—that is, to allow students to pray, think about an upcoming exam, or just daydream—they have been sustained.

Nevertheless, in a case from New Jersey that the Supreme Court declined to review on jurisdictional grounds, the U.S. Court of Appeals for that region upheld a district court finding that the state's statute was unconstitutional despite its facial neutrality. The law stated as its purpose that it was to be "one minute . . . to be used solely at the discretion of the individual student . . . for quiet and private contemplation and introspection."[4] However, the district court was influenced by three witnesses of the legislative hearings, the media coverage of them, and prior attempted bills on the same subject, who testified that this law also had an "entirely religious purpose." The court of appeals felt obliged to affirm the trial court's findings because they were "not clearly erroneous." Although these may have been correct decisions from a technically legal point of view, they are ones that nonpreferentialists, not to mention equal separationists, would likely see as examples of blatantly erroneous applications of the establishment clause.

During the past quarter-century a new and more complicated set of battles over school prayer has erupted involving prayers by chaplains or students at graduation ceremonies, and student-led prayers over the public address system in the school or at football games. In 1989 one of the first such cases, denied review by the Supreme Court, involved prayers said over the public address system at high school football games in Douglas County, Georgia, where that had been a tradition since 1947. The plaintiff, Doug Jager, was a Native American. In *Jager v Douglas County School District* a panel of the U.S. Court of Appeals, by a 2-1 vote, found this practice in violation of the establishment clause.[5]

Three years later, in a Texas case, a U.S. Court of Appeals panel upheld the policy of a school district to permit student-led prayers at graduation ceremonies so long as they were nondenominational.[6] By the time an appeal of that decision reached the Supreme Court, our highest Court was in the process of handing down a landmark ruling holding that prayers said by clergymen at high school graduations violated the First Amendment. That 5-4 decision, in *Lee v Weisman,* came as a surprise to many people and led to storms of protest claiming that the Court was exiling God from the public schools.[7] Justice Anthony Kennedy, writing for the majority, argued that the practice was a "coercive" promotion of religion because dissenting students, although technically free to do so, would not want to opt out of their graduation ceremony in order to avoid being made to feel like second-class citizens. Justices O'Connor and Souter, also part of the majority, preferred to view it as an "endorsement" of religion rather than coercion, but still unconstitutional. Justice Scalia, joined by Chief Justice Rehnquist and Justices Byron White and Thomas, wrote a scathing dissent in which he criticized the Kennedy opinion as "psychobabble" that "lays waste a tradition that is as old as public school graduation ceremonies themselves." To this Justice Souter responded with a lengthy scholarly review of the history of the separation of church and state in America.

Having established this new precedent, the Court remanded the Texas case to the lower courts for reconsideration of their decision in the light of its principles. The court of appeals then reaffirmed its earlier decision, contending that it was not incompatible with the *Lee v Weisman* precedent.[8] The following year the Supreme Court declined to review that second decision.[9] Thereupon Pat Robertson's conservative American Center for Law and Justice sent 300,000 letters to school districts across the country urging them to follow the example of the Texas case and allow students to say graduation prayers. The ACLU responded with its own letter to school districts nationwide, urging its view that the Texas case had been wrongly decided and reminding them of the legally accurate fact that a Supreme Court refusal to review a lower court decision means nothing one way or the other about its validity.

Even Congress and the Clinton administration felt that they had to get in on the act. Senator Jesse Helms proposed an amendment to a federal education funding bill that would deny funds to any school that "effectively prevents" students from praying on a voluntary basis. After Helms accepted a modifying adjective proposed by Senator Edward Kennedy that limited the provision to "constitutionally protected" voluntary prayer, the amendment passed by an overwhelming 75-22 vote.[10] However, that was all superseded five months later when Senator Nancy Kassenbaum offered another amendment, which also passed, allowing for the cutting off of funds only after a *judicial* finding that it was truly constitutionally protected voluntary prayer a school was forbidding. The following year, in 1995, President Clinton made a speech at a suburban Virginia high school, explaining that students were entirely free to engage in a variety of voluntary and private religious activity in the public schools but that any endorsement of it or participation in it by school officials was prohibited by the establishment clause.[11] He then ordered the Department of Education to publish guidance on the matter, which was done the following month. The four-page set of guidelines "stressed the extent to which student-initiated prayer or proselytizing can be accommodated so long as they are not disruptive, coercive or endorsed or organized by the school or teachers."[12]

Anyone who believed that these actions would settle the issue of student-initiated prayer once and for all was to be sorely disappointed. Shortly after the *Lee v Weisman* precedent was established, a panel of the Ninth U.S. Circuit Court of Appeals, in a 2-1 vote, declared that student-led prayer at an Idaho high school graduation, like clergy-led prayer, violated the First Amendment.[13] The plaintiffs had argued that, since a majority of the students had voted to have such a prayer, the school officials had violated the free exercise of religion in prohibiting it, and were not required by the establishment clause to forbid it, as the school claimed it was obliged to do. When the plaintiffs appealed to the Supreme Court, that Court granted review and then vacated the lower court's decision with the instruction to dismiss it as moot, presumably because the student in question had already said the prayer and graduated. The court of appeals, as was its obligation, obeyed that order.[14] Thus its original decision, which had been authored for the two-person majority by former Republican Congressman Charles Wiggins, has disappeared from the books. In that decision Judge Wiggins had written: "Elected officials cannot avoid constitutional mandates by putting them to a majority vote. The decision is made by a majority of the senior class and imposed on a minority."[15]

Further, and vastly complicating this matter, was a case that arose in Jackson, Mississippi, involving a "School Prayer Statute" adopted by the Mississippi legislature in 1994. That statute provided that "on public school property . . . invocations, benedictions or nonsectarian, nonproselytizing student-initiated voluntary prayer shall be permitted during compulsory or noncompulsory school-related assemblies, sporting events, graduation . . . and other school-related student events."[16] This law had been passed in response to an event at Jackson's high school where students had voted 490-96 to have students say a prayer each morning over the school's public address system. The principal had allowed it, and his superiors had suspended him for violating their policy against it. Pursuant to those occurrences, the executive director of the Mississippi ACLU, David Ingebretsen, who had a daughter in the school, filed a lawsuit challenging the law. A panel of the Fifth U.S. Circuit Court of Appeals, the same circuit in which the Texas practice of student-led prayer at graduations had been upheld, struck down the Mississippi law.[17] By a vote of 9-6 the entire circuit court refused to grant a rehearing *en banc,* and the U.S. Supreme Court also denied review.[18] Thus left standing were two seemingly contradictory decisions of the Fifth Circuit, one allowing student-led prayer at graduations but the other disallowing it over the school's intercom system.

No longer seeing fit to avoid the issue, the U.S. Supreme Court finally came to grips with it in 2000 with its 6-3 decision in *Santa Fe* [Texas] *Independent School District v Doe*.[19] Here again were student-led prayers for which a majority of the students had voted, but being said over the school's public address system at the opening of football games rather than when school was in session. The Court rejected the claim that this was constitutionally distinguishable from the clergy-led prayers at graduation that it had invalidated eight years previously. Admitting that students who would be offended by the prayers might avoid going to football games more willingly than skip their graduation ceremony, the Court pointed out that those events are still school-sponsored functions on school property. As for the argument that the saying of these prayers was student-led, and occurred only as the result of a majority vote of the student body, the Court replied that school officials were still involved in conducting the election, and that although "a majoritarian election might ensure that most of the students are represented, it does nothing to protect the minority. Indeed, it likely serves to intensify their offense." Illustrating the insensitivity of those who fail to appreciate this point, as well as the staying power of the "Christian America" mythology, was an eighteen-year-old high school senior in Alabama. After a federal court there had invalidated that state's law allowing student-led nonproselytizing, he complained: "Everyone around here is God-believing. Everyone around here believes in Jesus Christ, as far as I know. Having Jesus in our schools is something that we need. It gives us strength."[20]

Chief Justice Rehnquist's dissent in the *Santa Fe* case, joined by Justices Scalia and Thomas, was far less impassioned than Justice Scalia's had been in *Lee v Weisman*, but still reflected his nonpreferential leanings. Conceding the possibility that an "election could lead to a Christian prayer before ninety percent of the football games," he argued that that had not happened in this instance and that "If, upon implementation, the policy operated in this fashion . . . it will be time enough to invalidate it if that is found to be the case."

Interestingly, in the fall football season following the Court's ruling, a Texas group calling themselves "No Pray No Play" vowed to bring ten thousand Christians to Santa Fe to pray out loud in the grandstands before the game, which would, of course, have been their constitutional right. Only a handful showed up, however, and even they were drowned out by the loudspeaker's announcement of the arrival of one of the teams onto the field.[21]

The last wrinkle in this unfolding set of cases that we will consider here appears in two cases that arose in states governed by the Eleventh U.S. Circuit Court of Appeals. The first was in DeKalb County, Alabama, where a federal district court had issued a very broad injunction against religious speech by students in any sort of public context within the school on the assumption that it would be perceived as school-endorsed. The Eleventh Circuit Court of Appeals then unanimously vacated the injunction.[22] That decision was appealed to the Supreme Court, which accepted it for review, but then, after deciding the *Santa Fe* case, the justices remanded it to the lower court for reconsideration in the light of the new precedent. Thereupon the Eleventh Circuit reaffirmed its original decision and the Supreme Court declined review.[23] The circuit court reasoned that the original district court injunction "eliminated any possibility of *private* student religious speech under any circumstances other than silently or behind closed doors." The court continued: "So long as the prayer is *genuinely student-initiated,* and not the product of any school policy which actively or surreptitiously encourages it, the speech is private and protected." There was one caveat, however. In view of the fact that the district court had a "great deal of information concerning prior actions of school personnel indicating a majoritarian purpose to foster one particular religion," a monitor was appointed to assure that this would not continue. The court of appeals said it assumed that the school would now act in conformity with the nonestablishment principle, and that if it did not the monitor would call that to the attention of the district court.[24]

The second case originated in Duval County, Florida, where a public school policy allowed students to decide by majority vote whether they wanted to have any students speak at graduation and who would speak. Once chosen, such speakers were free to make either secular or religious statements, including prayers, if that is what they wished to do. The Eleventh Circuit, in an *en banc* ruling, affirmed a district court decision that this practice did not violate the establishment clause because there was no school involvement in it. Instead, those courts believed that such student behavior was simply an example of the free exercise of religion.[25]

On appeal, the Supreme Court, as it had done in the DeKalb case, remanded the circuit court decision for reconsideration in the light of the *Santa Fe* case.[26] As in the DeKalb case, the circuit court reaffirmed its earlier ruling, finding no inconsistency between it and the *Santa Fe* decision.[27] When this went back once more to the Supreme Court, that Court, again as in the DeKalb case, declined review.[28]

Pledging Allegiance to the Flag

Among the religious beliefs of Jehovah's Witnesses is a literal interpretation of a Bible passage in Exodus which commands that "Thou shalt not make unto thee any graven image . . . thou shalt not bow down thyself to them nor serve them." They regard the flag as such an image and therefore will not participate in any flag salute ritual. In the early 1940s the Minersville School District of West Virginia was requiring all of its teachers and students to salute the flag in a daily exercise. When the children of the Gobitis family, ages ten and twelve, were expelled from school for refusing to participate, their parents sued in federal court for a violation of religious freedom. After the district court and court of appeals ruled in their favor, the school district appealed to the Supreme Court, which reversed those decisions.[29] The majority argued that the guarantees of the First Amendment are not absolutes, but may be subject to "what society thinks necessary for the promotion of some great common end, or . . . which appears dangerous to the general good." They then asserted that the "religious liberty which the Constitution protects has never excluded legislation of general scope not directed against doctrinal loyalties of particular sects."

Following that decision the State Board of Education adopted a resolution requiring all the public schools of the state to include the flag salute ritual as part of their program of activities. Children's failure to conform would be dealt with by expulsion until they complied, and during their absence they could be prosecuted for delinquency! Again Jehovah's Witnesses filed a lawsuit, but this time with much greater success, winning their case by a 6-3 vote of the Supreme Court.[30] What had happened to cause the high court, in the course of merely three years, to reverse itself so dramatically? For infrequently does the Supreme Court reject its prior precedents, and rarely, if ever, after so few years have passed. It was due in part to a change in personnel and in part to a change of minds. Justice Stone, who had been the lone dissenter in *Minersville,* had been promoted to chief justice, and two of the justices in the majority had retired and been replaced, one of them by the persuasive and articulate Justice Jackson. Since three of the other members of the *Minersville* majority were still there and dissented from the *Barnette* decision, that left two other members of the earlier majority, Justices Black and Douglas, who had changed their position.

The newly appointed Justice Jackson wrote the *Barnette* opinion for the Court's six-person majority, and it is one of the most eloquent and frequently quoted statements in First Amendment jurisprudence. Among other precedent-setting principles, the Court asserted that it was not just the free exercise of religion that was at stake in the case, but freedom of speech as well, since the latter encompasses a freedom "not to speak." That would apply to nonbelievers as well. This was the Court's first unequivocal acknowledgement of a "right of silence" under the First Amendment. It also illustrates the point made earlier in this book about the close nexus between the free exercise of religion and freedom of speech.

Another major principle enunciated by the Jackson opinion was as follows:

> there is no doubt that, in connection with the pledges, the flag salute is a form of utterance. Symbolism is a primitive but effective way of communicating ideas. The use of an emblem or flag to symbolize some system, idea, institution, or personality, is a short cut from mind to mind.

That principle has served as the basis for many later Supreme Court decisions involving what we now call nonverbal communication, including not only flags but draft cards, crosses, and a wide variety of other nonlinguistic symbolic behavior. It was also, for its time, an unusually sophisticated understanding of what the processes of communication are all about.

Finally, there were these eloquent words by Justice Jackson about the limits of majoritarianism and the rights of minorities:

> If there is any fixed star in our constitutional constellation, it is that no official, high or petty, can prescribe what shall be orthodox in politics, nationalism, religion, or other matters of opinion or force citizens to confess by word or act their faith therein. . . . Those who begin coercive elimination of dissent soon find themselves eliminating dissenters. Compulsory unification of opinion achieves only the unanimity of the graveyard.
>
> It seems trite but necessary to say that the First Amendment to our Constitution was designed to avoid these ends by avoiding these beginnings.

The dissenting opinion in the *Barnette* case was a lengthy lecture on judicial restraint by Justice Felix Frankfurter, a statement that has also served as ammunition for those who advocate strict limits on judicial review. He confessed his own discomfort with the state's having imposed this particular requirement on a minority religion, but he believed that a nonelected Supreme Court should refrain from invalidating the laws of the democratically elected representatives of the people in state legislatures and the Congress unless their acts clearly violated the Constitution. He did not think this was such a case. Frankfurter's view about the appropriate relationship of the judicial and legislative branches of government was in the tradition of famous earlier justices like Oliver Wendell Holmes and Louis Brandeis and has an advocate on the present Supreme Court in the person of Justice Stephen Breyer.[31]

In contrast to Justice Frankfurter's consistent view in the two flag salute cases, Justice Black explained for himself and Justice Douglas their change of mind as follows:

> Reluctance to make the Federal Constitution a rigid bar against state regulation of conduct thought inimical to the public welfare was the controlling influence which moved us to concur to the *Gobitis* decision. Long reflection convinced us that although the principle is sound, its application in this particular case was wrong.

After-School Religious Club Meetings

In many communities across the nation, the auditorium of a public school is one of the few places, if not the only place, large enough or sufficiently convenient to accommodate meetings of large groups of people. Being public facilities, they can be made available, if the board of education so chooses, for rental or even free use to community groups when school is not in session. When they are thus made accessible they are considered by our courts to be "limited public forums," not "traditional public forums" like the public sidewalks, streets, and parks, which the Supreme Court has said must be open without discrimination to everyone.[32] As "limited public forums," whether an auditorium or classroom, their governing body may decide to allow their use for some purposes and groups and not others if this is done in a reasonable and viewpoint-neutral manner and the activity is open to the public on a nonexclusive basis.[33] For example, the privilege to use the facilities may be extended to groups for educational, recreational, entertainment, or athletic purposes but not for political or religious gatherings. They may, in other words, engage in what the Court has called "content" but not "viewpoint" discrimination.

If usage for religious purposes is permitted by the board of education's policy, this immediately raises the question as to whether that kind of indirect government support violates the establishment clause of the First Amendment. On the other hand, a refusal to allow facilities to be used for religious purposes, if all other kinds of usages are permitted, may be seen as hostility to, if not a violation of, the free-exercise-of-religion clause. Allowing such usage is not generally seen as an establishment problem if, for instance, a local church burns down and its congregation uses the school auditorium on a temporary basis while a new church facility is being built, or if occasional meetings by religiously oriented groups are held in class-room spaces. If those arrangements become permanent, however, some doubt about their constitutional propriety may arise, since the support for religion that is involved becomes so much more extensive.

The Supreme Court has made it absolutely clear in a unanimous deci-sion that if a school allows the use of its after-hours space for a particular subject matter it may not then disallow a meeting which proposes to ad-dress that subject from a religious standpoint. In that particular case the school had refused permission for an evangelical church group to show to primarily adult audiences a film series dealing with family issues and child-rearing, an otherwise allowable subject under the school's policy, because the films would be doing so from a religious point of view. The Court held that this was impermissible viewpoint discrimination.[34]

The Supreme Court had gone even further in an earlier case involving a state university, the University of Missouri at Kansas City, when it held that even though the school had discretion whether to limit the use of its facilities or not, once it had opened its forum for general use by all recog-nized student groups it could not engage even in content-based discrimina-tion without demonstrating a "compelling interest" in doing so.[35] The requirement of such a showing in order to place limits on First Amend-ment rights is known as a standard of "strict scrutiny." In a footnote to that Missouri *Widmar v Vincent* decision the Court also suggested the caveat that university students are less impressionable than younger children and therefore fully capable of appreciating that the mere fact of allowing a reli-gious meeting on campus did not imply the school's endorsement of that or any other kind of religion.

Three years after *Widmar,* Congress adopted "The Equal Access Act of 1984," which essentially made the principles of that decision applicable to public secondary schools. The law provided that *if* a high school permitted any non-curriculum-related extracurricular clubs to use its facilities after school, they could not discriminate on the basis of either their content or viewpoint, so long as a club was voluntary, student-initiated, did not in-volve employees of the school or government in a participatory manner, and was not conducted or controlled by non-school persons. A legal chal-lenge to that law reached the Supreme Court six years later, where it was upheld on the same basis as that used in the Missouri case.[36] As a result of that decision some high schools have eliminated *all* non-curriculum-

related after-hours clubs so that they will not have to allow student groups
espousing racist or bizarre cultish doctrines to meet in the building. Such
abolition does not apply to curriculum-related extracurricular activities,
like the work of the staff of the student newspaper, rehearsals for plays, or
meetings of a debate club.

No one could have guessed how much more complicated the issue could
still get. This occurred in the 1990s as a result of the activities of a Christian evangelical organization called the Good News Clubs, which sought access to elementary schools for the purpose of proselytizing children from
the ages of six to twelve. Many school districts, including Milford Central
in the state of New York, and Ladue, Missouri, a suburb of St. Louis, denied
their requests for classroom space immediately after school because outside
adult leaders would lead prayers, read Bible passages, give the children
candy for reciting Bible verses, and "invite" the "unsaved" children "to
trust the Lord Jesus to be your savior from sin." Good News challenged
those exclusions in federal court, claiming that the schools had violated
their freedom of speech. The argument of the schools, of course, was that
to allow such activities would violate the establishment clause and that excluding them was permissible under the "limited public forum" principle.

In the Milford case the district court issued a preliminary injunction that
enabled the club to meet at the school for about a year, but then vacated
that injunction and granted the school's motion for summary judgment to
exclude them.[37] The Second U.S. Circuit Court of Appeals sustained that
ruling in favor of the school,[38] but the Eighth Circuit decided in favor of
the Good News Club in Ladue.[39] The Supreme Court granted review to the
Milford case in order to resolve the difference between the two circuits,
and in 2001, by a 6-3 vote, the Court reversed the Second Circuit, thus giving a victory to the Good News Clubs.[40]

However, the facts in the Milford case were not only very complicated
but also incomplete, because both of the lower courts had decided it in a
summary manner. Therefore, there had never been a trial in which the
missing information could have been more thoroughly explored, and that
was a major objection to the majority's decision by the dissenting Supreme
Court justices. Facts that were clear, nevertheless, were as follows: (1) That
the school had a policy, allowed by state law, that permitted its facilities to
be used after school for educational instruction, the arts, and for civic,
recreational, and entertainment purposes "pertaining to the welfare of the
community"; (2) That the Boy Scouts, Girl Scouts, and 4-H Clubs had been
permitted to hold meetings in the school; and (3) That the school included

under the permitted purposes the teaching of "morals and character development to children," even from a "religious perspective." What was offered
as the basis for rejecting the application of the Good News Club was that
they admittedly would be conducting "religious instruction" or proselytizing, and that these fell "outside the limits of pure 'moral and character
development.'"

The Supreme Court majority's primary rationale for ruling in favor of
the Good News Club was that the school had, indeed, violated their freedom of speech by engaging in "viewpoint discrimination." Since the school
policy permitted other groups meeting in its facilities to discuss moral and
character development from a religious *perspective* it was discriminatory to
deny Good News the right to engage in religious *instruction*. "We disagree,"
the majority said, "that something that is 'quintessentially religious' or 'decidedly religious in nature' [phrases used by the lower courts] cannot also
be characterized properly as the teaching of morals and character development from a particular point of view."

The majority also rejected the school's argument that granting access for
meetings of the Good News Club would constitute a violation of the establishment clause. Since parents had to give permission for their children to
attend the club's meetings, the Court saw no risk of the children going because of peer pressure. Furthermore, since the meetings were to be held
after school hours, were not sponsored by the school, and were led by out-
siders, there was no danger that they would be perceived by either the parents or the children as endorsed by the school administration. On the
contrary, the majority argued that to disallow the meetings could be seen
as hostility to religion, and thus a violation of the government neutrality
required by the establishment clause.

In response, the dissenting justices saw no viewpoint discrimination in
the school's permitting the teaching about morals from a religious perspective but disallowing the conduct of proselytizing worship services. As to the
peer pressure and perception of endorsement issues, all three dissenters
objected vigorously to the lack of a fully developed record from the lower
courts as to the facts about these establishment questions. The dissent of
Justice Souter, speaking for himself and Justice Ginsburg, pointed out
these differences between the Milford situation and previous precedents in
which decisions went against the schools: (1) The audience here would be
six- to twelve-year-olds rather than either the high school students covered by the Equal Access Act of Congress or the "less impressionable"
young adults at the University of Missouri; (2) School let out at 2:54 P.M.

and Good News meetings began promptly at 3 P.M., following "regular school activities so closely that the Good News instructors must wait to begin until 'the room is clear' and 'people are out of the room,'" whereas the Scouts and 4-H Club met later in the afternoon; (3) When meetings had previously been held in a community church, only eight to ten children had attended, whereas that number had tripled during the year the school was the meeting site, thus suggesting that peer pressure or the physical convenience of the public school building might have been influential. Interestingly, one of the solutions suggested by some of the school administrators who found the majority's decision troublesome has been to require *any* outside groups that meet in the school building to do so only after 4:30 or 5:00 P.M., or in the evening, as had been the case in the showing of religious films to an adult audience.

Justice Stevens, writing his own separate dissent, tried to draw finer lines than any of the other justices between and among the kinds of religious speech that must be allowed and those that may be excluded. He then asserted what must be considered the greatest understatement of the day when he wrote: "This case is undoubtedly close."

We should not leave this topic without a brief look at what has now presumably become past history but was once a lively issue that is relevant here. During the 1940s and 1950s it was a practice of public schools in some communities to release from the last period of classes those students who, with parental permission, wished to attend weekly religious education courses conducted by nonschool personnel in another classroom of the same school building. The rest of the students would remain in their regular classroom or study hall, doing work that apparently was considered nonessential for their departed peers.

Vashti McCollum was an atheist living in Champaign, Illinois, whose child was enrolled in a school that had such a "released time" program. That program applied to the fourth through ninth grades, and included classes conducted separately by a Protestant leader, a Catholic priest, and a Jewish rabbi. Ms. McCollum filed a lawsuit against the practice and won her challenge by an 8-1 vote of the U.S. Supreme Court.[41] The Court strongly rejected the argument that because the program did not prefer one religion over another, providing equally for Protestants, Catholics, and Jews, it did not violate the establishment clause. The justices reminded school officials that the state is also forbidden by the establishment clause to prefer religion over nonreligion or to assist religious education generally.

Here was a clear example of the *Everson* rationale prevailing over a possible nonpreferentialist ruling.

The *McCollum* decision met with vehement public protests from religious leaders, who claimed it was impermissibly hostile toward religion. Four years later, whether influenced by those protests or not we cannot know, the Supreme Court backed off considerably from the *McCollum* decision. This time the released-time program at issue was conducted off the school premises. However, attendance was still monitored by the school to insure that the students would not simply be playing hooky during the last period of classes. A majority of six justices of the Supreme Court, although admitting that keeping track of attendance involved some entanglement between church and state, viewed permission to leave class and the school building with parental consent for religious education as essentially no different from not penalizing students who stay out of school for a day for the observance of religious holidays, like the Jewish Yom Kippur or a Catholic Holy Day of Obligation.[42]

The three dissenting justices took the position that despite the distinctions the majority tried to draw, this ruling simply could not be reconciled with the principles enunciated by the *McCollum* precedent. For them this was not even a "close case."

The Teaching of Evolution

The struggle over the teaching of Charles Darwin's theory of evolution in the public schools of America began with a dramatic incident in the small town of Dayton, Tennessee, about forty miles from Chattanooga. That story is not only in all of our history books but was dramatized by a now-classic stage play, "Inherit the Wind," later made into a popular movie.

It started when the secretary in the New York headquarters of the relatively newborn ACLU called to the attention of its executive director, Roger Baldwin, a newspaper clipping reporting the adoption in Tennessee of a law prohibiting the teaching of evolution in the state's public schools and universities. Baldwin immediately placed an ad in the *Chattanooga News*, offering to pay the expenses of anyone willing to test the constitutionality of that law.

John Scopes, who had graduated from the University of Kentucky in 1924, was hired that fall by the Rhea County Central High School in Dayton to coach their football team and teach algebra, chemistry, and physics. Yet he was also called upon, during his first year, to fill in temporarily in the biology course when its regular teacher, who was also the school principal, was ill. The textbook he used, which had been adopted by the state textbook commission six years earlier, contained an exposition of the theory of evolution.

Shortly after Baldwin's ad appeared, Scopes received a call from Fred Robinson, a pharmacist who owned Robinson's Drug Store, the social gathering place of the town. Robinson also happened to be chairman of the Rhea County School Board. He asked Scopes to come down to the drugstore to meet with a small group that included George Rappelyea, a local businessman who was eager to promote the local economy by garnering as much publicity for the town as he could. Robinson showed Scopes Baldwin's ad and asked if he would be willing to be the defendant in a test case of the new Tennessee law. Scopes said yes, and Robinson immediately went to the phone, called the *Chattanooga News,* and said, "I'm chairman of the school board here, and we've just arrested a man for teaching evolution." George Rappelyea then called the ACLU and got a promise that they would handle Scopes's defense. The story was picked up by the Associated Press and became national front-page news.[43]

To enhance the event's publicity potential, Rappelyea also sent a telegram to William Jennings Bryan, three-time presidential candidate and the country's most well known religious fundamentalist, asking him to enter the case for the prosecution, which he eagerly agreed to do. Meanwhile Chicago attorney Clarence Darrow, almost as well known, volunteered his services to the ACLU as an attorney for the defense. Darrow's flamboyant style and controversial career made Roger Baldwin and some of his colleagues a bit wary of using him, and they sounded out the more dignified and respectable Charles Evans Hughes, former Republican presidential candidate and later chief justice of the Supreme Court, and John W. Davis, former Democratic presidential candidate, as possible alternatives. Yet the ACLU's top legal officer, Arthur Garfield Hays, who himself participated in the case, wanted Darrow, as did Scopes, and that settled the matter.[44]

The most dramatic episode in that trial, highlighted in both play and film, was when Darrow got Bryan to take the witness stand and proceeded to make him the laughing stock of the nation by his withering examination of Bryan's simplistic and sometimes inconsistent literal interpretations of biblical passages. Thoroughly humiliated, as well as already vastly overweight and no doubt also suffering from the deadly August heat in Dayton that had forced the trial to be moved out of doors, Bryan died a week later.

What is less widely realized about the Scopes trial is that Darrow and his colleagues lost the case in the Dayton court. Scopes was found guilty by the jury and fined $100 by the judge. The law against the teaching of evolution remained untouched. The Tennessee Supreme Court did eventually overturn the conviction but solely on the technicality that under Tennessee law only a jury, not a judge, could impose a fine of more than $50. It was not until more than four decades later that the U.S. Supreme Court, in the case of *Epperson v Arkansas,* decided that such statutes were unconstitutional.[45] Yet the issue had been raised, and the battle for public opinion successfully begun, by twenty-five-year-old John Scopes and the ACLU, back in 1925.

Arkansas, like Tennessee, had adopted a statute in the mid-1920s that made it unlawful for a teacher in any public school or state university "to teach the theory or doctrine that mankind ascended or descended from a lower order of animals." However, effective for the 1965–66 school year, the Little Rock Central High School, on the recommendation of its biology teachers, had adopted a new textbook for the biology courses that, unlike the previous texts that had been used, included a chapter on evolution. This was the school, incidentally, that later became the site of a famous school desegregation battle between then-Governor George Wallace and the U.S. Department of Justice. Susan Epperson had begun teaching biology at Little Rock Central in 1964. Concerned that using the new textbook, which she wanted to do, might subject her to criminal punishment under the state law, she initiated a lawsuit to test the statute's constitutionality. A decision of the Arkansas Supreme Court upholding the law was appealed to the Supreme Court, which unanimously overturned that ruling.[46] The Court declared:

> Arkansas' law cannot be defended as an act of religious neutrality. Arkansas did not seek to excise from the curricula of its schools and universities all discussion of the origin of man. The law's effort was confined to an attempt to blot out a particular theory because of its supposed conflict with the Biblical account, literally read. Plainly, the law is contrary to the mandate of the First, and in violation of the Fourteenth, Amendment to the Constitution.

Fervent believers in the biblical story of creation, to whom the theory of evolution is anathema, are not ones to abandon their cause lightly. Frustrated by the unequivocal message of the Supreme Court that they could not succeed in banning evolution from the public schools, they decided to go for half a loaf. First in Arkansas, and then in Louisiana, creationist legislators introduced, and were successful in getting adopted, laws to require that if and when evolution was taught in the public schools of the state it had to be "balanced" by the presentation of an alternative theory they called "creation science." That theory had been developed and promoted by an Institute for Creation Research, an affiliate of the Christian Heritage College in San Diego, California, and the Creation Research Society, in Ann Arbor, Michigan. Members of the latter organization had to subscribe to the statement that "the bible is the written word of God, and because it is inspired throughout, all of its assertions are historically and scientifically true." The proponents of the legislation claimed that there was substantial scientific evidence to support creationism and that the gaps in the theory of evolution rendered that theory suspect. It was only fair and in the interest of academic freedom, they argued, to give "equal time" to creationism.

Quickly after the adoption of the Arkansas law, a coalition of mainstream religious organizations and prominent scientists, organized by the ACLU, filed suit against it in federal court. After a lengthy and expensive trial, the district court judge declared the statute to be in violation of the First Amendment.[47] In a strongly worded opinion based heavily on the testimony of the witnesses at the trial, he found that so-called creation science was more religion than it was science, and the attempt to impose it on the public schools flew in the face of the establishment clause. He said of the statute that its "concepts and wording . . . convey an inescapable religiosity," and that its ideas were "not merely similar to the literal interpretation of Genesis; they are identical and parallel to no other story of creation." The state's attorney general, who had never been a supporter of the law although obliged to defend it at trial, decided it would be futile to appeal this decision.

Meanwhile, a similar trial was about to take place in a Louisiana federal district court, challenging that state's "Balanced Treatment for Creation-Science and Evolution-Science in Public School Instruction" statute. The district court, the circuit court of appeals, and finally the Supreme Court all held the law to be in violation of the establishment clause of the First Amendment. They found that it did not truly further its alleged secular purpose of "protecting academic freedom," which they viewed as a sham, but rather that it had the primary purpose of advancing religion.[48] Only Chief Justice Rehnquist and Justice Scalia dissented from the Court's decision. They did so because they believed that the Court should have accepted at face value the claim that the legislature had a secular purpose in adopting the law. This was despite the fact that the bill's sponsor, state senator Bill Keith, had said during the legislative hearings, "My preference would be that neither [creation nor evolution] be taught."

Except for occasional efforts to get local school boards to eliminate the use of textbooks that discuss evolution, the anti-evolution advocates remained relatively quiescent for a number of years after the Supreme Court's *Edwards v Aguillard* ruling in 1987. However, in 2002 a new movement came upon the scene. Called the Intelligent Design Network, the group seeks to obtain "equal time" for their view of the creation of the earth, just as the creationists had tried unsuccessfully to do. A *New York Times* story reported that they were able to obtain a hearing before the Ohio State Board of Education in March 2002.[49] The report continued:

> Supporters of this theory acknowledge that the earth is billions of years old, not thousands, as a literal reading of the Bible suggests. They also accept that organisms change over time, according to commonly held principles of evolution. But they dispute the idea that the astounding complexity of the earth's plants and animals could just have happened through natural selection, the force that Darwin suggested drives evolution. An intelligent designer—perhaps the God of Genesis, perhaps someone or something else—had to get the ball rolling, they contend. . . . Opponents of intelligent design view it as a sophisticated version of the decades-old effort to force theism into the public schools.
>
> "It's a shrouded way of bringing religion into the schools," said Martha W. Wise, a state board member who is the lone opponent of intelligent design on the standards subcommittee. "Personally, I'm creationist. I believe in God the Father, Almighty, creator of heaven and earth," said Ms. Wise, a retired business executive. She emphasized, however, that her belief had no place in a science lesson. "I think intelligent design is a theology, and it belongs in another curriculum."
>
> "Intelligent design is a repackaging of the anti-evolution movement to try to withstand court challenges by avoiding the C-word," said Dr. Eugene Scott, executive director of the National Center for Science Education in Oakland, Calif., which promotes the teaching of evolution.

Religious Expression by School Officials

Drawing a line between the free exercise of religious expression and violations of the establishment clause by public school teachers and administrations is often quite difficult and is frequently perceived by members of the majority religious group in a community as making petty distinctions. Some kinds of religious expression by teachers and other school officials are rather clearly not violations of the separation of church and state, but others may come close to crossing the line, or actually do so.

It is generally accepted, for example, that teachers, even though they are in a position of authority and may be influential role models, may wear small symbols of their religious affiliation, like necklaces with the Christian cross or Jewish Star of David, as part of their personal mode of dress. Presumably such means of religious expression are no more likely to be viewed by their students as endorsed by the state than if they express a political opinion, though teachers of very young children should generally be cautious about doing the latter.

The wearing of more predominantly religious garb, however, has been seriously problematic. Catholic nuns, for example, who have taught in public as well as parochial schools in many parts of the country, had historically worn their religious habits in the public school classrooms, as they always did elsewhere in the past. As early as 1906 that practice was found by New York's highest court to be impermissible.[50] In New Mexico, until the middle of the twentieth century, not only did nuns wear their religious garb to class in several counties of the state but the public schools were staffed *entirely* by nuns, who also led prayers and gave religious instruction. The New Mexico Supreme Court eventually put an end to the operation of that system.[51]

In a case in Oregon, a Sikh teacher refused, when so ordered, to stop wearing white clothing and a white turban. She was suspended from her job on the basis of an Oregon statute prohibiting the wearing of religious garb by public school teachers while on duty. She challenged that action in court and lost the case. The Supreme Court of Oregon upheld the law's requirement if and when it was applied to "wearing religious dress as a regular and frequently repeated practice while teaching."[52] The U.S. Supreme Court dismissed an appeal.[53]

Finally, there were three cases in Pennsylvania on the same issue. The earliest court decision, back in 1894, held that the wearing of religious garb did *not* constitute prohibited "sectarian teaching."[54] The state legislature thereupon enacted a statute prohibiting the practice, and that law was upheld by the Pennsylvania Supreme Court against an argument that it constituted a "religious test."[55] Most recently, in a much more complicated Philadelphia case, a substitute teacher who was a devout Muslim covered her entire body, except for her hands and face. She claimed that a provision of Title VII of the 1964 federal Civil Rights Act required her employer, as it does all employers, to accommodate the free exercise of religion unless it imposes an "undue hardship" on the employer. She was supported in her claim to be allowed to wear her garb by the federal Equal Opportunity Employment Commission and the U.S. Department of Justice, who represented her cause in court. Nevertheless a three-judge panel of the Third U.S. Circuit Court of Appeals held that requiring the school district to accommodate this particular kind of religious expression would, indeed, impose an "undue hardship" on them and that they were thus entitled to enforce a policy that was, after all, authorized by state law.[56] An *en banc* hearing by the full court was denied and the decision was not appealed to the Supreme Court.

We have already discussed in the previous chapter the issue of Good Friday as a school as well as a local or state holiday, noting there that a circuit court of appeals, as recently as 1999, upheld a Maryland state law providing for school holidays on Good Friday, and that the Supreme Court declined to review that decision. What was not mentioned at that point was that this practice continues to be viewed by some as a questionable kind of accommodation to religion. One such critic is the highly respected and conservative chief judge of the Seventh U.S. Circuit Court of Appeals and former University of Chicago law professor, Richard Posner.

Judge Posner had written an opinion for that circuit in 1995, also denied review by the Supreme Court, that struck down a fifty-year-old state law mandating the closing of the state's public schools on Good Friday.[57] He said of the statute that the state "has accorded special recognition to Christianity beyond anything that has been shown to be necessary to accommodate the religious needs of the Christian majority." He went on to point out that "Christmas and Thanksgiving have accreted secular rituals, such as shopping, and eating turkey with cranberry sauce. . . . Likewise with Easter egg hunts for children, not to mention photo sessions with the Easter Bunny. Good Friday has accreted no secular rituals."

Finally, and perhaps most difficult of all the issues of religious observances by school officials, is the common practice of devoting one of the regular all-school assemblies just prior to the Christmas break to observing the season by singing Christmas carols. These may include everything from "Jingle Bells" and "Deck the Halls with Boughs of Holly" to "Silent Night." The problem from an establishment of religion point of view is that "Silent Night" includes the lines "Round yon virgin mother and child, Holy Infant so tender and mild," and "Christ our Savior is born," whereas "Jingle Bells" refers only to riding a one-horse sleigh. Requiring that the former be excluded from school assemblies while allowing the others strikes many as being picayune. Yet anyone who has been raised in the Jewish, Muslim, or Buddhist faith, or is an agnostic or atheist, is likely to testify that they feel like shriveling up when those words are sung. That is one of the reasons, among many, why the drawing of lines that may seem petty to some can be of paramount importance in a society that cherishes a secular state.

Textbook and Library Censorship

We must begin this section by describing a case that is about religious expression only in an attenuated sense. Yet it is the only word we have had from the U.S. Supreme Court on the subject of schoolbook censorship, and even then there is no majority opinion on which to rely.[58] That is because one of the five justices on the prevailing side, Justice White, concurred only in the decision to send the case back for trial to a district court where the judge had simply rendered a summary judgment. Justice White did not accept any of the plurality opinion, written by Justice Brennan, that was agreed to in whole or in part by the three other prevailing justices. To further complicate matters, each of the four dissenters wrote his or her own opinion, only two of which were agreed to by other dissenters.

The case essentially raised a freedom-of-speech issue, initiated by a group of students led by Steven Pico, who challenged an action by their school board in removing nine books from the school library because the board members viewed them as "anti-American, anti-Christian, anti-Semitic, and just plain filthy." The list included Kurt Vonnegut's *Slaughterhouse Five*, Bernard Malamud's *The Fixer*, Richard Wright's *Black Boy*, Eldridge Cleaver's *Soul on Ice*, Piri Thomas's *Down These Mean Streets*, Alice Childress's *A Hero Ain't Nothin' But a Sandwich*, Desmond Morris's *The Naked Ape*, and *Best Short Stories by Negro Writers*, edited by Langston Hughes. Besides the obvious prominence of African American writers and subject matter on the list, *The Naked Ape* is a zoologist's discussion of the development of humans from earlier forms of animal life (shades of the struggle over evolution).

Pico and his group of plaintiffs claimed that the school board's action violated their First Amendment right to receive ideas—a right described in Justice Brennan's plurality opinion as one that "is a necessary predicate to the *recipient's* meaningful exercise of his own rights of speech, press, and political freedom." Yet the district court ruled in favor of the school board without holding a trial on the merits of that claim. The judge had concluded, according to Justice Brennan's opinion, that it was within the school board's "broad discretion to formulate educational policy," and that the courts "should not intervene in 'the daily operation of the school systems' unless 'basic constitutional values' were 'sharply implicated.'" Curiously, that judge did not think such values were sufficiently involved to hear the students out.

A panel of the U.S. Circuit Court of Appeals reversed the district court and sent the case back for a trial, but, seeking to avoid that eventuality, the school board appealed the circuit court's ruling to the Supreme Court. A majority of the justices agreed with the court of appeals that a trial should be held and remanded the case for that purpose. At that point, however, the school board threw in the towel and allowed the books to go back on the library shelves.

Perhaps the members of the board feared that the nonbinding guidance provided to the lower courts by Justice Brennan's plurality opinion would undermine their position, for he had said that although school boards do have broad discretion to "transmit community values" to their students, they may not exercise that discretion "in a narrowly partisan or political manner." Presumably religious beliefs, and surely racism, would be included in one of those prohibited categories. If, on the other hand, their motivation for removing books was because they lacked "educational suitability" or were "pervasively vulgar," that, in the Supreme Court's plurality view, would be constitutionally permissible. Such questions of motivation could be determined only by a trial on the facts.

Justice White, who had provided the fifth vote for sending the case back down for trial, said he could not support the plurality opinion because he believed it was "premature . . . to issue a dissertation on the extent to which the First Amendment limits the discretion of the school board to remove books from the school library."

Chief Justice Burger, in the only dissenting opinion joined by all the other dissenters, objected entirely to the idea of submitting the question as to what books are to be in a school library to federal court review. "Were this to become law," he wrote, "this Court would come perilously close to becoming a 'super censor' of school board library decisions."

Although the religious beliefs of the school board members arguably may have played only a subsidiary role in the *Pico* case, the views expressed by Supreme Court justices concerning the discretion of school boards in making decisions about schoolbooks, and the limits imposed on that discretion by the First Amendment, have important implications for the cases we are about to consider. Because the Supreme Court has chosen not to review any of the multitude of lower court decisions on this subject, whether involving freedom of speech, the free exercise of religion, or the establishment clause, we will settle here for a small sampling of them to learn the kinds of arguments and pressures that may be involved.

In Hawkins County, Tennessee, a fundamentalist group of families requested that the public school not expose their children to certain reading materials that they found objectionable because that material taught about making one's own moral judgments, tolerance for other people's religious views, and critical thinking skills. The books to which they objected were a Holt, Rinehart, and Winston Reading Series for young people. They asked that their children be exempted not only from reading these materials but also from hearing them discussed in class. When their children were suspended from school for refusing to engage in those activities, the group brought suit against the school board, claiming that their free exercise of religion had been violated.

A federal district court judge ordered that they be allowed to "opt out" of those activities without penalty, but that decision was reversed by the U.S. Circuit Court of Appeals.[59] The latter court held that the free exercise of religion is not burdened by requiring children to be exposed to possibly disagreeable ideas. The appellate court noted that the parents could, if they found what the public school was doing too objectionable, educate the children at home, which was permitted by state law, or send them to a private school. The decision also commented that a school cannot accomplish educational objectives if it is required to become a "cafeteria" of choices. The Supreme Court declined to review that decision.

In Alabama, a district court judge by the name of Brevard Hand had achieved some national notoriety when he expressed the view that the U.S. Supreme Court was flatly wrong in making the establishment clause of the First Amendment applicable to the states.[60] Nevertheless, four years later he banned forty-four history, social studies, and economics textbooks from the public schools in his district because he said that they taught the "religion" of "secular humanism" in violation of that very same establishment clause.[61] He obviously accepted the Supreme Court's power as final arbiter of constitutional interpretation, but apparently also enjoyed the opportunity in this particular case to turn it to his advantage. His decision was reversed by the Eleventh U.S. Circuit Court of Appeals.[62] Judge Frank Johnson, who wrote the opinion for the circuit court, dismissed out of hand the idea that so-called secular humanism was a religion. Even if it were, he said, the books at issue would not constitute an establishment of religion in violation of the *Lemon* tests, since they merely espoused values like independent thought and tolerance for the view of others, did not have the purpose or effect of advancing religion, and did not involve any entanglement of church and state.

Finally, in the state of Washington, an objection was made by a parent to a public school's use of *The Learning Tree* by Gordon Parks, arguing that it violated both the establishment clause and the free exercise of religion. It is a novel about the experience of growing up in America in a working-class African American family and deals in only a minor way with religion. The school had denied the parent's request to remove the book from the curriculum but was willing to allow the student, Cassie Grove, to substitute another book and to leave the classroom when the Parks book was being discussed. Apparently unsatisfied with that resolution of the matter, the parent sued in federal court but lost the case. Like the court described previously which said that a school's curriculum cannot be made into a cafeteria, the court of appeals in the *Grove* decision held that the burden on Cassie's free exercise of religion was minimal, that the use of the book by the school did not constitute an establishment of religion, and that the kind of accommodation to religion the parent was seeking would be at odds with the school's educational objectives.[63] The Supreme Court declined to review that decision.[64]

Since all three of these cases occurred in the 1980s, one might be tempted to infer from their fate that this issue has been put to rest. That would be an unwarranted conclusion in view of the vigorous efforts, often successful, that Christian fundamentalists have engaged in during the past decade in many communities to take over local school boards by organizing and winning elections of their supporters. The objective of these efforts, of course, is to shape the curricula of the schools to express their own religious beliefs and to exclude any views that are incompatible with that expression. Those who value this country's adherence to the separation of church and state cannot, therefore, assume that it will be preserved without the "eternal vigilance" that "is the price of liberty."[65]

5

Public Funding of Religious Schools

❖❖❖❖❖

W hile it is an understatement to observe, as we have in the preceding chapter, that the Supreme Court has been relatively inactive with respect to school text and library book censorship, it would be almost impossible to overstate the extent to which it has rendered decisions on the subject of government financial support to religious schools. Yet, despite their abundance, those cases have left us with a confusing trail to follow. The respected legal historian Leonard Levy has said of them that "Sometimes the Justices make distinctions that would glaze the minds of medieval scholastics."[1] The authors of the most comprehensive recent legal case book on religious freedom make the following observation:

> Commentators on the cases applying the nonestablishment provision to religious education have not found them coherent. For example, Professor Choper [former dean of the Boalt School of Law at the University of California, Berkeley, and a respected First Amendment scholar] has written: "There is broad consensus that a central threat to the religious freedom of individuals and groups—indeed, in the judgment of many the most serious infringement upon religious liberty—is posed by forcing them to pay taxes in support of a religious establishment or religious activities." Jesse H. Choper, *Securing Religious Liberty* 16 (1995). The application of this general principle to the particular details of state and

federal programs of assistance to various aspects of religious education, however, has left Choper and others utterly bewildered.[2]

Before embarking on this perplexing journey through the school cases of the most recent decades it will be useful to take note of a few early precedents involving government financial aid to religion. As early as August 1789, "the same First Congress that a month later adopted the First Amendment took steps to adapt the Northwest Ordinance 'to the present Constitution of the United States.' No changes were made in the Ordinance's provision connecting schools and religion."[3] The Continental Congress, in that ordinance, had granted a huge acreage of land to the Ohio Company to be reserved and used for the support of religion. "In 1833 . . . Congress authorized the state of Ohio to sell the land appropriated 'for the support of religion' and to use the proceeds 'forever' for 'the support of religion.'"[4]

In 1811 President Madison vetoed a bill to reserve land for the Baptist Church in the Mississippi territory, but in 1832 Congress appropriated money for the American Board of Commissioners for Foreign Missions, a Congregationalist organization, to preach the gospel to the Cherokee Indians in Indian territory bordering on Georgia. The mission's agents, however, "transgressed a statute of the state of Georgia prohibiting the entry of white men into the Indian territory without the license of the state."[5] This led to the conviction for that offense of one of their number, the Reverend Samuel Worcester. "The Supreme Court of the United States in exonerating him in 1832 made no adverse comment on the federal legislation that had launched his evangelical enterprise."[6] The following year, 1833, Congress made a grant of $25,000 worth of land in the District of Columbia to Georgetown College, a Jesuit institution for the education of Catholic boys.[7]

Moving to the twentieth century and beyond the issue of schools for the moment, we find Congress adopting the Hill-Burton Act in 1946, designed to support the construction and services of hospital facilities in the country, which included in its coverage hospitals that are owned or operated by religious institutions. In order to accommodate the religious beliefs of the Catholic Church, an amendment was added in 1973 that allowed Catholic hospitals receiving government funding to refuse to perform sterilization procedures or abortions. That amendment was challenged in federal court by a woman in Oregon who had been refused a tubal ligation by a Catholic hospital in Eugene. A decision by the Ninth U.S. Circuit Court of Appeals, not reviewed by the Supreme Court, held that the law did not violate the establishment clause of the First Amendment.[8]

Financial Aid to Religious Grade Schools

The first case to be decided by the Supreme Court that was specifically addressed to the issue of government funding of religious grade schools involved the state of Louisiana, which was providing textbooks free of charge to all children, whether attending public, religious, or other private schools. The Court found that there was a legitimate public purpose to this practice, and quoted to this effect the opinion of the Supreme Court of Louisiana as follows:

> The appropriations were made for the specific purpose of purchasing school books for the use of the school children of the state, free of cost to them. It was for their benefit and the resulting benefit to the state that the appropriations were made. True, these children attend some school, public or private . . . sectarian or nonsectarian, and that the books are to be furnished to them . . . whichever they attend. The schools, however, are not the beneficiaries of these appropriations. They obtain nothing from them, nor are they relieved of a single obligation, because of them. The school children and the state alone are the beneficiaries.[9]

A decade later a similar rationale was employed when the Supreme Court, in the landmark *Everson* case, quoted at the end of chapter 1, upheld the use of taxpayers' money to provide busing for all children, whether their destination was a public or a parochial school. Then, beginning in the late 1960s and extending to the end of the century, there was a steady stream of cases accepted and decided by the Supreme Court. We will examine them in their chronological order.

In 1968 the Court decided *Board of Education v Allen,* which approved the loaning of secular textbooks by the state of New York to children in grades seven to twelve, whether in public or religious schools.[10] The six-person majority saw no essential difference between this practice and the provision of busing approved in *Everson.* However, Justice Black, who had written the strong separationist language for the Court in *Everson,* concluding that busing alone did not violate that principle, now penned a strong dissent. "It is true," he said, "that the New York law does not as yet formally adopt or establish a state religion. But it takes a great stride in that direction and coming events cast their shadows before them."

There had been four dissenters in *Everson* and three in *Allen,* but in 1971, in another landmark decision that has already been referred to, *Lemon v Kurtzman,* all of the justices joined in striking down a Pennsylvania statute, and all but one of them joined in striking down a Rhode Island statute, both of which involved the provision of government funding for the salaries of teachers of secular subjects in nonpublic grade schools.[11] In Pennsylvania the schools themselves were reimbursed by the state "for the cost of teachers' salaries, textbooks, and instructional materials in specified secular subjects." In Rhode Island the statute authorized "state officials to supplement the salaries of teachers of secular subjects in nonpublic elementary schools by paying directly to a teacher an amount not in excess of 15% of his current annual salary." This was the case in which Chief Justice Burger, writing for the Court, enunciated the famous three-pronged *Lemon* test for determining whether a law or practice violates the establishment clause. It was clear to the Court that going so far as to pay for teachers' salaries, whether by way of reimbursement to the schools or directly to the teachers, was going well beyond what had been allowed in *Everson* and *Allen.*

There then followed two cases from the state of New York in which the strict separationist point of view again prevailed. The first involved per-student cash grants that were made to religious and other nonpublic schools to cover the cost of administering examinations, some of which were prepared by the state and some by the school's teachers. Because the law made no distinction between the two, and the internal tests might, as the Court put it, "be drafted with an eye, unconsciously or otherwise, to inculcate students in the religious precepts of the sponsoring church," eight of the justices voted to invalidate the law.[12]

The other case dealt with a New York statute that provided per-student money grants "to maintain and repair school facilities"; "[r]eimbursements of $50 to $100 per nonpublic school pupil to parents with income of less than $5,000"; and a "tax credit per nonpublic school pupil for parents with income of $25,000 or less."[13] All but one of the justices agreed that the grants for maintaining and repairing school facilities violated the establishment clause, and all but three of them found the other two provisions to be unconstitutional as well. This time Chief Justice Burger was one of those three dissenters, protesting that "government aid to individuals generally stands on an entirely different footing from direct aid to religious institutions."

During the next twenty-five years (1975–2000), the Court continued to decide cases on this subject once every two to eight years. The decisions were usually by votes of either 5-4 or 6-3, with the Court so divided that there were many plurality, concurring, and dissenting opinions written in which the various justices selected out particular sections of each of the laws being adjudicated for their approval or rejection. Often there were justices who approved *all* of the provisions and others who opposed them all.

In the first of these cases, in 1975, a Pennsylvania statute was at issue that authorized the loaning of secular textbooks to nonpublic as well as public school students, as well as the provision of other secular instructional materials to the schools. Following the precedent established in *Allen,* a majority of the Court upheld the loaning of the textbooks but found the provision of other instructional material to be violative of the First Amendment.[14]

Two years later the Court decided a case from Ohio, whose law included six categories of financial aid to nonpublic as well as public school pupils, their parents, or the schools. By votes of 6-3 a majority sustained four of those sections and invalidated the other two.[15] The items that were approved were (1) the loaning of secular textbooks to the students or their parents; (2) the costs of administering standardized tests in whose preparation nonpublic personnel were not involved; (3) speech, hearing, and psychological diagnostic services on school premises; and (4) career guidance and remedial services, so long as they were performed off-campus. The majority struck down (1) the provision of instructional equipment like projectors, tape recorders, maps, and science kits; and (2) paying for transportation for field trips. Those justices who tended to be supportive of all or some provisions believed that it was possible to maintain a sufficient distinction between secular activities and those that were potentially too religious. The justices who leaned in the opposite direction worried about religious indoctrination creeping into a program and about the "serious potential for divisive conflict over the issue of aid to religion." For some of the latter group it did not matter if the aid went directly to the students' parents or to the school, because in either case they saw it as supporting "the religious roles of the schools."

The next decision was simply a reaffirmation, for New York, of the state's right to reimburse nonpublic schools for the cost of administering state-mandated examinations.[16] That was followed by a ruling sustaining a Minnesota statute that permitted parents, whether their children were in public or private schools, to take a state tax deduction of up to $700 per child for the expenses of tuition, textbooks, and transportation to school.[17] The majority of the Court believed that the program served the secular purpose of a well-educated citizenry and was therefore permissible under the *Lemon* criteria. The four dissenters were disturbed by the fact, among other things, that 96 percent of the families who were actually eligible for this aid were the parents of parochial school students.

In the following case, however, there were five votes for invalidating a program of the Grand Rapids School District in Michigan that provided remedial and enrichment education to nonpublic elementary school children in math, reading, art, music, and physical education *on the school premises* by public school teachers. Also struck down was the school district's after-school program in the arts and Spanish, taught by public employees, again in the nonpublic school building.[18] The majority of the justices felt that although the purposes of these programs might have been secular, they in fact risked the possibility of religious indoctrination. They noted that "40 of the 41 schools in this case are . . . 'pervasively religious.'" They were, in fact, almost all Catholic or Protestant. Justice Brennan wrote for the majority:

> First, the teachers participating in the programs may become involved in intentionally or inadvertently inculcating particular religious tenets or beliefs. Second, the programs may provide a crucial symbolic link between government and religion, thereby enlisting—at least in the eyes of impressionable youngsters—the powers of government to the support of the religious denomination operating the school. Third, the programs may have the effect of directly promoting religion by impermissibly providing a subsidy to the primary religious mission of the institutions affected.

Shortly thereafter, with the same five justices in the majority and the same four in the minority, the Court reiterated one of the propositions that had been a part of the Ohio *Wolman v Walter* decision eight years previously, and ruled that remedial education taught by public employees, to which nonpublic as well as public school students were entitled under Title I of the federal Elementary and Secondary Education Act of 1965, had to be held off-campus, albeit in nearby mobile units, if it were not to violate the establishment clause.[19] It was the view of the majority that there was too much "entanglement" of church and state, in violation of the third prong of the *Lemon* standards, if the classes were held in the religious school building.

With the arrival of the 1990s there was a turn in the Court's prevailing position. The first indication of this change came with a decision on the quite narrow question of whether a deaf child, who was entitled to be accompanied to school by a sign-language interpreter under the federal Individuals with Disabilities Education Act, could have that interpreter accompany him to a Catholic high school. In this particular instance, the child, James Zobrest, had originally been in a school for the deaf, but had attended a public school in grades six through eight, where he was accompanied by a government-funded interpreter. His parents transferred him to the Catholic high school for the ninth grade and sought to have this assistance continued. The Supreme Court held in favor of the parents, operating on the premise that the primary beneficiary of the aid was the child, not the school.[20]

Then, in 1997, in the case of *Agostini v Felton,* a five-person majority of the Court explicitly rejected the precedent established twelve years previously that required remedial classes for religious school students to be taught in a mobile unit off-campus.[21] However, in reaching this conclusion the Court went much further than the particular issue at hand, turning its back as well on several of the Court's earlier decisions. Writing for the majority, Justice O'Connor made these broad pronouncements:

> As we have repeatedly recognized, government inculcation of religious beliefs has the impermissible effect of advancing religion. Our cases subsequent to *Aguilar* have, however, modified in two significant respects the approach we use to assess indoctrination. First, we have abandoned the presumption erected in *Meek* and *Ball* that the placement of public employees on parochial school grounds inevitably results in the impermissible effect of state-sponsored indoctrination or constitutes a symbolic union between government and religion. . . . Second, we have departed from the rule relied on in *Ball* that all government aid that directly aids the educational function of religious schools is invalid. . . .
>
> A number of our Establishment Clause cases have found that the criteria used for identifying beneficiaries . . . might themselves have the effect of advancing religion by creating a financial incentive to undertake religious indoctrination. . . . This incentive is not present, however, where the aid is allocated on the basis of neutral, secular criteria that neither favor nor disfavor religion, and is made available to both religious and secular beneficiaries on a nondiscriminatory basis. Under such circumstances, the aid is less likely to have the effect of advancing religion. . . .
>
> Not all entanglements . . . have the effect of advancing or inhibiting religion. Interaction between church and state is inevitable . . . and we have

always tolerated some level of involvement between the two. Entanglement must be "excessive" before it runs afoul of the Establishment Clause.

This revised point of view prevailed again in 2000 when the Court majority withdrew its previous objections to the use of taxpayer monies to supply secular instructional materials and equipment, such as computers, maps, projectors, and television sets, to religious as well as public schools.[22] Although this time there were six justices who voted to allow the particular financial aid at issue, two of them, Justices O'Connor and Breyer, were unwilling to join with the reasoning of the other four, thus rendering the latter only a plurality opinion. The principle objection of these two separately concurring justices to the plurality opinion written by Justice Thomas was essentially the same as one of the objections articulated by Justice Souter in his dissenting opinion. Justice Souter had written that the plurality opinion "appears to take evenhandedness neutrality and in practical terms promote it to a single and sufficient test for the establishment constitutionality of school aid."

Yet Justice Souter's lengthy and passionate dissent, joined by Justices Stevens and Ginsburg, had much more than that to say about the First Amendment issue:

> For more than 50 years, this Court has been attempting to draw these lines. . . . In all the years of its effort, the Court has isolated no single test of constitutional sufficiency. . . . I believe the Court commits error in failing to recognize the divertibility of funds to the service of religious objectives. . . . Government aid corrupts religion. . . . Government establishment of religion is inextricably linked with conflict. . . . If we looked no further than evenhandedness, and failed to ask what activities the aid might support, or in fact did support, religious schools could be blessed with government funding as massive as expenditures made for the benefit of their public school counterparts, and religious missions would thrive on public money. . . . The plurality's new criterion is unequalled in the history of Establishment Clause interpretation. . . . There is no mistaking the abandonment of doctrine that would occur if the plurality were to become a majority.

There is one final issue that logically belongs in this section of the book but will be postponed until the end of the chapter because it can be better understood against the background of matters to be discussed in the next section. It is the question of state or federal government funds being used for school vouchers, a method of aiding the parents of students attending religious and other private schools to pay for their children's tuition, more particularly with respect to programs that are designed to help only economically disadvantaged families.

Financial Aid to Private Higher Education

This is going to be a much shorter story than that of the elementary and secondary schools, primarily because college and university students are thought to be less impressionable, more discriminating about what constitutes or does not constitute the endorsement of ideas by school administrators, and more capable of resisting possible attempts to influence their religious beliefs than younger people. Thus, there have been far fewer challenges to government financial aid for higher education, with the result of only a small handful of Supreme Court decisions.

Probably the most extensive government financial support for higher education in our history, albeit it in the form of financial aid for students rather than for colleges and universities themselves, was the so-called G.I. Bill, which provided to veterans of World War II all of their tuition expenses plus a monthly cost-of-living cash stipend. Obviously, many of those veterans chose to attend private universities, most of which were originally founded by religious organizations and many of which, particularly the Catholic ones, were still governed by religious institutions. No one, to this author's knowledge, ever questioned the constitutionality of the G.I. Bill on establishment-of-religion grounds.[23]

The next most significant move of Congress in providing financial support to institutions of higher education, whether public or private, was Title I of the Higher Education Facilities Act of 1963. That law authorized substantial funds for the construction of college and university buildings and facilities if they were to be used solely for secular purposes. The law was sustained by the Supreme Court in 1971, with the exception of one provision.[24] The item that the Court struck down as insufficiently protective of the separation of church and state was a provision that would have allowed the schools to convert the funded facilities to sectarian uses after a period of twenty years.

Only three more decisions of the Supreme Court during the ensuing fifteen years dealt with financial aid to religious schools of higher education, all of them involving state rather than federal programs. The first entailed revenue bonds issued by South Carolina to aid in the construction of buildings for institutions of higher learning if they were to be used for secular purposes. Similar to the federal program already upheld, this state statute was also approved by the Supreme Court.[25]

Going one step further, the Court next rejected a challenge to a Maryland program that made grants for *any* secular purpose to private institutions of higher education, except for those offering degrees only in theology.[26] A five-person majority found that this program passed muster under all three prongs of the *Lemon* tests. The four dissenters expressed a concern, among others, that the government carrot of providing funds for secular purposes might "tempt religious schools to compromise their religious mission" in order to avoid being seen by the courts as so "pervasively sectarian" as to disqualify them from government financial aid.

Finally, a case arising in the state of Washington involved a state program providing financial aid for higher education to persons who were visually impaired. When one such student sought to use this assistance to study to become a minister at the Inland Empire School of the Bible in Spokane, the state agency administering the program denied his request and was upheld by the state's Supreme Court. A unanimous U.S. Supreme Court reversed that decision, arguing that "any aid provided under Washington's program that ultimately flows to religious institutions does so only as a result of the genuinely independent and private choices of aid recipients."[27] This decision was somewhat surprising, not because there was a lack of precedent for the concept of differentiating aid to a student from aid to an institution itself in the grade school cases we have already reviewed, but because in this instance that principle was accepted unanimously. Again, it was probably the fact that it was higher education rather than the lower grades at issue that made the difference.

There is one other Supreme Court decision affecting financial aid to higher education that must now be mentioned, although it involved the question of tax exemption rather than government monetary appropriations. Bob Jones University in Greenville, South Carolina, is a fundamentalist Christian institution whose president believed that the Bible called for a separation of the races. In pursuit of that belief, the school prohibited any interracial dating and would expel any students who violated the rule. Prior to 1971 it had even refused admission entirely to African Americans, but then began admitting them if they were already married to other African Americans. After 1975 and a U.S. Circuit Court of Appeals decision prohibiting racial discrimination in *admissions* by private schools,[28] later affirmed by the Supreme Court,[29] the university admitted all African

Americans, regardless of their marital status, but continued the policy against interracial dating.

Before 1970, the U.S. Internal Revenue Service (IRS) had been granting even to those schools with racially discriminatory policies the tax exemption allowed by law for private charitable and educational institutions. When that IRS policy was challenged in a case from Mississippi, the IRS reversed itself and denied further tax exemption to Bob Jones on the grounds that its racial discrimination was incompatible with "public policy." That decision was challenged by the university, which claimed that the IRS lacked authority to deny the exemption and that their doing so violated the school's free exercise of religion. A federal district court in South Carolina agreed with them but was overruled by the circuit court of appeals, a decision that was then sustained by the Supreme Court.[30] Chief Justice Burger wrote the Court's opinion:

> When the Government grants exemptions or allows deductions all taxpayers are affected: the very fact of exemption or deduction for the donor means that other taxpayers can be said to be indirect and vicarious "donors." Charitable exemptions are justified on the basis that the exempt entity confers a public benefit. . . . The institution's purpose must not be so at odds with the common community conscience as to undermine any public benefit that might otherwise be conferred. . . . The governmental interest at stake here is compelling. The Government has a fundamental, overriding interest in eradicating racial discrimination in education. . . . That governmental interest substantially outweighs whatever burden denial of tax benefits places on petitioners' exercise of their religious beliefs.

Justice Lewis Powell agreed with the Court's judgment as to Bob Jones University but wrote a separate concurring opinion to express some reservations about the majority opinion's treatment of the "public benefit" question. He said that what was troubling to him was "the element of conformity that appears to inform the Court's analysis. The Court asserts that an exempt organization must 'demonstrably serve and be in harmony with the public interest.' . . . In my opinion, such a view . . . ignores the important role played by tax exemptions in encouraging diverse, indeed often sharply conflicting, activities and viewpoints."

Justice Rehnquist was the sole dissenter, taking the position that neither the IRS nor the courts had the authority to deny a tax exemption of this sort. He argued that this was solely a matter for Congress to decide, and that since Congress had failed to act, even when asked to do so by the administration, the courts should not have intervened.

Equal Access to University Activities Funds

In the section of chapter 4 on after-school religious club meetings the case of the Good News Clubs versus the public school district of Milford, New York, was described. That case involved a clash between the claim by the Good News group that it had a free-speech right of after-school access to school facilities on the same basis as groups that did not engage in religious proselytizing and the school's argument that to allow the use of its facilities for proselytizing purposes would constitute an establishment of religion in violation of the First Amendment. Although the freedom-of-speech clause was used as the basis for the Good News claim, they might just as well have added that the rejection by the school was also a violation of their free exercise of religion. It will be recalled that the Supreme Court ruled in favor of the Good News Clubs on the grounds that denying them the facility constituted impermissible viewpoint discrimination under the freedom-of-speech clause, and that allowing the use of the facility would not violate the establishment clause.

The same opposing arguments had been presented to the Supreme Court five years earlier, but in a somewhat different context and with different subject matter. The setting was a public institution of higher education, the University of Virginia, instead of a public elementary school, and what was being sought by the religious student group was not a meeting room but financial aid from the Student Activities Fund for the printing costs of their publication. There was no question about the fact that the requesting students were a duly recognized campus organization or that funds had previously been allocated by the Student Council for subsidizing publications of other recognized student organizations. Unlike at some colleges, at the University of Virginia such allocated funds were paid directly by the university to the service providers, rather than to the student groups themselves. This was not really an issue in the case, though it did make it clear that the denial of funds was government action subject to First Amendment scrutiny. Also undisputed was the fact that the guidelines under which the Student Activities Fund was administered permitted the funding of publications that included religious subject matter but excluded those that promoted a particular religious ideology.

In another of its 5-4 votes the Supreme Court majority, as in the Good News case to be decided later, found that the denial of funds for the printing of the publication at issue—one that clearly and forcefully espoused Christian doctrine—constituted viewpoint discrimination in violation of the First

Amendment's freedom-of-speech clause.[31] Furthermore, the majority rejected the university's argument that it would be violating the establishment clause if it were to allow this kind of financial aid. They compared the situation to the one faced in the University of Missouri case discussed in chapter 4, where the Court had ruled that the university, having created a limited public forum for its students, could not then deny them a meeting room for religious devotional exercises. "A central lesson of our decisions," Justice Kennedy wrote for the majority, "is that a significant factor in upholding government programs in the face of Establishment Clause attack is their neutrality toward religion. . . . The governmental program here is neutral toward religion."

As she was to do later when the Court, in 2000, upheld the supplying of computers and other instructional equipment to religious grade schools, Justice O'Connor wrote a separate concurring opinion, agreeing with the majority's final judgment in the particular case at hand but expressing her concerns about relying so exclusively on the neutrality principle. She would have looked beyond that to other establishment clause considerations, and in so doing noted that "the aid to religion at issue here is the result of petitioner's private choice. No reasonable observer is likely to draw from the facts before us an inference that the State itself is endorsing a religious practice or belief."

For the four dissenters, speaking through Justice Souter, there was a significant difference between providing a meeting room and paying out funds for a publication that promoted religious doctrine. The majority's argument, he wrote,

> is as unsound as it is simple, and the first of its troubles emerges from an examination of the cases relied upon to support it. . . . Each case drew ultimately on unexceptionable Speech Clause doctrine treating the evangelist, the Salvation Army, the millenialist or the Hare Krishna like any other speaker in a public forum. It was the preservation of free speech on the model of the street corner. . . . The analogy breaks down entirely, however, if the cases are read . . . to cover more than forums for literal speaking. . . . The forum cases cannot be lifted to a higher plane of generalization without admitting that new economic benefits are being extended directly to religion in clear violation of the principle barring direct aid.

In other words, the dissenters were saying that there is a substantial and constitutionally significant difference between a school's providing meeting spaces where groups may choose to proselytize and paying those groups' bills to promote religious doctrines. It is of interest to note that the ACLU national board of directors, after an intense debate over whether to file an *amicus* brief in this case and, *if so, on which side,* finally decided to advocate the position taken by the four dissenters.

School Vouchers

We return now to the question of school vouchers, an issue whose prominence in public debate has had its ups and downs for a very long time. Many parents who send their children to parochial schools have complained for years about what they have often called "double taxation," referring to the fact that in addition to supporting the public schools with their taxes they are spending money for private school tuition. They are, of course, doing that as a matter of personal choice, and this argument also overlooks the fact that people who have no children are also being taxed to support their community's public schools without any direct benefit to themselves.

In more recent years the chorus of support for providing government financial aid to send children to private schools has grown much louder because of the disastrous state into which so many public schools have fallen, particularly in large inner cities. Although the development of magnet and charter schools within the public system has offered an alternative for some students, the desire to enhance "school choice," as it is frequently called, beyond the public sector has grown. In response, critics of school vouchers have expressed alarm that such programs will not only divert sorely needed resources from the public schools but will breach the wall of separation of church and state even more seriously than it has already been compromised. Nevertheless, local experiments on a limited basis have already been tried, and legal challenges are working their way through the courts.

One of the earliest experiments was begun in 1990 in Milwaukee, Wisconsin, where vouchers were made available to low-income families to send their children to private schools. As originally designed, the plan excluded religious schools. In 1995, however, religious schools were added to the Milwaukee Parental Choice Program, so long as the students who attended those schools were allowed to be excused from religious activities. That revised plan was temporarily enjoined by the state supreme court until a full trial on its merits could be held. Both the trial and appellate courts invalidated the program, but in 1998 the state supreme court reversed those decisions and held that the program passed muster on the basis of the *Lemon* tests.[32] It was viewed by that court as having the valid secular purpose of providing a better education for the children of poor families, as not having the primary effect of advancing religion, and as not involving excessive entanglement with the religious schools that the students attended. The U.S. Supreme Court declined to review that ruling.

In 1995 the public school system in Cleveland, Ohio, created a program similar to Milwaukee's, in that it was targeted to low-income families, but it included religious schools from the outset. Challengers failed to persuade a trial judge in the state courts to enjoin the plan, but a state court of appeals reversed that decision and held that the program violated two provisions of the state constitution.[33] Section 7, Article I, of the state constitution reads that "No person shall be compelled to attend, erect, or support any place of worship, or maintain any form of worship, against his consent; and no preference shall be given, by law, to any religious society; nor shall any interference with the rights of conscience be permitted." Section 2, Article VI, reads that "The general assembly shall make such provisions, by taxation, or otherwise . . . [as] will secure a thorough and efficient system of common schools throughout the state; but no religious or other sect, or sects, shall ever have any exclusive right to, or control of, any part of the school funds of this state."

The Ohio Supreme Court, vastly complicating the case, reversed part of that decision and affirmed it in part.[34] It ruled that the program did not violate the establishment clause of the U.S. Constitution, except insofar as it gave priority for selection to families that belonged to religious groups supporting particular sectarian schools. Also, the court ruled that the program did not violate either of the state constitution's provisions quoted previously. The court affirmed, however, the lower court ruling that the program violated the one-subject rule.

Thereupon a new law was adopted by the legislature that was limited to the single subject of the Cleveland voucher plan. This time the challengers decided their chances would be better in a federal court, and that proved to be correct. They succeeded in persuading a district court judge to enjoin the program, and that decision was affirmed by the Sixth U.S. Circuit Court of Appeals.[35]

Meanwhile, in 1999, the legislature of the state of Florida adopted the first statewide voucher program. It provided what it called "opportunity scholarships" that students could use at either public or private schools, and the law explicitly included both sectarian and nonsectarian private institutions in its coverage. In March 2000, a state court judge enjoined the program. He found it to be in violation of the state's constitutional provision "that declares education a 'fundamental value' of the state and says it is a 'paramount duty' to provide a 'uniform, efficient, safe, secure and high quality system of free public schools.'"[36] A state court of appeals, however, held that the trial court had erred in finding the law in violation of the state constitution. The appellate court interpreted the constitutional requirement that the legislature fund public schools as not meaning that it might not fund private schools in addition.[37] The case was sent back to the trial court for reconsideration of other issues raised by the law's challengers, and the Florida Supreme Court declined to review that decision.[38]

In 1997 the U.S. House of Representatives got into the act in adopting, by a vote of 203-202, a voucher plan for the District of Columbia. President Bill Clinton had opposed it, but was saved from the necessity of a veto when the Senate declined to act on it. Later that year a more general voucher bill was introduced in the House, but was soundly defeated when thirty-five Republicans joined with all but four Democrats in voting against it. During the presidential election campaign of 2000, George W. Bush made school vouchers one of the planks in the platform he proposed for enactment if elected. However, after he took office he discovered that there was not sufficient political support for his administration to pursue the matter. Thus, it was dropped out of the first major education bill he proposed and that was enacted by the Congress.

Whether or not school vouchers would be viewed as constitutionally acceptable by the U.S. Supreme Court remained an open question. There was language in two of the opinions of Justice O'Connor, a swing voter on establishment clause issues, that foreshadowed how she, and perhaps even a majority, might vote. The first was the majority opinion she wrote in *Agostini v Felton,* approving of the on-site provision of remedial education for religious school students. She said then:

> In *Witters v. Washington Department of Services for the Blind* . . . we held that the Establishment Clause did not bar a State from issuing a vocational tuition grant to a blind person who wished to use the grant to attend a Christian college and become a pastor, missionary, or youth director. Even though the grant recipient would use the money to obtain religious education, we observed that the tuition grants were "made available generally without regard to the sectarian-nonsectarian, or public-nonpublic nature of the institution benefited." . . . The grants were disbursed directly to students, who then used the money to pay for tuition at the educational institution of their choice. In our view, this transaction was no different from a State's

issuing a paycheck to one of its employees, knowing that the employee would donate a part or all of the check to a religious institution. In both situations, any money that ultimately went to religious institutions did so "only as a result of the genuinely independent and private choices of" individuals. . . . The same logic applied in *Zobrest*, where we allowed the State to provide an interpreter . . . because the . . . neutral eligibility criteria ensured that the interpreter's presence in a sectarian school was a "result of the private decision of individual parents" and [could] not be attributed to *state* decision making.[39]

Three years later, in *Mitchell v Helms*, the decision that upheld the loaning by the government of instructional equipment like computers to religious as well as public schools, Justice O'Connor joined only in the final judgment to make it a majority. She then explained her own position in a concurring opinion:

> I write separately because, in my view, the plurality announces a rule of unprecedented breadth for the evaluation of Establishment Clause challenges to government school-aid programs. Reduced to its essentials, the plurality's rule states that government aid to religious schools does not have the effect of advancing religion so long as the aid is offered on a neutral basis and the aid is secular in content. The plurality also rejects the distinction between direct and indirect aid, and holds that the actual diversion of secular aid by a religious school to the advancement of its religious mission is permissible. . . . We decided *Witters* and *Zobrest* on the understanding that the aid was provided directly to the individual student who, in turn, made the choice of where to put that aid. . . . This characteristic of both programs made them less like a direct subsidy, which would be impermissible under the Establishment Clause, and more akin to the government issuing a paycheck to an employee who, in turn, donates a portion of that check to a religious institution. . . . I do not believe that we should treat a per-capita-aid program the same as the true private-choice programs considered in *Witters* and *Zobrest*. [The amount of equipment loaned in the case about which she was now writing was based on the size of a participating school's enrollment.] . . . First, when the government provides aid directly to the student beneficiary, that student can attend a religious school yet retain control over whether the secular government aid will be applied toward the religious education. . . ."The fact that aid goes to individuals means that the decision to support religious education is made by the individual, not the State" [quoting her own concurring opinion in *Witters*]. . . .
>
> Second, I believe the distinction between a per-capita school-aid program and a true private-choice program is significant for purposes of endorsement. . . . In terms of public perception, a government program of direct aid based on the number of students attending each school differs meaningfully

from the government distributing aid directly to individual students who, in turn, decide to use the aid at the same religious schools. . . .

Finally, the distinction between a per-capita-aid program and a true private-choice program is important when considering aid that consists of direct monetary subsidies. . . . If, as the plurality contends, a per-capita-aid program is identical in relevant constitutional respects to a true private-choice program, then there is no reason that, under the plurality's reasoning, the government should be precluded from providing direct money payments to religious organizations (including churches) based on the number of persons belonging to each organization. And, because actual diversion is permissible under the plurality's holding, the participating organizations (including churches) could use that aid to support religious indoctrination. To be sure, the plurality does not actually hold that its theory extends to direct money payments. . . . That omission, however, is of little comfort. In its logic—as well as its specific advisory language . . . the plurality opinion foreshadows the approval of direct monetary subsidies to religious organizations, even when they use the money to advance their religious objectives.[40]

Although it is difficult to follow the fine lines drawn by Justice O'Connor in these lengthy excerpts, and even to understand fully why her disagreement with the reasoning of her colleagues in the plurality did not lead her to disagree with their conclusion as well, it is important to attempt to do so because of the significance it had for a major Supreme Court ruling on school vouchers that was in the offing.

That landmark decision came two years later in the case of the Cleveland voucher program, which, as we have seen, had been found unconstitutional by both a federal district court and the U. S. Sixth Circuit Court of Appeals. The Supreme Court, in still another of its "conservative" versus "liberal" 5-4 splits, reversed the decision of the lower courts and held the Cleveland program to be allowable under the Establishment Clause.[41]

In an opinion written by the chief justice, the majority decided that because the vouchers could be used at nonreligious as well as religious private schools, the program was neutral as to religion. The fact that in actuality 96 percent of the families using the vouchers sent their children to Roman Catholic schools did not lead the majority to conclude, as the minority did, that the program had the effect of advancing religion in violation of the effects prong of the *Lemon* test. As in some of the cases described earlier, the majority argued that the program did not constitute an aid to religion because the families using the vouchers were free to choose between sending their children to a religious or a nonreligious private school. The aid, it was maintained, was therefore to them as individuals and would support religion only indirectly as a result of their choice.

Justice Souter, writing for the four dissenters in a lengthy and scholarly historical review of the relevant precedents, claimed that the majority was relying on a "verbal formalism" in describing the program as being neutral with respect to religion and was ignoring the reality of how the program was operating mainly to support parochial schools. Families receiving the voucher checks were simply signing them over to schools that were devoted to the promotion of their religion. The limited number of nonreligious private schools that were in fact available in Cleveland made the so-called choices of those using the vouchers something of a fantasy. In additional dissents, Justices Stevens and Breyer expressed their particular concern about the divisiveness among religious groups that the Court's precedent might engender.

Apparently because of the thoroughness and potency of the Souter essay and the relative brevity of Chief Justice Rehnquist's opinion for the majority, Justice O'Connor chose to write a long concurring opinion that tried to refute each of Justice Souter's arguments. In view of her earlier attempts to walk a fine line in distinguishing permissible from impermissible use of public funds that might aid religion, she presumably felt a need to justify her joining the majority in this instance.

Although most of the points made in the various majority and dissenting opinions had been foreshadowed in earlier financial aid decisions, the impact of this decision on Establishment Clause jurisprudence was much more profound and could have consequences far beyond those earlier cases. That is because it not only opened the door for school boards, city councils, state legislatures, and even the Congress to start proliferating a wide range of school voucher programs, but might have ramifications for other kinds of public support to religiously sponsored services. Whether that actually happens will depend on how politically popular or unpopular school voucher and other such programs are with the voting public, since they must ultimately be decided by the nation's legislatures.

6

Historical Issues of Religious Expression versus Competing Social Interests

❖❖❖❖❖

If President James Madison were alive today he would no doubt be seen as a wild-eyed extremist about the separation of church and state. Devoted believer that he was in Christianity and in a vigorous free exercise of religion, he viewed the slightest establishment of religion by government as entirely incompatible with the ability to exercise that freedom without inhibition. He thought that government should not even be involved in the incorporation of religious organizations, and vetoed a bill adopted by Congress in 1811 to give corporate status to the Anglican Church in Alexandria, Virginia.[1] That view, of course, never gained any later acceptance in this country, nor did his opposition to the government financing of chaplains for legislatures or the military. His belief that church property should not be tax-exempt was rejected unanimously by the U.S. Supreme Court in the *Walz v Tax Commission of the City of New York* case described in chapter 2.[2] Indeed, the only challengers in that important case were the ACLU and the atheist organization of Madalyn Murray O'Hair. We will now turn to a handful of other twentieth-century tax exemption cases, the first of several issues to be discussed in the ensuing sections of this chapter in which the courts have been called upon to decide whether, in some instances, competing social interests outweigh the right to the free exercise of religion or, in other instances, if special exceptions for religion violate the establishment clause.

Tax Exemptions

When Congress adopted the first federal income tax in 1913, as it was permitted to do by the Sixteenth Amendment to the Constitution that had been ratified in February of that year, it included an exemption for educational, charitable, scientific, and religious organizations. In a Supreme Court decision three years later, the Court rejected a challenge by a stockholder of the Union Pacific Railroad who complained that the decision of Congress to establish different rates for different categories of people and organizations was not authorized by the Sixteenth Amendment.[3] The Court replied that the language of the Sixteenth amendment, which empowered the Congress to impose taxes on incomes, "from whatever source derived . . . and without regard to any census or enumeration," allowed distinctions to be made, for example, for "certain enumerated organizations or corporations, such as labor, agricultural, or horticultural organizations." Although charitable, educational, and religious organizations were not specifically named in that list, it was clear from the rationale of the entire decision that they were implicitly included. This case gave an early indication that a legislature may, in its discretion, exempt religious organizations and individuals along with other nonprofit institutions from obligations like taxation that are imposed generally on the rest of society.

Many years later, an Amish group, about whom we will have much to say in this chapter, challenged the requirement to pay social security taxes, arguing that it was sinful for them to pay for, or to receive, social security benefits because their religion demanded that they care for their own elderly people. A unanimous Supreme Court, in an opinion written by Chief Justice Burger, held that the government's interest in maintaining a compulsory social security system outweighed the Amish desire to exercise their religious freedom in this particular matter.[4] The Court obviously believed that an accommodation to religion was not required here.

The establishment, rather than free exercise, clause, was at issue when the state of Texas was challenged for exempting from its sales tax "periodicals that are published or distributed by a religious faith and that consist wholly of writings promulgating the teaching of the faith and books that consist wholly of writings sacred to a religious faith." A majority of the

Supreme Court found the law in question to be a violation of the establishment clause.[5] Three of the five justices in the majority objected to the fact that the law singled out religion for this exemption, arguing that if it had given similar benefits to secular publications or nonreligious groups it might have passed constitutional muster. The other two justices in the majority suggested in a concurring opinion, without definitively committing themselves, that the case might have been different if the exemption had been defended on the basis of the free exercise clause rather than maintaining that it did not violate the establishment clause. The three dissenters objected strongly to what they felt was a departure from the *Walz* precedent that had allowed tax exemptions for church property, and described the majority's decision as a "judicial demolition project." They argued that the Court in *Walz* had "rejected an Establishment Clause challenge that was in all relevant respects identical" to the Texas case.

It was not long, however, until the Court did address the question of whether the free-exercise clause required an exemption for religious activity from a general state sales tax. The very next year, a challenge to a California statute that required *all* retailers to pay a sales tax "for the privilege of selling tangible personal property at retail" was decided by the Supreme Court. The plaintiff was Jimmy Swaggart Ministries. Jimmy Swaggart was a fundamentalist evangelical preacher who had been unmasked as a hypocrite when it was revealed in 1987 that he had himself consorted with New Orleans prostitutes while condemning fellow evangelist Jim Bakker for *his* extramarital sexual encounters with a former church secretary. Swaggart had said that Bakker, who was driven from his television pulpit and served five years in prison for defrauding his followers of 158 million dollars, was a "cancer affecting the body of Christ."

The Swaggart Ministries argued that the California sales tax requirement violated both the free exercise and establishment clause provisions of the First Amendment. In a unanimous opinion, written for the Supreme Court by Justice O'Connor, both claims were rejected.[6] As to the free-exercise clause, Justice O'Connor's opinion said:

> We . . . conclude that the collection and payment of the generally applicable tax in this case imposes no constitutionally significant burden on appellant's religious practices or beliefs. The Free Exercise Clause accordingly does not require the State to grant appellant an exemption from its generally applicable sales and use tax.

As to the establishment clause issue, she wrote:

Appellant also contends that application of the sales and use tax to its sale of religious materials violates the Establishment Clause because it fosters "an excessive government entanglement with religion." . . . First, we note that the evidence of administrative entanglement in this case is thin. . . . Second, even assuming that the tax imposes substantial administrative burdens on appellant, such administrative and record keeping burdens do not rise to a constitutionally significant level. . . . Accordingly . . . we find no excessive entanglement between government and religion in this case. . . .

These tax exemption decisions lend some credence to the view of the "equal separationists" that religious organizations can and should be treated no better and no worse than other nonprofit institutions that contribute to the benefit of society. Paradoxically, they also suggest the contrary possibility, alluded to by some of the justices in the Texas case, that because of the First Amendment's free-exercise-of-religion clause a religious institution or practice may be given a deference or allowed an accommodation that the government does not afford to other nonprofit organizations.

Polygamy

The classic and earliest major instance of a clash between the free exercise of religion and competing social interests in the United States, and one that led to the first landmark decision of the Supreme Court on that issue, dealt with the practice of polygamy by members of the Mormon Church. In 1862 Congress adopted the Morrill Act, which made polygamy a criminal offense. The law lay dormant during the Civil War and even to this day has only infrequently been enforced. Indeed, there are said to be several thousand polygamous marriages still in existence in Utah and the adjacent states. However, in 1874 the secretary to Brigham Young, George Reynolds, a bigamist, was convicted of violating the law, and his conviction was upheld by a unanimous Supreme Court in *Reynolds v United States*.[7] That historic case has served until the present day as the leading precedent delineating the point at which compelling social interests may outweigh the free exercise of religion.

The alleged social interests in prohibiting polygamy have been numerous. The practice was denounced in 1865 by the Speaker of the U.S. House of Representatives as "barbarism," and has been described by others since then as a form of slavery for the women involved.[8] In what would now be considered a grossly ethnocentric and racially prejudicial statement, the Supreme Court said in *Reynolds:* "Polygamy has always been odious among the northern and western nations of Europe, and, until the establishment of the Mormon Church, was almost exclusively a feature of the life of Asiatic and of African people." Yet just as that statement in this day and age may itself be characterized as "odious," we have also come to understandings about equal rights for women that make polygamy appear to be in even more serious conflict with enlightened public policy than in the nineteenth century.

More important to the concerns of this book, however, is the premise on which the Supreme Court decided the *Reynolds* case. Stated in the opinion in its most succinct form, it was that "Laws are made for the government of actions, and while they cannot interfere with mere religious belief and opinions, they may with practices." The Court had harked back to Thomas Jefferson, who wrote "that it is time enough for the rightful purposes of civil government for its officers to interfere when principles break out into overt acts against peace and good order."[9] Continuing its reference to the man who inspired the religion clauses of the First Amendment, the Supreme Court asserted:

> Coming as this does from an acknowledged leader of the advocates of the measure [the First Amendment], it may be accepted almost as an authoritative declaration of the scope and effect of the amendment thus secured. Congress was deprived of all legislative power over mere opinion, but was left free to reach actions which were in violation of social duties or subversive of good order.[10]

Although this premise appears indisputable as a general proposition, the matter is not quite as simple in application as it seems. The problem is that many religious practices are such an integral part of a religious faith that to say one may believe in them, and even verbally advocate them, but not actually engage in them is like trying to split Siamese twins. The advocate of free exercise can legitimately argue that it is not very useful to be able to believe in something if one is not permitted to act upon that belief. That argument becomes particularly potent when the alleged harm to society of the action in which the religionist wishes to engage is not clearly evident. Thus a polygamist may claim that if his wives are not dissatisfied with the relationship and do not believe themselves to be exploited, society has no business intervening. The fact that this particular practice has been winked at, and is still winked at, so commonly by our law enforcement officials would seem to lend some credence to this argument. I am by no means arguing for polygamy, or any other form of religious practice that deviates so substantially from society's norms, but only suggesting, as have many respected legal scholars, that the *Reynolds* case may have been wrongly decided, and that the free-exercise clause of the First Amendment should sometimes shield actions, especially if they are only symbolic ones, as well as opinions and beliefs. We will encounter that question again and again throughout the remainder of this chapter.

The Draft and Conscientious Objection

The issue of compulsory military service and its possible conflict with pacifist religious beliefs is one of long standing. As early as 1789, James Madison proposed a constitutional amendment that "No person religiously scrupulous of bearing arms shall be compelled to render military service in person." Because the constitutions of several of the states already provided for such an exemption from conscription, it was not thought necessary to make it part of federal law, so the proposed amendment was not adopted.[11]

It was not until the Civil War that conscription was resorted to as a means of raising an army, and then it was done by both the Union and the Confederacy. In perhaps the same spirit as the language of the proposed Madison constitutional amendment, with its reference to military service "in person," it was possible during the Civil War for people to buy their way out of the military by paying someone else to serve in their place.

No such buy-out provision was included in the Selective Service Act of 1917, which drafted soldiers for World War I. That law did, however, provide an exemption from combat duty for members of "any well-recognized sect or organization at present organized and existing whose existing creed or principles forbid its members to participate in war in any form." Refusal to serve could lead one to prison, as it did for one year for Roger Baldwin, founder of the ACLU. The ACLU, begun after the war in 1920, was an outgrowth of a predecessor group known as the American Union Against Militarism, in which Baldwin was involved, which had opposed U. S. entry into the war and gave assistance to conscientious objectors.

Several legal challenges to the constitutionality of the 1917 law wound up in the U.S. Supreme Court, which summarily dismissed those challenges in 1918, finding that the congressional power to raise armies provided for in the Constitution necessarily encompassed a power to conscript.[12] This did not mean that Congress could not, if it so chose, exempt conscientious objectors from that general obligation, but that would be a matter of its discretion.

World War II broke out in Europe in 1939 and, in preparation for any possible involvement in it by the United States, Congress enacted the Selective Service Act of 1940. As in World War I, Congress decided to exempt anyone from "combatant training and service . . . who, by reason of religious training and belief, is conscientiously opposed to participation in war in any form." Those granted such exemptions would be assigned to noncombat duty in the military or, if they objected to that, would "be assigned to work of national importance under civilian direction."

It was not necessary, under the 1940 law, to be a member of a "well-recognized sect," so long as one's objection was based on "religious training and belief." Also unlike the World War I act, the draft law remained on the books when the war was over. Although no one was actually drafted until the war in Vietnam, young men still had to register when they reached the age of eighteen.

In 1948 Congress amended the law to specify that "religious training and belief means an individual's relation to a Supreme Being." Yet in 1965 the Supreme Court, arguably taking considerable liberty with that language of Congress, interpreted the meaning of that amendment as follows: "The test might be stated in these words: A sincere and meaningful belief which occupies in the life of its possessor a place parallel to that filled by God. . . . This construction avoids imputing to Congress an intent to classify different religious beliefs, exempting some and excluding others, and is in accord with the well-established congressional policy of equal treatment for those whose opposition to service is grounded in their religious tenets."[13]

Then came the Vietnam War and with it widespread objection to it by people who were not necessarily either pacifists or religious, but who regarded that particular war as profoundly immoral. Many refused to even register for the draft, much less serve if called. Congress, responding to the Supreme Court's decision just described, adopted still another amendment to the Selective Service Act in 1967. This time they deleted the term "Supreme Being" from the 1948 version, but specified that "religious training and belief" does *not* pertain to "essentially political, sociological, or philosophical views, or a merely personal moral code." Apparently the authors of that amendment were trying to walk a fine line between giving carte blanche to avoid service in Vietnam to those who were politically or philosophically motivated, yet respecting the Supreme Court's concern that in so doing they not discriminate among religions or between religion and its secular equivalents.

Those who admittedly were not *total* pacifists but sought conscientious objector status nonetheless because of their opposition to the war in Vietnam then ran afoul of the provision that had been in all of the draft laws since World War I, which limited exemptions to those who objected to "war in any form." Two such men, Guy Gillette and Louis Negre, went to court, claiming that the distinction between conscience objection to all war and to a particular war, if the latter was based on religious beliefs or deeply held equivalents, violated the neutrality required by the establishment clause. The U.S. Supreme Court rejected that claim.[14] It made no difference to the Court that Gillette's objection was "spurred by deeply held moral, ethical, or religious beliefs" and Negre's was classically religious. Negre, in fact, had studied for the Catholic priesthood and been influenced by Catholic scholars who distinguished between just and unjust wars, as well as the pronouncement by the Second Vatican Council in 1966 that "Any act of war aimed indiscriminately at the destruction of entire cities or of extensive areas along with their population is a crime against God and man himself."[15] The fact remained, said the Court, that Congress limited its dispensation to those "conscientiously opposed to participation in war in any form," and that "This language, on a straightforward reading, can bear but one meaning; that conscientious scruples relating to war and military service must amount to conscientious opposition to participating personally in any war and all war." It should be noted that, given the intensity of passions about the Vietnam War, if the Court had ruled otherwise the Congress might simply have eliminated all conscientious objector exemptions.

We cannot leave the topic of conscientious objection to war without describing three cases decided by the Supreme Court that did not involve the draft, but rather an oath required by the Immigration and Naturalization Service of persons seeking naturalization as American citizens. In the first case, decided by the Supreme Court in 1929, an application for naturalization by a Hungarian immigrant was rejected because she declared that "I am not willing to bear arms."[16] In a 6-3 vote the Court ruled against her, stating that it was "a fundamental principle of the Constitution" that citizens had a duty to defend their country by arms.

Two years later the Court again decided against an applicant, this time a Canadian who was a Baptist minister teaching theology at Yale University. He refused to take the required oath because he said he "could not put allegiance to the government of any country before allegiance to the will of

God."[17] The chilling language of the majority opinion, written by Justice George Sutherland, was unequivocal about society's interest in overriding the free exercise of religion in this matter. He wrote that "we are a Nation with the duty to survive; a Nation whose Constitution contemplates war as well as peace; whose government must go forward upon the assumption, and safely can proceed on no other, that unqualified allegiance to the Nation and submission and obedience to the laws of the land, as well those made for war as those made for peace, are not inconsistent with the will of God."

That opinion elicited an equally strong dissent written by Chief Justice Charles Evans Hughes, joined by the most distinguished possible trio of other justices—Oliver Wendell Holmes, Louis Brandeis, and Harlan Fiske Stone:

> The essence of religion is belief in a relation to God involving duties superior to those arising from any human relation. . . . The battle for religious liberty has been fought and won with respect to religious beliefs and practices, which are not in conflict with good order, upon the very ground of the supremacy of conscience within its proper field. . . . There is abundant room for enforcing the requisite authority of law . . . without demanding that either citizens or applicants for citizenship shall assume by oath an obligation to regard allegiance to God as subordinate to allegiance to civil power. The attempt to exact such a promise . . . has been the cause of many deplorable conflicts. The Congress has sought to avoid such conflicts in this country by respecting our happy tradition. In no sphere of legislation has the intention to prevent such clashes been more conspicuous than in relation to the bearing of arms. It would require strong evidence that the Congress intended a reversal of its policy in prescribing the general terms of the naturalization oath. I find no such evidence.

Fifteen years later these dissenters were vindicated in a 5-3 vote that favored the application of a Seventh-Day Adventist to become a citizen without having to take the prescribed oath.[18] The majority opinion, written by Justice Douglas, declared that "The bearing of arms, important as it is, is not the only way in which our institutions may be supported and defended, even in times of great peril. . . . Nor has Congress expressly made any such finding [the promise to bear arms] a prerequisite to citizenship. To hold that it is required is to read it into the Act by implication. But we could not assume that Congress intended to make such an abrupt and radical departure from our traditions." Those words precisely tracked the concluding sentences of the Hughes dissent quoted just previously, and made clear that at least on this question the social interest patriotically trumpeted by Justice Sutherland in 1931 was insufficient to trump the free exercise of religion.

The reader may recall that in chapter 2 a statement by Professor Laurence Tribe was quoted asserting that those who wrote and adopted the First Amendment "clearly envisioned religion as something special."[19] That is to say that they believed religion, like speech and press, was entitled to greater freedom from government control than other kinds of social behavior. The cases and decisions that have been discussed in this section are illustrative and supportive, to one degree or another, of that constitutional interpretation.

Sacraments

The use of wine as a sacrament in religious services has a long history in the major religions of America. It is used by Catholics in the celebration of Mass, by many Protestants in celebrating Holy Communion, and by Jews as one of the rituals of weddings and the Seder meal. This posed something of a problem when the Eighteenth Amendment to the Constitution was adopted in 1919, for it prohibited "the manufacture, sale, or transportation of intoxicating liquors within . . . the United States and all territory subject to the jurisdiction thereof for beverage purposes." It went on to provide that "Congress and the several States shall have concurrent power to enforce this article by appropriate legislation." This was promptly followed by congressional passage of the Volstead Act, which criminalized not only the manufacture and sale of any beverage containing more than one-half of one percent alcohol, but its possession as well. Obviously this law would apply to wine, which is clearly an alcoholic beverage, unless some accommodation were made for its uses as a religious sacrament. Thus a politically sensitive Congress included the following section in the Volstead Act: "Nothing in this title shall be held to apply to the manufacture, transportation, possession or distribution of wine for sacramental purposes, or like religious rites."

Unfortunately, religious sects less politically powerful in the United States than Catholics, Protestants, and Jews have not always been so favored by the discretionary powers of Congress or state legislatures in receiving exemptions for other kinds of rituals that may engage them in conflict with federal or state laws. The most prominent and controversial case of this sort to be decided by the U.S. Supreme Court occurred when

the Court, by a 6-3 vote in 1990, permitted the state of Oregon to deny unemployment benefits to members of the Native American Church who had
been dismissed from their jobs because they had used peyote in their religious ceremonies.[20] Unlike a number of other states, Oregon's ban on the
use of peyote made no exception for the sacramental use of that drug.
When confronted with the argument that it was a violation of the free-
exercise-of-religion clause of the First Amendment for Oregon to deny unemployment benefits that would otherwise have been available to them
just because they had used an illegal drug as part of a religious ritual, the
majority rejected that claim.

Justice Scalia wrote an opinion for five members of the six-person majority, which took the position that because the state statute prohibiting the
use of peyote was a law of general applicability not aimed at religion in
particular, it did not violate the free exercise clause and had to be obeyed.
The premises on which that opinion were based were so anathema to Justice O'Connor, who still voted with the majority for her own reasons, that
she wrote a separate concurring opinion that reads more like a dissent. In
fact, the three actual dissenters, Justices Brennan, Marshall, and Harry
Blackmun, joined that opinion in addition to issuing a dissent of their own.
The significance of the disparity between the Scalia and O'Connor opinions
is so great that we must look at those differences in considerable detail.
There are three critical matters on which they diverge.

The first has to do with where the line should be drawn between belief
and action for the purpose of adjudicating free exercise claims. Here is
what the Scalia opinion says on that point:

> The free exercise of religion means, first and foremost, the right to believe
> and profess whatever religious doctrine one desires. Thus the First Amend-
> ment obviously excludes all "governmental regulation of religious *beliefs* as
> such." . . . But the "exercise of religion" often involves not only belief and
> profession but the performance of (or abstention from) physical acts: assem-
> bling with others for a worship service, participating in sacramental use of
> bread and wine, proselytizing, abstaining from certain foods or modes of
> transportation. It would be true . . . that a state would be "prohibiting the
> free exercise [of religion]" if it sought to ban such acts or abstentions only
> when they are engaged in for religious reasons, or only because of the reli-
> gious belief they display. . . .
>
> Respondents in the present case, however, seek to carry the meaning of
> 'prohibiting the free exercise [of religion]' one large step further. They con-
> tend that their religious motivation for using peyote places them beyond
> the reach of a criminal law that is not specifically directed at their religious

practice, and that is concededly constitutional as applied to those who use the drug for other reasons. . . . We do not think the words must be given that meaning. . . . We have never held that an individual's religious beliefs excuse him from compliance with an otherwise valid law prohibiting conduct that the State is free to regulate.

To this, the O'Connor response was as follows:

Because the First Amendment does not distinguish between religious belief and religious conduct, conduct motivated by sincere religious belief, like the belief itself, must therefore be at least presumptively protected by the Free Exercise Clause . . .

The Court today, however, interprets the Clause to permit the government to prohibit, without justification, conduct mandated by an individual's religious beliefs, so long as that prohibition is generally applicable. . . . A person who is barred from engaging in religiously motivated conduct is barred from freely exercising his religion. It is difficult to deny that a law prohibiting religiously motivated conduct, even if the law is generally applicable, does not at least implicate First Amendment concerns.

The Court responds that generally applicable laws are "one large step" removed from laws aimed at specific religious practices. . . . The First Amendment, however, does not distinguish between laws that are generally applicable and laws that target particular religious practices. Indeed, few States would be so naïve as to enact a law directly prohibiting or burdening a religious practice as such. . . . If the First Amendment is to have any vitality, it ought not to be construed to cover only the extreme and hypothetical situation in which a State directly targets a religious practice.

The second fundamental difference had to do with the standard of scrutiny that should be used by the courts for evaluating allegations by the government that competing social interests justify limitations on an uninhibited free exercise of religion. On this issue the Scalia opinion had the following to say:

Respondents argue that even though exemption from generally applicable criminal laws need not be automatically extended to religiously motivated actors, at least the claim for a religious exemption must be . . . justified by a compelling government interest. . . .

The "compelling government interest" requirement seems benign, because it is familiar from other fields. But using it as the standard that must be met before the government may accord different treatment on the basis of race . . . or before the government may regulate the content of speech . . . is not remotely comparable to using it for the purpose asserted here. What it produces in those other fields—equality of treatment, and an unrestricted flow of contending speech—are constitutional norms; what it would produce here—a private right to ignore generally applicable laws—is a constitutional anomaly.

Justice O'Connor's reply to that argument, although nuanced, was firm:

To say that a person's right to free exercise has been burdened, of course, does not mean that he has an absolute right to engage in that conduct. Under our established First Amendment jurisprudence, we have recognized that the freedom to act, unlike the freedom to believe, cannot be absolute. . . . Instead, we have respected both the First Amendment's textual mandate and the governmental interest in regulation of conduct by requiring the Government to justify any substantial burden on religiously motivated conduct by a *compelling state interest* [italics mine] and by means narrowly tailored to achieve that interest. . . . The compelling interest test effectuates the First Amendment's command that religious liberty is an independent liberty, that it occupies a preferred position, and that the Court will not permit encroachments upon this liberty, whether direct or indirect, unless required by clear and compelling government interests "of the highest order." . . .

Legislatures, of course, have always been "left free to reach actions which were in violation of social duties or subversive of good order." . . . Yet because of the close relationship between conduct and religious belief, "[i]n every case the power to regulate must be so exercised as not, in attaining a permissible end, unduly to infringe the protected freedom." . . . We have consistently asked the Government to demonstrate that unbending application of its regulation to the religious objector "is essential to accomplish an overriding government interest" . . . or represents "the least restrictive means of achieving some compelling state interest."

The third issue on which there was deep disagreement dealt with the fundamental question in a democracy of majority rule versus minority rights. On this question, Justice Scalia and his four brethren expressed the following astonishing view:

Values that are protected against government interference through enshrinement in the Bill of Rights are not thereby banished from the political process. Just as a society that believes in the negative protection accorded to the press by the First Amendment is likely to enact laws that affirmatively foster the dissemination of the printed word, so also a society that believes in the negative protection accorded to religious belief can be expected to be solicitous of that value in its legislation as well. It is therefore not surprising that a number of States have made an exception to their drug laws for sacramental peyote use. . . . But to say that a nondiscriminatory religious-practice exemption is permitted, or even that it is desirable, is not to say that it is constitutionally required, and that the appropriate occasions for its

creation can be discerned by the courts. It may fairly be said that leaving accommodation to the political process will place at a relative disadvantage
those religious practices that are not widely engaged in; but that unavoidable consequence of democratic government must be preferred to a system
in which each conscience is a law unto itself or in which judges weigh the
social importance of all laws against the centrality of all religious beliefs.

In other words, Justice Scalia was saying that if religious groups that are
small in number and have little political clout want to protect their right to
engage in unpopular religious practices, they must persuade legislators,
who always have one eye on the next election, to let them violate norms
that a majority of the population holds dear. So much for minority rights!

Justice O'Connor's rejoinder to that view pulled no punches:

> the Court today suggests that the disfavoring of minority religions is an "un-
> avoidable consequence" under our system of government and that accom-
> modation of such religions must be left to the political process. . . . In my
> view, however, the First Amendment was enacted precisely to protect the
> rights of those whose religious practices are not shared by the majority and
> may be viewed with hostility. The history of our free exercise doctrine
> amply demonstrates the harsh impact majoritarian rule has had on unpopu-
> lar or emerging religious groups such as the Jehovah's Witnesses and the
> Amish. . . . The compelling interest test reflects the First Amendment's man-
> date of preserving religious liberty to the fullest extent possible in a pluralis-
> tic society. For the Court to deem this command a "luxury" . . . is to
> denigrate "The very purpose of a Bill of Rights."

If one wonders why Justice O'Connor, despite her profound disagreement
with the thinking of her four brethren in the majority on fundamental issues, finally voted with them as she did, an answer of sorts is to be found in
only four sentences of her opinion. In her opening two sentences she writes:

> Although I agree with the result the Court reaches in this case, I cannot join
> its opinion. In my view, today's holding dramatically departs from well-set-
> tled First Amendment jurisprudence, appears unnecessary to resolve the
> question presented, and is incompatible with our Nation's fundamental
> commitment to individual religious liberty.

However, she then ends her opinion with the following surprising
conclusion:

> I would therefore adhere to our established free exercise jurisprudence
> and hold that the State in this case has a compelling interest in regulating
> peyote use by its citizens and that accommodating respondents' religiously

motivated conduct "will unduly interfere with the fulfillment of the governmental interest." Accordingly, I concur in the judgment of the Court.

Justice O'Connor was not the only one who was distressed about the majority opinion in the Oregon case. Religious groups across the entire spectrum, from the mainstream to the fringes, along with organizations like the ACLU and legal groups that were usually its bitter opponents, like the American Center for Law and Justice, were appalled. They joined forces to persuade the Congress to adopt a law that would essentially overturn the Court's decision and restore the "compelling interest" test to its previous role. Congress responded favorably with the Religious Freedom Restoration Act (RFRA) of 1993, passed unanimously by the House of Representatives and by a 97-3 vote of the Senate. Four years later, noting that twenty-eight states had legislation on their books exempting the ceremonial use of peyote by Native Americans from their anti-drug laws but that twenty-two others, like Oregon, did not, Congress adopted the American Indian Religious Freedom Act. It provided that "Notwithstanding any other provision of law, the use, possession, or transportation of peyote by an Indian for bona fide traditional ceremonial purposes in connection with the practice of a traditional Indian religion is lawful, and shall not be prohibited by the United States or any State." Thus, regardless of whether a "compelling interest" test or any other test might be used to adjudicate other kinds of conflict between the free exercise of religion and competing social interests, at least the use of peyote by Native Americans, like the use of wine as a religious sacrament, was insulated from any further penalties in the United States.

That did not end the story, however, with respect to the "compelling interest" test, because the Supreme Court still had a turf war it wanted to fight. It found a somewhat unlikely vehicle with which to do so, for the case it used involved a zoning issue in the little city of Boerne, Texas, where the Catholic archbishop of San Antonio applied for a building permit to enlarge the small Mission-style church there. The church was in a growing parish and was no longer big enough to accommodate those who wanted to worship there. The permit was denied because the church was in a historic preservation district where the proposed structural changes were not to be allowed. The archbishop filed a lawsuit in federal court claiming that the city's refusal to grant the requested permit violated the Religious Freedom Restoration Act. When the case got to the U.S. Supreme Court, *amicus curiae* briefs were filed in support of the church by the same broad array of organizations that had sponsored the RFRA. By a 6-3 vote the Court held that the RFRA was unconstitutional.[21]

The Court based that decision on a finding that Congress had exceeded its powers in adopting the RFRA, thus substituting its own judgment for that of the Court in deciding that the compelling interest test was the one that was constitutionally required in evaluating government limitations on the free exercise of religion. Congress had used as its authority for adopting the law in question, Section 5 of the Fourteenth Amendment, which provides that Congress could, "by appropriate legislation," enforce the constitutional guarantee that no state shall "deprive any person of life, liberty, or property, without due process of law; nor deny to any person within its jurisdiction the equal protection of the laws." Yet the Supreme Court refused to accept that justification:

> Legislation which deters or remedies constitutional violations can fall within the sweep of Congress's enforcement power. . . .
>
> It is also true, however, that "[a]s broad as the congressional enforcement power is, it is not unlimited." . . . Congress's power under Section 5, however, extends only to "enforc[ing]" the provisions of the Fourteenth Amendment. . . . Legislation which alters the meaning of the Free Exercise Clause cannot be said to be enforcing the Clause. Congress does not enforce a constitutional right by changing what the right is. It has been given the power "to enforce," not the power to determine what constitutes a constitutional violation. . . . If Congress could define its own powers by altering the Fourteenth Amendment's meaning, no longer would the Constitution be "superior paramount law, unchangeable by ordinary means." It would be "on a level with ordinary legislative acts, and like other acts . . . alterable when the legislature shall please to alter it." . . . Shifting legislative majorities could change the Constitution and effectively circumvent the difficult and detailed amendment process.

As if "shifting majorities" on the Supreme Court itself do not do essentially the same thing! But then, as its final declaration of triumph in this turf war, the Court declared:

> Our national experience teaches that the Constitution is preserved best when each part of the government respects both the Constitution and the proper actions and determinations of the other branches. When the Court has interpreted the Constitution, it has acted within the province of the Judicial Branch, which embraces the duty to say what the law is. . . . Broad as the power of Congress is under the Fourteenth Amendment, RFRA contradicts vital principles necessary to maintain separation of powers and the federal balance.

It is beyond the scope of this book and its subject matter to enter into a debate about the appropriate separation of powers in our federal government. Quite possibly on the question of the RFRA's enactment by Congress the majority of the Supreme Court had it right. It is perhaps relevant and significant to note that among the three dissenters in the *City of Boerne* case, two of whom were not yet on the Court when the *Smith* peyote precedent was established, none chose to directly challenge the position taken by the majority on the issue of congressional versus judicial power. Instead, all of them focused their concerns on the way the earlier peyote case had been decided. Justice O'Connor, the only one of the three who had participated in the Oregon decision, put it this way:

> The Court's analysis of whether RFRA is a constitutional exercise of Congress's Section 5 power . . . is premised on the assumption that *Smith* correctly interprets the Free Exercise Clause. This is an assumption that I do not accept. I continue to believe that *Smith* adopted an improper standard for deciding free exercise claims.

To Justice O'Connor's last sentence this author would say a hearty "Amen," and add my continuing puzzlement over why she finally voted as she did to support the denial of unemployment benefits to the Native Americans who had ingested peyote in Oregon.

The territorial dispute between the Supreme Court and Congress stirred up by the RFRA and ensuing *City of Boerne* decision was not the only separation of powers matter brought to public attention by the use or lack of use of the compelling interest test in free exercise cases. Another basic feature of the structure of our government is its federalism, leaving the states, their legislatures, and their courts with considerable room to deviate from national policies in either more liberal or more conservative directions. A significant result of the Supreme Court majority's decision to strike down the RFRA, with its concomitant backing away from the compelling interest test, is that a substantial number of states proceeded to adopt their own versions of religious freedom "restoration." As of mid-2001, nine state legislatures had passed statutes requiring that the compelling interest test be used in their state courts in free-exercise-of-religion cases, and in six others the same result was achieved by decisions of their supreme courts.[22]

It should be noted, at the same time, that there has also been a downside to this variation in state regulations regarding religious freedom. In addition to restoring the compelling interest test, there has been a widespread granting to religious organizations of exemptions from generally applicable laws, as some had previously done with respect to peyote. This has led to actions by some religious institutions that are fundamentally contrary to the public interest, such as unlicensed and substandard daycare centers and nursing homes, child abuse at boarding schools, and dangerous lack of physical safety precautions.[23] To employ a tired but apt cliché, "Good things can sometimes be carried too far."

Much more distant from the mainstream of social norms than the use of peyote is the practice of animal sacrifice, and that issue, too, has been adjudicated by the Supreme Court. The case arose in the city of Hialeah, Florida, when a religious sect known as the Santeria wanted to engage in this practice. Noonan and Gaffney, in their casebook on *Religious Freedom*, explain:

> The sacrifice of animals as part of religious rituals has ancient roots. . . . Animal sacrifice is mentioned throughout the Old Testament . . . and it played an important role in the practice of Judaism before destruction of the second Temple. . . . Sacrifices [as part of the Santeria ceremonies] are performed at birth, marriage, and death rites, for its cure of the sick, for the initiation of new members and priests, and during an animal celebration.[24]

The citizens of Hialeah were not pleased, to say the least, at the prospect of a Santeria church opening in their community, much less at its practicing animal sacrifice. So the city council adopted a set of ordinances prohibiting the killing of animals, either privately or in public, if the animal was not intended for use as food. They declared this practice to be "contrary to the public health, safety, welfare and morals of the community."

The Santeria filed suit in federal court, claiming a violation of the free exercise clause, and lost their case at both the district court and court of appeals level. The Supreme Court, however, unanimously reversed those decisions.[25] Unlike the Oregon ban on the use of peyote, these ordinances were not laws of general applicability. As the Court said, "The city concedes that 'neither the State of Florida nor the City has enacted a generally applicable ban on the killing of animals.' . . . Each of Hialeah's ordinances pursues the city's governmental interests only against conduct motivated by religious belief." Indeed, it was obvious to at least two of the justices that the Hialeah laws were motivated by hostility to the Santeria. "The record on this," they agreed, "compels the conclusion that suppression of the central element of the Santeria worship service was the object of the ordinances. . . . No one suggests . . . that city officials had in mind a religion other than Santeria." Yet two other justices, in a separate concurring opinion, objected to that particular observation, "because it departs from the opinion's general focus on the object of the *laws* at issue to consider the subjective motivation of the *lawmakers*."

The sharp disagreements among the justices who wrote opinions in the *Smith* peyote and the *City of Boerne* religious freedom cases raise issues that go far beyond differing interpretations of the provisions of the First Amendment. It is the matter referred to in our earlier discussion of the Jehovah's Witnesses pledge-of-allegiance case involving the Frankfurter/Holmes/Brandeis philosophy of judicial restraint. To what extent should the federal courts defer to the democratically elected legislative branch of government, thus leaving to the political process decisions that may affect constitutional rights? And to what extent should they allow the states to engage in practices that may be insensitive to the interests of the country as a whole or to the rights of those who are not in a political majority within their own jurisdiction?

Those questions do not always elicit consistent answers from the justices who sit on the Supreme Court. Some who claim to believe in judicial restraint often depart from that position, and some who lean toward judicial activism sometimes find themselves advocating restraint. A dramatic instance of such an about-face occurred in what is surely one of the most controversial decisions in the Court's history, *Bush v Gore,* handed down on 12 December 2000.[26]

Justice Scalia, for example, who had decided that the right of Native Americans to use peyote in their religious rituals should be left to a majoritarian political process, was unwilling to let the political process play out in a hotly contested presidential election. Rather, he felt that the Court should intervene in a way that effectively decided who would be the president of the United States. Chief Justice Rehnquist, who, as we saw earlier, has been a strong proponent of giving more latitude to the states than to the federal government with respect to provisions of the Bill of Rights, did not hesitate to hold in *Bush v Gore* that the Florida Supreme Court's rulings on matters of state law concerning the counting of votes would not be allowed to be the final word.

Justice Stevens, in the most impassioned of the four dissenting opinions, went so far as to intimate that political preferences may have motivated his colleagues of the majority. He said that "Although we may never know with complete certainty the identity of the winner of this year's presidential election, the identity of the loser is perfectly clear. It is the nation's confidence in the judge as an impartial guardian of the law."

In the days and weeks after *Bush v Gore,* four of the justices, two from the majority (Scalia and Thomas) and two of the dissenters (Ginsburg and Breyer) gave public speeches in which they attempted to shore up the credibility of the Court. In a speech to high school students just two days later, Justice Thomas said that "it was a mistake for anyone to believe that politics played a role in any of the court's deliberations and decisions."[27] Following that there were lectures to law school audiences by Justice Scalia at the University of San Diego, by Justice Ginsburg at the University of Melbourne, Australia, and by Justice Breyer at the University of Kansas.[28] Justices Scalia and Ginsburg spoke only in general terms about the collegiality of the justices, with the implication that each of them, no matter whose side they were on, made a conscientious effort to apply the rule of law as they saw it. Justice Scalia added that "if you can't disagree without hating each other, you better find another profession other than the law."[29]

Justice Breyer was more direct in describing *Bush v Gore* by claiming that "it isn't ideology and it isn't politics."[30] It would be comforting to believe that to be true, but it may be wiser for us to remember Ripley's famous skepticism to "believe it or not."

7

Current Issues of Religious Expression
versus Competing Social Interests

❖❖❖❖❖

The issues discussed in the preceding chapter, where religious expression has had to compete with conflicting societal interests, have by and large become settled matters as far as the United States Supreme Court is concerned. By contrast, most of those to be described in this chapter are questions that are still very much in dispute and are likely to remain so for a long time to come. They pose very close questions, as we shall see.

Public Education, Health, and Safety

An early case in which the Supreme Court established a precedent that has sometimes been followed and sometimes been circumvented or ignored involved a Jehovah's Witness, Sarah Prince, who had her nine-year-old daughter out selling the group's *Watch Tower* publication in Massachusetts. State law, however, prohibited children from selling newspapers and magazines on the street. Ms. Prince was therefore found guilty of aiding a minor to violate the law. In her defense she contended that her conviction violated her free exercise of religion, as well as her right to raise her child as she saw fit.

With only one dissent, the Supreme Court held that "the family itself is not beyond regulation in the public interest, as against a claim of religious liberty. . . . Parents may be free to become martyrs themselves. But it does not follow that they are free, in identical circumstance, to make martyrs of their children."[1]

However, the Court came to quite a different conclusion three decades later in its landmark ruling in *Wisconsin v Yoder.*[2] In that case members of the Old Order Amish religion sought to keep their children "down on the farm" [my quotation marks] after they completed the eighth grade of public school. As the Supreme Court described it, "They believed that by sending their children to high school, they would not only expose themselves to the danger of censure of the church community, but . . . also endanger their own salvation and that of their children."

Wisconsin's compulsory school-attendance law, however, required all children to attend either a public or a private school until they reached the age of sixteen. Thus the Amish parents, who had kept their fourteen- and fifteen-year-olds at home, were convicted of violating the statute. The question before the Supreme Court was whether enforcing that state law against them was a violation of the free exercise of their religion.

In a surprising decision that was a far cry, in both substance and tone, from the polygamy ruling of the previous century and the *Smith* decision that was to come eighteen years later, the Court, with only one dissent, agreed that Wisconsin was in violation of the free-exercise clause. The majority's opinion spoke at considerable length, and with great sympathy, about the religious values at stake:

> the traditional way of life of the Amish is not merely a matter of personal preference, but one of deep religious conviction. . . . Their way of life in a church-oriented community, separated from the outside world and "worldly" influences, their attachment to nature and the soil, is a way inherently simple and uncomplicated, albeit difficult to preserve against the pressures to conform. . . . As the record so strongly shows, the values and programs of the modern secondary school are in sharp conflict with the fundamental mode of life mandated by the Amish religion. . . . Wisconsin law affirmatively compels them, under threat of criminal sanction, to perform acts undeniably at odds with fundamental tenets of their religious beliefs. . . . Wisconsin concedes that under the Religion Clauses religious beliefs are absolutely free from the State's control, but it argues that "actions," even though religiously grounded, are outside the protection of the First Amendment. But our decisions have rejected the idea that religiously grounded conduct is always outside the protection of the Free Exercise Clause.

As for the competing social interest alleged to be involved, the Court said:

There is no doubt as to the power of a State, having a high responsibility for education of its citizens, to impose reasonable regulations for the control and duration of basic education. . . . A State's interest in universal education, however highly we rank it, is not totally free from a balancing process when it impinges on other fundamental rights and interests, such as those specifically protected by the Free Exercise Clause of the First Amendment and the traditional interest of parents with respect to the religious upbringing of their children. . . .

The State advances two primary arguments in support of its system of compulsory education. It notes . . . that some degree of education is necessary to prepare citizens to participate effectively and intelligently in our open political system if we are to preserve freedom and independence. Further, education prepares individuals to be self-reliant and self-sufficient participants in society. We accept these propositions.

However, the evidence adduced by the Amish in this case is persuasively to the effect that an additional one or two years of formal high school for Amish children . . . would do little to serve those interests. . . .

The State [also] attacks respondents' position as one fostering "ignorance" from which the child must be protected by the State. No one can question the State's duty to protect children from ignorance but this argument does not square with the facts disclosed in the record. Whatever their idiosyncrasies as seen by the majority, this record strongly shows that the Amish community has been a highly successful unit within our society even if apart from the conventional "mainstream."

One's enthusiasm for the *Yoder* decision, if one is so inclined, should be tempered a bit by the point made in Justice Douglas's dissent. He notes that what has been vindicated in the case are the rights of the *parents*, which may not necessarily be identical to the interests of the *child*. He points out that although one of the children involved had "testified that her own religious views are opposed to high-school education," the views of the other children were unknown. Not only in this case, but in many others that do not even involve the free exercise of religion, the question of what rights, if any, minors have when they are in conflict with their parents, is an important and exceedingly difficult one to answer. Our society wisely places a very high value on the sanctity of the family, and the legal right of parents to make decisions for their children until the age of eighteen, but we should not overlook the point made by the Supreme Court in the *Prince* case that parents should not have the right to make martyrs of their children. That would be troubling even in the case of the Amish if just one of the children in their community thoughtfully and conscientiously wanted to be free to be more "worldly."

That question can become a matter of life and death when health and medical decisions are made on religious grounds by parents on behalf of minors. There have been scores, if not hundreds, of cases of this sort in state courts involving Jehovah's Witnesses, who do not believe in blood transfusions, and Christian Scientists, who rely on the spiritual treatment of illnesses. Since governmental requirements that parents provide for the health and medical care of their children, and violations thereof, are a matter of state law, which varies widely, we can deal here with only three examples that illustrate the issues involved.

Although there are a multitude of state court decisions, old and recent, on the matter, there is only one relevant U.S. Supreme Court decision, and even that one has been largely overtaken by the passage of time. Back in 1905 the Supreme Court rejected a challenge to a Massachusetts compulsory-vaccination law, and held that it was justified by the governmental interest in preventing epidemics.[3] The reason that decision has become somewhat outdated is that all but two states have since chosen to allow exemptions from compulsory vaccinations for people who object to them on either religious or medical (e.g. allergic reactions) grounds. Furthermore, many Christian Scientists themselves do not object to the vaccination of their children.

The cases that have been much more difficult than those involving vaccinations are those in which children have actually died as result of parental objections to medical treatment. Although, again, many state laws, like this one in Massachusetts, provide that "remedial treatment by religious means" does not constitute child neglect, this has not stopped some states, including Massachusetts itself, from prosecuting parents, usually on a charge of involuntary manslaughter, when their refusal to allow life-saving medical procedures has eventuated in a child's death.

An instance of this sort occurred in Massachusetts when Christian Scientists David and Ginger Twitchell relied on a practitioner of their faith to deal with their two-year-old son's obstruction of his bowel. When the child died five days later, the Twitchells were charged with involuntary manslaughter. They argued in their defense that they had relied on the state law that recognized spiritual means of remedial treatment as acceptable parental care. The trial court ruled that that exemption did not apply when parental conduct is "wanton and reckless," and sentenced the

Twitchells to ten years of probation and monitoring by the state of medical care for their other children. Yet the state's Supreme Judicial Court reversed that decision on the grounds that these parents had, in good faith, relied on the advice of a church pamphlet, that in turn had relied on an opinion of the state's attorney general, that the state law's exemption was absolute.[4]

A similar case in some respects arose in Minnesota, where an eleven-year-old boy with diabetes fell into a coma and was treated by a Christian Science practitioner with prayer rather than insulin. His Christian Scientist mother and stepfather were indicted for manslaughter, but the case against them was dismissed on the grounds that the Minnesota law, like that of Massachusetts, generally provides protection from prosecution for parents who rely on spiritual treatment of their children because of their religious beliefs.[5] The U.S. Supreme Court declined to review that decision.[6]

Then, however, the boy's biological father sued the Christian Science Church for civil damages, and a jury awarded him $5.2 million in compensatory damages and $9 million in punitive damages for the wrongful death of his child. Those awards were reduced to $1.5 million by a Minnesota court of appeals.[7] The Minnesota Supreme Court declined to review that decision, as did the U.S. Supreme Court.[8]

A third case of relevance here, but considerably more complicated, occurred in Chicago, where a young woman, Earnestine Gregory, who was seventeen and a half years old, was suffering from nonlymphatic leukemia, a malignant disease of the white blood cells. She and her family were devout Jehovah's Witnesses who were willing for her to be treated for the leukemia with chemotherapy and other medical procedures but objected to the use of blood transfusions. It was the opinion of doctors that without blood transfusions along with the chemotherapy she would die within a month, but that with them there was an 80 percent chance for a remission of the disease.

Earnestine's mother refused to give her consent to the blood transfusions, arguing that her daughter was mature enough to make that decision herself. A child psychiatrist who interviewed Earnestine found her to be an exceptionally "mature minor," who realized the fatal consequences of refusing blood transfusions. Nevertheless, she and her mother continued to deny consent for them. The hospital thereupon obtained a ruling from a trial court judge that the mother was guilty of "medical neglect," and appointed a temporary guardian who would authorize the transfusions. The girl, still objecting but not able to make her wishes binding because she was not yet legally an adult, asked that she at least be sedated during the transfusions, and that was done.

By the time an appeal of the lower court's decision reached the Illinois Supreme Court, Earnestine had turned eighteen and was thus able to have her wishes respected. The Court could, therefore, have found the case to be moot, as a dissenting justice said it should have done, but a majority felt it important to establish a precedent for the future. They said that since the girl was a "mature minor," and also just months short of her eighteenth birthday, her right to refuse treatment should have been respected. They also ordered the lower court to void the finding of "medical neglect" against the mother, since they believed she was justified in wanting the decision to be left to her mature daughter. The Court recognized that there is a strong public interest in the preservation of life and the prevention of suicide, much greater than with respect to other health care matters, but that a "mature minor" should have the same right as an adult to the free exercise of religious beliefs that may conflict with that societal interest.[9]

When adults are making health decisions for themselves rather than for their minor children the problem of the free exercise of religion versus competing social interests becomes much easier. Presumably the scales should be, and usually are, weighted in favor of free exercise. There have, however, been difficult cases in which hospitals and their doctors have been faced with situations in which a Jehovah's Witness who was not conscious would die if not given a blood transfusion, and the patient's next of kin refused permission for it. Or, alternatively, the patient herself or himself had previously specified that he or she did not want blood transfusions but had failed to make clear that this extended even to life-threatening moments.

In a case in New Jersey a husband gave his consent to a blood transfusion for his Jehovah's Witness wife, but upon recovery she sued the hospital for having done it.[10] In Michigan, an anesthesiologist who did a blood transfusion on a Jehovah's Witness to deal with excessive bleeding during surgery was later sued for battery by the recovered patient.[11] Similarly, in Washington, D.C., a doctor and hospital who had obtained a court order to administer a blood transfusion to save the life of a Jehovah's Witness were sued by that patient after her recovery, apparently because she believed that it was better to be dead than to live as a sinner. Consistently in such cases courts have ruled against Jehovah's Witness plaintiffs.

Turning from issues of education and medical treatment to those of public safety and health, we again encounter the Old Amish religion and a handful of cases in which their religiously motivated practices have clashed with competing social interests.

The most visible of these occurred when fourteen members of the Old Amish sect in Minnesota refused to display on the back end of their horse-drawn buggies the reflective fluorescent orange-red triangle required by state law for slow-moving vehicles. Their objection was that a display of such "loud colors" and of such a "worldly" contraption violated their religious beliefs. Criminal charges were brought against them, and the trial court judge refused to dismiss the case. That decision was appealed to the Minnesota Supreme Court, which held that, although the state had a compelling interest in highway safety, that interest could be served by the alternative of a lighted lantern and outlining the edges of the buggy with silver reflecting tape, which the Amish had proposed to do.[12] The state appealed that ruling to the U.S. Supreme Court, which, having decided the *Smith* peyote case in the meanwhile, vacated the Minnesota court's decision and sent it back to them for reconsideration in the light of that new precedent.[13] The Minnesota Supreme Court, in its second bite of the apple, reaffirmed its earlier ruling in favor of the Amish.[14] The Minnesota court skillfully circumvented the disliked *Smith* precedent by relying on the state constitution's own free-exercise-of-religion provision rather than the federal First Amendment, thus keeping the case outside the jurisdiction of the U.S. Supreme Court.

Two other cases would be humorous if they were not so serious to the Amish. In Sparta, Wisconsin, two Old Amish members (one of whom, incidentally, was named Yoder) had gone to jail for six days for refusing to pay fines for having unlicensed privies on their property that did not meet the county's outhouse code. That code also required that screens be put on outhouses to keep out flies, that they have adequate ventilation and sufficient space between seat openings, and that they be kept a certain distance from dwellings and water sources. The Amish men said they did not want to do that, asserting that they wanted to be left alone to live simple lives in accordance with their religious beliefs.[15] When a non-Amish man who had been prosecuted previously for having a substandard and unlicensed privy complained to the trial court judge that it was unfair for him to have to comply with the regulations if the Amish did not, the judge ordered the county to start enforcing the law uniformly. Thereupon the county prosecutor told the press that he hated doing so because the Amish were "very nice people." At the same time he asked the local ACLU to defend them. The ACLU of Wisconsin declined to take the case because they felt that in the light of the *Smith* precedent they could not mount an effective defense. They suggested, instead, that the Amish should help lobby for the Religious Freedom Restoration Act, a suggestion that would surely fall on deaf ears for a sect that did not want to get involved in worldly affairs.

The other case occurred in Lancaster, Pennsylvania, where a member of the Old Amish Church built a house on his fifteen-acre farm without a sewer system, thus violating a state regulation that required every new house to have such a system. He said that, on religious grounds, he believed it to be an "unnecessary modern convenience." He spent fifteen days in the county prison as a result, but ultimately won his case on appeal. He had been willing to build a privy, if he could get a permit for it, but he was unwilling to install the septic system with an electric pump that the township officials were insisting he must have.[16]

Private Employment

As indicated in the discussion in chapter 4 of the wearing of religious garb by public school teachers, Title VII of the Civil Rights Act of 1964, as amended, has several sections that provide certain exemptions for religious organizations. Section 703 (e) (1) allows religious employers to hire people on the basis of their religion, sex, and national origin where those criteria are "*bona fide* occupational qualifications" reasonably necessary to the operation of their enterprise. Section 703 (e) (2) allows religious schools, if they so choose, to limit the hiring of employees to persons of their own faith. Section 2, according to Noonan and Gaffney's casebook, is the "most important exemption for religious employers. . . . In the 1964 version of the Act, Section 702 exempted only the *religious activities* of religious employers from the statutory prescription against religious discrimination in employment. In 1972 Congress amended this provision, extending the exemption to *all activities* of religious organizations."[17]

Apart from the provisions dealing with religious employers, Title VII requires that *all* employers are not only prohibited by Section 703 (a) (1) from discriminating in their hiring practices on the basis of race, color, religion, sex, or national origin, but they also must, under the terms of Section 701 (j), make "reasonable accommodation" for the free exercise of religion unless it imposes "undue hardship" on them.

There have been four significant Supreme Court decisions dealing with employment discrimination by private employers. Two of them were based only on the free exercise clause of the First Amendment, while the other two were involved with Title VII.

The earliest of the four came about when a member of the Seventh-Day Adventist Church was fired by an employer in South Carolina because she refused to work on Saturdays, her Sabbath. When she applied for unemployment compensation the state's Employment Security Commission turned her down because state law disqualified anyone from unemployment benefits if they failed "without good cause" to accept "suitable work when offered" by their employer. After the state courts upheld that decision, she appealed to the U.S. Supreme Court, which reversed the state courts.[18]

The Court said:

> We turn first to the question whether the disqualification for benefits imposes any burden on the free exercise of appellant's religion. We think it clear that it does. . . . Not only is it apparent that appellant's declared ineligibility for benefits derives solely from the practice of her religion, but the pressure upon her to forego that practice is unmistakable. The ruling forces her to choose between following the precepts of her religion and forfeiting benefits, on the one hand, and abandoning one of the precepts of her religion in order to accept work, on the other hand. . . .
>
> We must next consider whether some compelling state interest enforced in the eligibility provisions of South Carolina's statute justifies the substantial infringement of appellant's First Amendment right. It is basic that no showing of merely a rational relationship to some colorable state interest would suffice; in this highly sensitive constitutional area, "[o]nly the gravest abuses, endangering paramount interests, give occasion for permissible limitation. . . . No such abuse or danger has been advanced in the present case.

It should be noted, in passing, how different the standard used here by the Court was from the one to be enunciated twenty-seven years later in *Smith*.

A second unemployment compensation case occurred in Indiana, where a Jehovah's Witness refused to accept his employer's transfer from his job fabricating sheet steel to one working on the manufacture of army tanks. He said that his pacifist religious beliefs forbade him to engage in such work, and he was thereupon fired. He, too, was denied unemployment benefits by the state's Employment Security Division, and that decision was upheld by the state's supreme court, which held that his unemployment was "voluntary" and not for "good cause." The U.S. Supreme Court, following the precedent it had established in the South Carolina case, reversed the Indiana Supreme Court.[19]

The third and fourth cases both involved Title VII, one of them with respect to a nonreligious employer and the other involving the Mormon Church.

An employee of Trans World Airlines, who was a member of the Worldwide Church of God, was fired when he refused an assignment to work on Saturdays, his Sabbath day. He filed suit in federal court with a claim that his employer had violated Title VII. The Supreme Court, in a 7-2 vote, decided that TWA would have suffered "undue hardship" by accommodating this employee's religious beliefs and thus had not violated the Civil Rights Act.[20] Turning the free exercise clause somewhat upside down, the majority said that accommodating this employee would have meant that "the privilege of having Saturday off would be allocated according to religious beliefs." The two dissenters, Justices Marshall and Brennan, felt that because TWA had made no effort to find a substitute to do the Saturday work, it had not made a "reasonable accommodation" for a religious belief. They were not persuaded that giving him Saturday off would have caused the company "undue hardship."

Finally, we return to the establishment clause and to a question as to whether Title VII's provision allowing religious organizations to discriminate in employment on the basis of religion was a violation of that clause. The case began when a man who was employed as an assistant building engineer at a gymnasium owned and operated by the Mormon Church was dismissed from his job for his failure to become a member of that church. He charged that insofar as the exemption given to religious organizations in the Civil Rights Act that allowed discrimination on the basis of religion was applicable to nonreligious jobs, like his, it violated the First Amendment. The Supreme Court held that the provision in question was an acceptable accommodation of the free exercise of religion by a religious *organization* and that it did not violate the establishment clause.[21]

The fact that there were no dissenters in this case is better explained by the concurring opinion of Justice Brennan, joined by Justice Marshall, than by the majority opinion, which simply justified the decision by describing, one by one, how Title VII passed each of the three *Lemon* tests. Justice Brennan wrote:

> These cases present a confrontation between the rights of religious organizations and those of individuals. Any exemption from Title VII's prescription

on religious discrimination necessarily has the effect of burdening the religious liberty of prospective and current employees. . . .

At the same time, religious organizations have an interest in autonomy in ordering their internal affairs, so that they may be free to "select their own leaders, define their own doctrines, resolve their own disputes, and run their own institutions. . . . They exercise their religion through religious organizations and these organizations must be protected by the [Free Exercise] [brackets his] clause." . . . Determining that certain activities are in furtherance of an organization's religious mission, and that only those committed to that mission should conduct them, is thus a means by which a religious community defines itself. . . .

The authority to engage in this process of self-definition inevitably involves what we normally regard as infringement on free exercise rights.

Faith-Based Social Services

When Republican candidate George W. Bush proposed in the presidential election campaign of 2000 that the federal government should engage in large-scale financial support for faith-based social services, his Democratic opponent, Al Gore, readily agreed with the idea. It was not until after the election and the new president's appointment of a team of experts to draw up specific plans for such a program that serious opposition began to develop. Not only opponents, but supporters as well, came from unexpected sources. Many conservative religious leaders expressed reservations about the program's potential for government interference with their religious activities, and many liberal African American church officials were excited about the possibility of receiving government funds to support and enhance their efforts to help the homeless, drug addicts, ex-convicts, and so on.

Yet even more interesting is the fact that what was being proposed and contested was not as new as many of the participants in the debate seemed to appreciate. There were, to be sure, some troubling new elements in the program being proposed by the administration, which will be discussed shortly, but the basic concept of providing government funding to religious organizations to support their social service work was not only not new but had already been adjudicated by the U.S. Supreme Court. That decision dealt with the Adolescent Family Life Act (AFLA) adopted by Congress back in 1981, the first year of the Reagan administration, to respond to the problem of pregnancy and child bearing by unwed adolescents. In a 5-4

ruling the Supreme Court held that the law did not violate the establishment clause.[22]

The majority had this to say about the statute:

> the AFLA states that "grants may be made only to projects or programs
> which do not advocate, promote, or encourage abortion." . . . A number of
> grantees or subgrantees were organizations with institutional ties to reli-
> gious denominations. . . . It is clear from the face of the statute that the
> AFLA was motivated primarily, if not entirely, by a legitimate secular pur-
> pose—the elimination or reduction of social and economic problems caused
> by teenage sexuality, pregnancy, and parenthood. Appellees cannot, and do
> not, dispute that, on the whole, religious concerns were not the sole moti-
> vation behind the Act. . . . There simply is no evidence that Congress's "ac-
> tual purpose" in passing the AFLA was one of "endorsing religion."
>
> . . . . the more difficult question is whether the primary effect of the chal-
> lenged statute is impermissible. . . . A fairly wide spectrum of organizations
> is eligible to apply for and receive funding under the Act, and nothing on
> the face of the Act suggests it is anything but neutral with respect to the
> grantee's status as a sectarian or purely secular institution.
>
> . . . . this Court has never held that religious institutions are disabled by
> the First Amendment from participating in publicly sponsored social welfare
> programs. . . . Of course we have said that the Establishment Clause does
> "prohibit government-financed and government-sponsored indoctrination
> into the beliefs of a particular religious faith" . . . and we have struck down
> programs that entail an unacceptable risk that government funding would
> be used to "advance the religious mission" of the religious institution receiv-
> ing aid.

The four dissenters were not so sanguine about how this law was actually working in practice. They cited one example where government funding had gone to a faith-based social service program, wondering if
"Congress ever envisioned that public funds would pay for a program during a session of which parents and teenagers would be instructed: 'You
want to know the church teachings on sexuality. . . . You are the church.
You people sitting here are the body of Christ. The teachings of you and
the things you value are, in fact, the values of the Catholic Church.'"

Both before and after passage of the federal AFLA, many state and local
governments were using public financing to support social services of religiously oriented institutions. Catholic Charities, Lutheran Charities, and
the Salvation Army, for example, were all running extensive social service
programs across the country, and were the recipients of considerable funding from all levels of government.

Then, in 1996, the Personal Responsibility and Work Opportunity Reconciliation Act, more popularly known as the Welfare Reform Bill, was adopted by Congress. Section 104 (j) of that law, known as the "Charitable Choice" provision, permitted states to fund faith-based social services using block grants given to them by the federal government. For reasons that are not entirely clear, surprisingly few states and religious institutions took advantage of the "charitable choice" opportunity. Some had never even heard of it. A report by the Center for Public Justice in September 2000 found that "37 states had not implemented charitable choice rules that require removing the restrictions on financing for religious groups."[23]

Yet when the debate over the Bush administration's proposal gathered steam during the summer of 2001, with the House of Representatives enacting the "Community Solutions Act" as proposed by the administration and the media paying a great deal of attention to the issue, the extent to which activities of this kind had already been going on came to light. It became clear how widespread government funding for faith-based social services already was through a variety of channels—from the Agency for International Development (AID) at the federal level to state and city grants or contracts for services involving a broad range of religious organizations from Catholic and Lutheran Services to the Hare Krishna, the Church of Scientology, and the Nation of Islam. The Hare Krishna had received millions from Philadelphia to operate shelters for the homeless and halfway houses for recovering addicts and parolees.[24] The Nation of Islam and Charles Colson's religiously oriented Prison Fellowship had been running very effective rehabilitation programs for prisoners with the help of taxpayer monies, and the Church of Scientology got state money in Oklahoma for the treatment of drug addicts.[25] It has been estimated that, counting all levels of government, the Salvation Army had gotten nearly $300 million annually for its soup kitchens, daycares, drug treatment centers, and battered women shelters, and that Catholic Charities, perhaps the largest religious social service provider in the country, had received as much as $2.3 billion. Jewish Family Services had been a beneficiary, and Philadelphia had given money to the Muslims as well as the Hare Krishna.[26] The state of New Jersey had paid for the cost of operating a Lutheran Home for children in Jersey City, and the U.S. State Department had contracted with several religious agencies to resettle refugees from abroad.[27]

As far back as 1976 the federal Department of Health, Education, and Welfare (HEW) gave seventy-seven acres of land and an abandoned army hospital situated on it to Valley Christian College, a school affiliated with the Assemblies of God church. The property, appraised at $577,500 was given to the college free of charge. HEW's authority came from the Federal Property and Administrative Services Act of 1949, which allows surplus public property to be donated for the "public benefit." A legal challenge to this action by Americans United for Separation of Church and State was rejected by the Supreme Court in a 5-3 decision, holding that Americans United lacked standing to sue because they suffered no direct injury. The dissenters argued that their status as taxpayers entitled them to standing.[28]

In the summer of 2001 the press also began reporting instances where there was little regard by some faith-based social service programs for separating the offering of their help from religious proselytizing, which was supposedly forbidden. One story revealed that Samaritan's Purse, a religious group that had received $200,000 from the Agency for International Development to assist earthquake victims in El Salvador, was conducting half-hour prayer meetings before showing people how to build the metal and plastic shelters they were providing to them. The program's director in El Salvador said that "We are first a Christian organization and second an aid organization. We can't really separate the two. We really believe Jesus Christ told us to do relief work."[29] When the international director for Samaritan's Purse was questioned about this he told the press that it was against the organization's policy and had been done by "a few overenthusiastic people."[30] A lawsuit had to be filed against Jobs Partnership in Washington County, Texas, a group that was using part of the $8,000 grant it had received from the state to buy Bibles for its clients, requiring them to read Scriptures, and advising them to find jobs through a relationship with Jesus.

The person appointed by President Bush immediately after his inauguration to direct his Office of Faith-Based and Community Initiatives was John DiIulio, a professor of political science at the University of Pennsylvania and acknowledged expert on the subject, who also happened to be a Democrat and Catholic. In speeches he gave around the country, he insisted that religious activities would be kept separate from social services, although the program proposed by the administration would allow religious symbols to be displayed at social service sites and religious activities to be conducted at the same time and place, so long as nobody was coerced into participation in them.

Senator Joseph Lieberman, who was an enthusiastic supporter of expanding faith-based social services but was concerned about some of the provisions of the administration's plan, said "I love John DiIulio," and offered to work with him to straighten out the wrinkles.[31] DiIulio also had the assistance as his top volunteer advisor of Stephen Goldsmith, a former mayor of Indianapolis, also a long-time advocate of faith-based social services. After a talk with clergymen by Goldsmith in Augusta, Georgia, in February 2001, there were quite different reactions from the African American and white ministers who were present. A black preacher who directed a social service program in a poor neighborhood of Augusta said, "I'm a minister, but if I have to remove the Bible, remove the cross from the wall, remove the Ten Commandments to get that government money, I'll do it. If God is in me, that's good enough."[32] However, one of the white ministers had a very different view. "When there's work to be done," he said, "I would rather see my church come up with the money and the people to do it. If we rely on the government, it compromises our witness."[33]

There were at least four major concerns felt by opponents and skeptics about the Bush/DiIulio plan, as well as about many of the similar programs that had preceded it. The first, and most important, was that it is virtually impossible without excessive government entanglement with religious institutions to monitor the separation of proselytizing from the rendering of social services if the group in question is not inclined, either consciously or unconsciously, to do it themselves. Even if they abstain from actively promoting their religion to the people they are serving, the religious symbols that may be omnipresent, and the possible on-site, simultaneous, and supposedly noncoercive religious activity that is allowed by law, may influence those being helped to "voluntarily" embrace the religion of their helpers. That may indeed be the intent of some, though certainly not all, of the providers of such services.

A second major source of concern had to do with the employment policies of the institutions offering the social services. Although the law passed by the House of Representatives forbade them from discriminating against potential *clients* on the basis of race, religion, gender, or national origin, it specifically permitted them, as we have seen, to hire as their *service providers* only members of their faith. It even allowed them to discriminate in their hiring on the basis of sexual orientation, if that was a central tenet of their faith, and thus evade state or local laws that prohibit such discrimination.

It is not at all apparent why a service provider doing drug counseling, passing out food, managing a shelter for battered women, or providing housing for the homeless needs to be of the same faith as someone who is engaged in the organization's religious education activities or the conduct of prayer meetings. Justice Brennan, concurring in the Supreme Court's decision to sustain such an employment policy in the case of the Mormon Church versus their gymnasium's assistant building engineer, made an argument of sorts on this point:

> ideally, religious organizations should be able to discriminate on the basis of religion only with respect to religious activities, so that a determination should be made in each case whether an activity is religious or secular. . . . What makes the application of a religious-secular distinction difficult is that the character of an activity is not self-evident. As a result, determining whether an activity is religious or secular requires a searching case-by-case analysis. This results in considerable ongoing government entanglement in religious affairs.[34]

This is an interesting point, but not entirely persuasive when one considers the kinds of service providers just identified.

A third concern was the pragmatic, economic one that to the extent taxpayer money is used to subsidize social services offered by religious institutions, effective as they may be, it may divert resources from private, secular organizations that are doing, or could do, just as good a job, and from public agencies that do, or could, perform the same services. It may even encourage governmental bodies to neglect their obligations in this area because they feel that religious organizations are handling the task adequately.

Finally, there were two kinds of worries expressed by many religious leaders themselves about government funding of faith-based social services. The first, and the one of most widespread concern, was that accepting government money for their services might open the door to undesirable government intrusion in their affairs. As the white minister at the Augusta, Georgia, meeting said, it is better that they raise the money themselves for their charitable activities than take handouts from the state. That way they are also as free as they want to be to combine their social services with the promotion of their faith.

The other concern, which was voiced by conservative religious spokesmen like Jerry Falwell and Pat Robertson, is that since the government may not discriminate on the basis of religious faith among applicants for the available funds, groups that they regard with abhorrence, like the Hare Krishna, Church of Scientology, and Nation of Islam, may have as much chance of being funded as religious institutions that are more acceptable in their eyes. The fact that such groups have often operated very successful programs makes that possibility a reality.

Given all of these problems, the Senate withheld action on the House bill, Professor DiIulio resigned to return to academia, and the terrorist attack of 11 September 2001 temporarily moved the matter onto a back burner. Yet in November President Bush sent a letter to Senate leaders, asking them to adopt a drastically slimmed-down version of his plan that eliminated its most controversial elements.[35] Senator Lieberman, along with Republican Senator Rick Santorum, then went to work with the White House to fashion a bill that might be able to gain bipartisan support. A compromise was reached and a bill entitled the "Charity Aid, Recovery and Empowerment Act" was introduced by the two senators in February 2002.[36] It provided for easier and more generous income tax deductions for the voluntary contributions of individuals to faith-based social service agencies but still allowed for the groups offering those services to identify themselves with their religious sponsorship. As Senator Lieberman put it, "You can't be discriminated against in applying for a grant to do social service work if you have a cross on the wall or a mezuzah on the door or if you praise God in your mission statement. And that's the way it ought to be."[37]

Most importantly, the provision in the original administration proposal as adopted by the House that would have allowed agencies receiving government funding to violate anti-discrimination laws by hiring only members of their own faith or by excluding gay or lesbian employees was deleted from the compromise bill. With that controversial issue finessed, the proponents of government financial aid to faith-based social services hoped to garner sufficient support to pass the new bill in both houses of the Congress. The legislation languished during 2002, however, as Congress became preoccupied with more pressing matters such as the creation of a new Department of Homeland Security and a proposal authorizing the president to use U.S. military power against Iraq to enforce United Nations resolutions.

Not to be deterred from its continuing desire to channel funding to faith-based social services, the administration bypassed the Congress and created a Center for Faith-Based and Community Initiatives in the Department of Health and Human Services by executive order. That center then proceeded to use the charitable choice provision of the 1996 bill and other legislation already on the books to make "demonstration grants" from a "Compassion Capital Fund" to community social services, some of which were operated by universities but others of which were under the auspices of religious institutions. For example, one-million-dollar grants were announced in October 2002 to the Christian Community Health Fellowship,

Catholic Charities of Central New Mexico, and Mennonite Economic Development Associates. Five hundred thousand dollars even went to Operation Blessing International, run by Pat Robertson, the man who had earlier criticized such programs as opening a "Pandora's box."

Then, in April 2003, a "Charity Aid, Recovery and Empowerment Act" passed the Senate by a 95-5 vote, stripped of all of its most controversial provisions and leaving only new tax incentives for private donations to faith-based social services. Passage by the House of Representatives appeared likely.

8

Religious Expression and Political Life

❖❖❖❖❖

There can be no doubt about the many enormously valuable contributions made to our American democracy by religious organizations and advocates. They range from the central role that churches and religious leaders played in the nineteenth-century struggle against slavery to the twentieth-century civil rights movement. Furthermore, the concept of church-state separation that is such a fundamental principle of our democracy has been greatly strengthened by the Baptists in the American colonies and early states who dissented from the established religions; by liberal Catholic theologians like Pope John XXIII and Father John Courtney Murray[1]; by lawyer-authors like the late Leo Pfeffer,[2] who also represented the American Jewish Congress in major First Amendment cases; by political leaders like our first Roman Catholic president, John F. Kennedy, and the born-again Southern Baptist but strict separationist President Jimmy Carter[3]; and even by the dogged and sometimes maddening behavior of Jehovah's Witnesses that led to so many landmark U.S. Supreme Court decisions.

At the same time, we cannot overlook the people put to death by the Salem witch trials; the anti-Catholicism and anti-Semitism of cross-carrying Ku Klux Klan members; the attempts to drive massive holes through the already perforated wall of separation by groups like the Christian Coalition and the currently dominant wing of the Southern Baptist church; the sexual repression promulgated by fundamentalists who have labeled homosexuality a sin and made masturbation a practice about which one should feel guilty; and the catalogue of "papal sins" so devastatingly described by the distinguished lay Catholic scholar Garry Wills.[4]

Where does this all lead with respect to the question of the appropriate role for religious expression in the political life of our nation? Our starting point must again be the First Amendment, but this time focusing on the interaction that exists between the free exercise and establishment clauses. James Madison, good Christian and fervent believer in a vigorous free exercise of religion, saw clearly that any establishment of religion meant a diminution in free exercise, the two being entirely incompatible. Even before the adoption of the Bill of Rights he and his fellow founders inserted Article VI into the Constitution itself, which provided that "no religious Test shall ever be required as a Qualification to any Office of Public Trust under the United States." That nonestablishment principle was extended to the states by the Supreme Court in 1967, in striking down a provision of the Maryland Constitution that required "a declaration of belief in the existence of God" to hold public office in that state.[5] The challenger in that case was a man who had been denied a commission to serve as a Notary Public because he refused to declare his belief in God.

On the free-exercise side of the coin was a historic case in Tennessee, where the state constitution had disqualified ministers from serving in the state legislature. When an ordained minister of the Baptist Church sought and won election to a state constitutional convention, he challenged that restriction, lost his case in the state supreme court, but won a reversal of that decision in the U.S. Supreme Court.[6] The Supreme Court noted that thirteen states had once had similar exclusions of clergymen from various public offices, "primarily to assure the success of a new political experiment, the separation of church and state." Yet as the "disestablishment experiment" proved to be a sturdy part of our history, all but Maryland and Tennessee abandoned those limitations. The Maryland provision had been struck down by a federal district court in 1974,[7] leaving only Tennessee to be corrected by the U.S. Supreme Court. The Court proclaimed in the Tennessee case that "the right to the free exercise of religion unequivocally encompasses the right to preach, proselyte, and perform other similar religious functions. . . . The American experience provides no persuasive support for the fear that clergymen in public office will be less careful of anti-establishment interests or less faithful to their oaths of civil office than their unordained counterparts."

It should be noted at this point that Father Robert F. Drinan, a Jesuit priest and professor of law who served ably for several years as a Democratic Congressman from Massachusetts, left the House of Representatives not because of any American legal ban but because of orders from the Vatican, which thought it inappropriate for its clergymen to serve in legislative office.

Not only as legislators but also as lobbyists, preaching from the pulpit, or advocating causes in the public forum, religious leaders have played an important part in shaping public policy, sometimes for good and sometimes for ill. The only legal inhibition on them is that insofar as they function as organizational spokespersons and take advantage of the general tax-exempt status of nonprofit associations under Section 501 C(3) of the Internal Revenue Code they are supposedly not to expend a "substantial amount" of the organization's income (defined variously as about 20 percent) on legislative lobbying and are supposedly not to participate whatsoever in political campaigns on behalf of particular candidates for public office. I have qualified the previous sentences with the word "supposedly" because these rules are often ignored with no adverse consequences. As an officer of the National Council of Churches and former ACLU national board member, Dean Kelley, once said:

> Churches are bound by their sense of mission, their consecrated obedience to God, to speak out on issues where the well-being of persons is at stake, to proclaim what they believe is the right and moral course for the whole of society and what will benefit everyone. . . . Churches were doing this sort of thing before there were legislatures or lobbies, and they will continue to do so—despite whatever odds or obstacles—as long as there are churches.[8]

Judge John Noonan has expanded on this point as follows:

> Crusades do, when successful, establish as the law of the land what begins as the religious perception of a moral requirement. Employing religion as a political institution, they mold the morals of the country. They lead to the enactment into law of religious-moral doctrine. At the same time they flourish because of the First Amendment. The government is not empowered to restrain them. They respond to imperatives that transcend the secular state. They are expressions of the demands of conscience. They have played a major part in the American experiment of Free Exercise.[9]

I am inclined to be somewhat more restrained in my endorsement of the free exercise of religious expression in our nation's political life. Although I can be enthusiastic about its vast benefits, I am more concerned than Kelley and Noonan apparently are about its sometimes verging on a violation of the spirit, if not the letter, of the establishment clause. I would make a distinction between two categories of religious expression. Religious advocacy that *opposes* and seeks to *abolish* laws and practices that violate religious principles or consciences runs no danger, as I see it, of establishing a religion, and should be entirely free. Examples that come immediately to mind are the militant anti-slavery rhetoric of a preacher like Theodore Parker, and the civil rights movement, inaugurated by the Southern Christian Leadership Conference at a meeting in the Ebenezer Baptist Church in Atlanta and led by the Reverend Martin Luther King Jr. This freedom should not, and of course does not, extend to the deadly violence of a religious fanatic like John Brown, hero though he may have been regarded by some in the anti-slavery movement. He had his counterpart, to be sure, in the fanatics who murdered anti-slavery publisher Elijah Lovejoy in Alton, Illinois, and the present-day crazies killing doctors who perform abortions.

The second, and very different, kind of religious expression is advocacy that seeks to *impose* the controversial religious values of some, even if they constitute a majority of the community, on the rest of the state or nation by enacting them into law. If successful, this not only verges on the establishment of religion but may cross the line into de facto establishment. Prime examples of this, in my view, were two Catholic-motivated state laws in Connecticut and Massachusetts. The Connecticut statute, which prohibited doctors from writing prescriptions for contraceptives for married couples, was struck down by the U.S. Supreme Court in 1965.[10] Reluctant to ground its decision in the establishment clause, the Court based its ruling on a right of privacy that it found implied in several provisions of the entire Bill of Rights—a decision that has been severely criticized by "strict constructionists" for "inventing" a new constitutional right, but that has nevertheless become thoroughly incorporated into Supreme Court doctrine.

In the wake of that decision Massachusetts enacted a law that respected the privacy of married couples but made it illegal to exhibit, sell, or give away contraceptive devices to the unmarried general public. When Bill Baird violated that law he was arrested by the Boston police after Catholic groups had lodged a complaint. Again invoking the right of privacy rather than the establishment clause, the Supreme Court also struck down this Massachusetts statute.[11]

I would argue, further, that the Comstock Act, enacted by Congress in 1873 at the behest of Anthony Comstock and his New York Society for the Suppression of Vice, outlawing the sending of so-called obscene material through the U.S. mails, was another instance of a de facto establishment of religion, imposing on our entire society the values of perhaps predominant religious groups. The same can be said, I believe, of the prohibition against polygamy discussed in the previous chapter.

A more sensitive and complicated example is the issue of abortion, which finds debates about a woman's right to choose *within* various religious denominations as well as between them and religious nonbelievers. Presumably it was the political clout of the Catholic Church, which is officially opposed to abortion, that resulted in the original enactment of state prohibitions against it. Yet for those, like the Church and other so-called pro-lifers, who believe that abortion constitutes murder, secular arguments can be and frequently are invoked to support their position and thus undercut any claim that its prohibition constitutes an establishment of religion. For so-called pro-choice people, on the other hand, who do not believe that abortion is the same as murder, legal prohibitions against it do constitute a de facto establishment of religious values. The Supreme Court, however, made no reference to the establishment issue when it ruled against abortion restrictions in *Roe v Wade*, once more relying on the right of privacy as the basis for its decision.[12]

However, the Court could not avoid the establishment issue seven years later when confronted with a case involving the Hyde Amendment, adopted by Congress in 1976 in response to *Roe v Wade*. Congressman Henry Hyde, a Roman Catholic, introduced the bill, which prohibited any federal funding of abortions. Planned Parenthood of New York City obtained an injunction against enforcement of the law from federal district court judge John Dooling, who was also a Catholic.[13] Judge Dooling's opinion flirted with the possibility of accepting the violation-of-establishment-clause argument made to him by the plaintiffs, but ultimately ruled in favor of Planned Parenthood on the grounds of the privacy right of a woman who needed financial help to obtain an abortion. He wrote:

> Religious motivation and allegiance to religiously perceived principle on the part of many legislators, on both sides of the issue, are easy and necessary inferences from the record and the legislative history. . . . What finally influenced the votes of the decisive number of legislators cannot be said with

any confidence to be religious motivation or religious conviction. . . . What can be said is that an organized effort of institutional religion to influence the vote . . . on religious grounds was made. . . . The narrow votes in both houses are open to the inference that in one or the other way the religious factor was decisive of the issue for enough legislators to affect the outcome of the voting. . . .

The repeated use during the debates of "human life" terminology extended at times to referring to the immortal soul of the fetus. . . . Much of this language is seen in the Roman Catholic literature already referred to. . . .

The debates were often bitterly controversial, even inflamed. . . . Remarkably, the issue cut across party lines, so that the lobbying effort had to be more personal than organizational. . . . No measure of the effect of the lobbying is possible. . . .

A woman's conscientious decision . . . to terminate her pregnancy . . . is an exercise of the most fundamental of rights, nearly allied to her right to be, surely part of the liberty protected by the Fifth Amendment, doubly protected when the liberty is exercised in conformity with religious belief and teaching protected by the First Amendment. To deny necessary medical assistance for the lawful and medically necessary procedure of abortion is to violate the pregnant woman's First and Fifth Amendment rights.

The Supreme Court reversed Judge Dooling, upheld the Hyde Amendment, and could not resist commenting on his discarded temptation to find an establishment clause violation.[14] "It is well settled," wrote Justice Potter Stewart for the five-person majority, "that 'a legislative enactment does not contravene the Establishment Clause if it has a secular legislative purpose, if its principal or primary effect neither advances nor inhibits religion, and if it does not foster an excessive entanglement with religion.' . . . Applying this standard, the District Court properly concluded that the Hyde Amendment does not run afoul of the Establishment Clause. . . . That the Judaeo-Christian religions oppose stealing does not mean that a State or the Federal Government may not, consistent with the Establishment Clause, enact laws prohibiting larceny."

For reasons that are not apparent, the dissenting Justices Brennan, Marshall, Blackmun, and Stevens made no mention in any of their several opinions of the establishment clause issue. Presumably this was because the case was decided by the majority's rejection of the right-of-privacy argument, after giving short shrift to the establishment question in the paragraph quoted previously, and it was on that matter that the dissenters necessarily focused their fire.

Given the diversity of religious beliefs and organizations in the United States, the presence of significant numbers of nonbelievers and nonpracticing religionists, and the firmly established constitutional underpinnings for the separation of church and state, it is difficult to imagine any circumstance in which our nation would become a theocratic state. It is important to the preservation of our way of life, however, that we remind ourselves of what it is like to live in a theocracy where there is no separation between the making of laws to govern violent or socially harmful conduct and judgments as to what is morally acceptable. As I have said previously:

> theocratic societies . . . make no distinction between morality and law. They think they know for certain what is good and what is bad for people . . . and do not hesitate to write those judgments into law. A free society, by contrast, does not regard the moral judgments of either its majority or its political and religious leaders as infallible. Hence it refrains from coercive measures to enforce them, except where that is necessary to insure that the exercise of one person's freedom and autonomy does not clearly and demonstrably interfere with the freedom and autonomy of others.[15]

We have witnessed the worst of theocratic societies in Afghanistan under Taliban rule, where a perverted version of the Islamic faith led to everything from the exclusion of women from education and jobs to the banning of music and the destruction of invaluable and historic Buddhist statues. The ayatollahs of Iran have been somewhat less repressive because of widespread vocal opposition to some of their edicts but have nevertheless imposed a heavy yoke of regressive morality upon their people. In Saudi Arabia, where 80 percent of the cabinet ministers have an M.A. or Ph.D. from American universities, those leaders have allowed fundamentalist Muslim mullahs to control the education of the young, and they live with laws that make proselytizing for any faith other than the Muslim religion an imprisonable offense.[16]

The governments of Algeria, Egypt, Turkey, and Pakistan have been able to maintain secular states only by the use of military power to keep religious fundamentalists from seizing the government and making those countries over into Muslim theocracies. In Israel, a genuine democracy in a secular state, the electorate is so closely divided between conservative and liberal political parties that smaller religious parties have been able to hold an inordinately influential balance of political power. That power has enabled them to impose many of their orthodox Jewish moral values on a Jewish population at least half of which does not share their views.

Although we in the United States are fortunately far from such possibilities, there have been troubling tendencies in recent years, strongly reinforced by the terrorist attacks of 11 September 2001, for religious expression to exceed the boundaries that a healthy separation between church and state requires. In the presidential election campaign of 2000, Democratic vice-presidential candidate Joseph Lieberman, an Orthodox Jew, stirred up considerable controversy when he proclaimed in a speech at Notre Dame University in October that, with respect to church-state matters, "We have gone far beyond what the Framers had imagined in separating the two." He went on to urge that political leaders be freer and more forthcoming about discussing matters of their faith in public discourse. Criticism of his remarks quickly came from, among many others, the Anti-Defamation League, the leading Jewish organization devoted to monitoring and fighting anti-Semitism. The senator's running mate, Al Gore, had already been doing what Lieberman advocated, while Republican presidential candidate George W. Bush had even gone so far as to say that his favorite philosopher was Jesus, and to make the federal funding of faith-based social services a major campaign pledge. After becoming president he nominated former senator John Ashcroft to be the attorney general—an outspoken adherent to fundamentalist Christian doctrine and fervent opponent of abortion, who nevertheless promised during his Senate confirmation hearings to enforce the law of the land evenhandedly whether or not it ran counter to his religious beliefs. How diligently he would or could fulfill that promise remains to be seen.

We have referred earlier to the insensitivity of the clergymen who delivered the prayers at the inauguration of George W. Bush as president by invoking the name of Jesus Christ—something that had not been done at presidential inaugurations for many years. We also noted the widespread efforts, particularly in the South, to defy court rulings with respect to prayer at public school events. In February 2002, a federal district court judge in Tennessee struck down a practice that had been going on for fifty-one years in the Rhea County public schools—the very county in which the Scopes trial had occurred—in which eight hundred children from kindergarten to the fifth grade were being given thirty-minute Bible classes taught by students from nearby Bryan College, named after William Jennings Bryan. Although students who objected were free to engage in alternative activities at the same time, parental consent was not required for those who did participate.[17]

In the wake of the terrorist attacks on the World Trade Center and the Pentagon, new efforts have been made to bring prayer to public school events, to post the Ten Commandments in the schools and on public buildings, and to otherwise enhance the role of religious expression in public life. In Virginia the House of Delegates approved a bill that would allow the public schools in the state to post the Ten Commandments accompanied by the First Amendment, the Declaration of Independence, and the Virginia Constitution.[18] Christian talk radio shows and conservative religious lobbying groups rallied to the support of a bill introduced in Congress by Republican Representative Walter B. Jones Jr. of North Carolina, entitled the "House of Worship Political Speech Protection Act," which would revoke the law requiring the Internal Revenue Service to deny tax exemption to religious organizations that endorse or oppose candidates for public office.[19]

From October 2001 through February 2002, newspapers repeatedly reported instances of renewed religiosity. In Greenbrier, Arkansas, according to the *New York Times:*

> The prayer circle formed at midnight, just before Friday night's kickoff between the Greenbrier Panthers and the Searcy Lions. Boosted over the public school's loudspeakers Jayla Johnston's soft voice filled the stadium. "In the name of Jesus . . . Our Father who are in heaven . . ."
>
> In the stands, teachers, relatives and friends bowed their heads and joined in, swelling the sound of prayer. Judy Jolley, a parent, felt goosebumps, and her eyes glistened with tears. "I think it's time for us to turn back to God," she said afterward. "We need his blessings desperately right now."
>
> With the pregame prayers, the Greenbrier Independent School District appeared to defy the most recent Supreme Court ruling banning prayer at public school events over a public address system. . . . Debbie Lessard, a mother of two, said: September 11 woke a lot of people up. A lot of Christian people. It's time we speak up."[20]

In Harvey, Illinois, a suburb just south of Chicago, a group of students at Thornton Township High School urged other students to join them in prayer at a weekly after-class sermon by a junior, Jason Clark.[21] As the *New York Times* reported:

> Mr. Clark and most of the teenagers who pray with him . . . call themselves Prayer Warriors for Christ. The metaphor is spiritual, but it fits on a political level, too, for the residents here who see the battlefield as the wall between church and state.

They include Harvey's mayor, Nickolas Graves, and City Council members who recently have called for voluntary prayer in the public schools in this city of thirty-three thousand, where community and church leaders have asked Harvey officials to petition the state for the right to pray openly in school.

Mr. Graves and Harvey's aldermen have pressed their case in light of the Sept. 11 attacks, and the subsequent national embrace of public prayer. . . .

Illinois is among the dozen states that allow voluntary moments of silence in the schools. But Harvey officials pushing for prayer contend that the law, which permits a moment of silence at a teacher's discretion, does not go far enough.

"What we want is actual prayer," said Alderman Ronald J. Waters. "I happened to have been around on Sept. 11. The next day at some of those schools, there was open prayer all through the schools. Even the president is asking for prayer."

In December 2001 the *Chicago Tribune* carried the following story:

Chattanooga, Tenn. On a recent Sunday, 3,000 people showed up at a downtown sports arena for a Ten Commandments rally that had the fervor of an old-fashioned tent revival. Declaring themselves Christian soldiers in a war against evil, they prayed, waved American flags and poured thousands of dollars into collection buckets.

It was a carefully crafted scene that is being played out across America as Christian conservatives energized by the spiritual revival brought on by the Sept. 11 terrorist attacks campaign to post the Ten Commandments in public buildings throughout the country. The biblical laws, which some Christians insist should be established as American doctrine, have become a weapon in a long-standing battle to erase the line separating church and state. . . .

"Sept. 11 was a point of demarcation for a renewed interest in this movement," said Charles Wyson, president of Ten Commandments Tennessee, the advocacy and fund-raising group that sponsored the Chattanooga rally. "There is a defiance and an unwillingness on the part of God's people to be ruled by groups like the ACLU (American Civil Liberties Union). Everyone is tired of their feeble arguments, including the courts, and we're not listening to them any more."

Across the nation, clergy are leading student assemblies in prayer, schools are requiring a moment of prayer, and government meetings are opening with religious devotionals. Several local governments face lawsuits for erecting the Ten Commandments in public venues.[22]

Although these events are not necessarily representative of the feelings and behavior of Americans as a whole, they do resonate favorably with a significant number of people. Clearly September 11 generally aroused a turning to religion for sustenance and awakened new pressures for religious expression in our political life. It remains to be seen whether the form that it takes as time passes erodes to the detriment of our free society the separation of church and state that has served us so well for over two hundred years. It is my hope that the future of religious expression in the United States is not such that James Madison, the Father of our Constitution and primary sponsor of the First Amendment, will turn over in his grave.

Appendices

❖❖❖❖❖

M ost of the documents in these appendices are extensive excerpts from lengthier original versions. Omissions of textual material are indicated by ellipses. Footnotes have also been omitted. All of these materials are in the public domain and may be quoted freely.

Appendix 1. Roger Williams's
Bloudy Tenent of Persecution, 1644
[Part of the Preface Summarizing His Argument]

The Argument

First, That the blood of so many hundred thousand souls of Protestants and Papists, spilt in the Wars of present and former Ages, for their respective Consciences, is not required nor accepted by Jesus Christ the Prince of Peace. . . .

Fifthly, All Civil States with their Officers of justice in their respective constitutions and administrations are proved essentially Civil, and therefore not Judges, Governors or Defenders of the Spiritual or Christian State and Worship.

Sixthly, It is the will and command of God that (since the coming of his Son, the Lord Jesus) a permission of the most Paganish, Jewish, Turkish, or Antichristian consciences and worships, be granted to all men in all Nations and Countries: and they are only to be fought against with the Sword which is only (in Soul matters) able to conquer, to wit, the Sword of God's Spirit, the Word of God. . . .

Eighthly, God requireth not an uniformity of Religion to be inacted and inforced in any civil state, which inforced uniformity (sooner or later) is the greatest occasion of civil War, ravishing of conscience, persecution of Christ Jesus in his servants, and of the hypocrisy and destruction of millions of souls. . . .

Tenthly, An inforced uniformity of Religion throughout a Nation or civil state confounds the Civil and Religious, denies the principles of Christianity and civility, and that Jesus Christ, is come in the Flesh.

Eleventh, The permission of other consciences and worships than a state professeth, only can (according to God) procure a firm and lasting peace (good assurance being taken according to the wisdom of the civil state for uniformity of civil obedience from all sorts).

Twelfthly, lastly, True civility and Christianity may both flourish in a state or Kingdom, notwithstanding the permission of divers and contrary consciences, either of Jew or Gentile.

Appendix 2. The General Laws and Liberties of the Massachusetts Colony, 1646

Although no human power be Lord over the faith and consciences of men, yet because such as bring in damnable heresies, tending to the subversions of the Christian faith, and destruction of the souls of men, ought duly to be restrained from such notorious impieties; it is therefore ordered and declared by the Court;

That if any Christian within this jurisdiction, shall go about to subvert and destroy the Christian faith and religion, by broaching and maintaining any damnable heresies; as denying the immortality of the soul, or resurrection of the body, or any sin to be repented of in the regenerate, or any evil done by the outward man to be accounted sin, or denying that Christ gave Himself a ransom for our sins, or shall affirm that we are not justified by His death and righteousness, but by the perfections of our own works, or shall deny the mortality of the fourth commandment, or shall openly condemn or oppose the baptizing of infants, or shall purposely depart the congregation at the administration of that ordinance, or shall deny the Ordinance of magistracy, or their lawful authority to make War, or to punish the outward breaches of the first table, or shall endeavor to seduce others to any of the errors or heresies above mentioned; every such person continuing obstinate therein, after due means of conviction, shall be sentenced to banishment. . . .

It is ordered and enacted by the authority of this Court, That no Jesuit or spiritual or ecclesiastical person (as they are termed) ordained by the authority of the Pope or see of Rome, shall henceforth at any time repair to, or come within this jurisdiction; And if any person shall give just cause of suspicion, he shall be committed to prison, or bound over to the next Court of Assistants, to be tried and proceeded with, by banishment or otherwise as the Court shall see cause.

And if any person so banished, be taken the second time within his jurisdiction, upon lawful trial and conviction, he shall be put to death. Provided this law shall not extend to any such Jesuit, spiritual or ecclesiastical person, as shall cast upon our shores by shipwreck or other accident, so as he continue no longer than till he may have opportunity of passage for his departure; nor to any such as shall come in company with any messenger hither upon public occasions, or merchant, or master of any ship belonging to any place, not in enmity with the State of England, of ourselves, so as they depart again with the same messenger, master, or merchant. . . .

It is ordered by this court and the authority thereof, That what person or persons soever professing the Christian religion, above the age of 16 years, that shall within this jurisdiction, wittingly and willingly, at any time after the publication of this order, deny either by word or writing, any of the Books of the Old Testament . . . or New . . . to be the written and infallible word of God . . . he shall be adjudged for his offense after legal conviction, to pay such a fine as the court which shall have cognizance of the crime shall judge meet, not exceeding the sum of fifty pounds, or shall be openly and severely whipped by the executioner, whether constable or any other appointed, not exceeding forty strokes, unless he shall publicly recant. . . .

And it is further ordered and enacted, That if the said offender after his recantation, sentence or execution, shall the second time publish, and obstinately, and pertinaciously maintain the said wicked opinion, he shall be banished or put to death as the Court shall judge. . . .

This Court doth order and enact, That every person or persons of the cursed sect of Quakers, who is not an inhabitant of but found within this jurisdiction, shall be apprehended (without warrant) where no magistrate is at hand by any constable, commissioner, or selectman, and conveyed from constable to constable until they come before the next magistrate, who shall commit the said person or persons to close prison, there to remain without bail until the next Court of Assistants where they shall have a legal trial by a special jury, and being convicted to be of the sect of the Quakers, shall be sentenced to banishment upon pain of death.

Appendix 3. Maryland Act Concerning Religion, 1649

Forasmuch as in a well governed and Christian commonwealth, matters concerning religion and the honor of God ought in the first place to be taken into serious consideration and endeavored to be settled, *be it therefore ordered and enacted,* by the Right Honorable Cecelius, Lord Baron of Baltimore, Absolute Lord and Proprietary of this province, with the advice and consent of this General Assembly, that whatsoever person or persons within this province and the islands thereunto belong shall henceforth blaspheme God, or shall deny the Holy Trinity—the Father, Son, and the Holy Ghost—or the Godhead of any of the said three Persons of the Trinity or the unity of the Godhead, or shall use or utter any reproachful speeches, words, or language concerning the said Holy Trinity, or any of the said three Persons thereof, shall be punished with death and confiscation or forfeiture of all his or her lands and goods to the Lord Propietary and his heirs. . . .

And be it further likewise enacted, by the authority and consent aforesaid, that every person and persons within this province that shall at any time hereafter profane the Sabbath or Lord's Day called Sunday, by frequent swearing, drunkenness, or by any uncivil or disorderly recreation, or by working on that day when absolute necessity does not require it, shall for every such first offense forfeit 2s. 6d., or the value thereof, and for the second offense 5s. or the value thereof, and for the third offense and so for every time he shall offend in like manner afterward, 10s., or the value thereof. And in case such offender and offenders shall not have sufficient goods or chattels within this province to satisfy any of the said penalties respectively hereby imposed for profaning the Sabbath or Lord's Day called Sunday as aforesaid, that in every such case the party so offending shall for the first and second offense in that kind be imprisoned till he or she shall publicly in open court before the chief commander, judge, or magistrate of that county, town, or precinct where such offense shall be committed acknowledge the scandal and offense he has in that respect given against God and the good and civil government of this province, and for the third offense and for every time thereafter shall also be publicly whipped.

And whereas the enforcing of the conscience in matters of religion has frequently fallen out to be of dangerous consequence in these commonwealths where it has been practised, and for the more quiet and peaceable government of this province, and the better to preserve mutual love and amity among the inhabitants thereof, be it, therefore, also by the Lord Proprietary, with the advice and consent of this assembly, ordained and enacted (except as in this present act is before declared and set forth) that no person or persons whatsoever within this province, or the islands, ports, harbors, creeks, or havens thereunto belonging, professing to believe in Jesus Christ, shall from henceforth be in any way troubled, molested, or discountenanced for or in respect of his or her religion, nor in the free exercise thereof within this province or the islands thereunto belonging, nor in any way compelled to the belief or exercise of any other religion against his or her consent, so as they be not unfaithful to the Lord Proprietary, or molest or conspire against the civil government established or to be established in this province under him or his heirs.

And that all and every person and persons that shall presume contrary to this act and the true intent and meaning thereof directly or indirectly either in person or estate willfully to wrong, disturb, trouble, or molest any person whatsoever within this province professing to believe in Jesus Christ for, or in respect of, his or her religion or the free exercise thereof, within this province other than provided for in this act, that such person or persons so offending shall be compelled to pay treble damages to the party so wronged or molested, and for every such offense shall also forfeit 20s. in money or the value thereof, half thereof for the use of the Lord Proprietary, and his heirs, Lords, and Proprietaries of this province, and the other half for the use of the party so wrong or molested as aforesaid. Or if the party so offending shall refuse or be unable to recompense the party so wronged, or to satisfy such fine or forfeiture, then such offender shall be severely punished by public whipping and imprisonment, during the pleasure of the Lord Proprietary, or his lieutenant or chief governor of this province, for the time being without bail or mainprise.

And be it further enacted, by the authority and consent aforesaid, that the sheriff or other officer or officers from time to time to be appointed and authorized for that purpose, of the country, town, or precinct where every particular offense in this present act contained shall happen at any time to be committed and whereupon there is hereby a forfeiture, fine, or penalty imposed, shall from time to time distrain and seize the goods and estate of every such person so offending as aforesaid against this present act or any part thereof, and sell the same or any part thereof for the full satisfaction of such forfeiture, fine, or penalty as aforesaid, restoring unto the party so offended the remainder or overplus of the said goods or estate after such satisfaction so made as aforesaid.

The freemen have assented.

THOMAS HATTON
Entered by the Governor William Stone.

Appendix 4. John Locke's Letter Concerning Toleration, 1689

Honoured Sir,

Since you are pleased to inquire what are my thoughts about the mutual toleration of Christians in their different professions of religion, I must needs answer you freely that I esteem that toleration to be the chief characteristic mark of the true Church. For whatsoever some people boast of the antiquity of places and names, or of the pomp of their outward worship; others, of the reformation of their discipline; all, of the orthodoxy of their faith—for everyone is orthodox to himself—these things, and all others of this nature, are much rather marks of men striving for power and empire over one another than of the Church of Christ. Let anyone have never so true a claim to all these things, yet if he be destitute of charity, meekness, and good-will in general towards all mankind, even to those that are not Christians, he is certainly yet short of being a true Christian himself. "The kings of the Gentiles exercise leadership over them," said our Saviour to his disciples, "but ye shall not be so." The business of true religion is quite another thing. It is not instituted in order to the erecting of an external pomp, nor to the obtaining of ecclesiastical dominion, nor to the exercising of compulsive force, but to the regulating of men's lives, according to the rules of virtue and piety. Whosoever will list himself under the banner of Christ, must, in the first place and above all things, make war upon his own lusts and vices. It is in vain for any man to usurp the name of Christian, without holiness of life, purity of manners, benignity and meekness of spirit. "Let everyone that nameth the name of Christ, depart from iniquity." "Thou, when thou art converted, strengthen thy brethren," said our Lord to Peter. It would, indeed, be very hard for one that appears careless about his own salvation to persuade me that he were extremely concerned for mine. For it is impossible that those should sincerely and heartily apply themselves to make other people Christians, who have not really embraced the Christian religion in their own hearts. If the Gospel and the apostles may be credited, no man can be a Christian without charity and without that faith which works, not by force, but by love. Now, I appeal to the consciences of those that persecute, torment, destroy, and kill other men upon pretence of religion, whether they do it out of friendship and kindness towards them or no? And I shall then indeed, and not until then, believe they do so, when I shall see those fiery zealots correcting, in the same manner, their friends and familiar acquaintance for the manifest sins they commit against the precepts of the Gospel; when I shall see them persecute with fire and sword the members of their own communion that are tainted with enormous vices and without amendment are in danger of eternal perdition; and when I shall see them thus express their love and desire of the salvation of their souls by the infliction of torments and exercise of all manner of cruelties. For if it be out of a principle of charity, as they pretend, and love to men's souls that they deprive them of their estates, maim them with corporal punishments, starve and torment them in noisome prisons, and in the end even take away their lives—I say, if all this be done merely to make men Christians and procure their salvation, why then do they suffer whoredom, fraud, malice, and such-like enormities, which (according to the apostle) manifestly relish of heathenish corruption, to predominate so much and abound amongst their flocks and people? These, and such-like things, are certainly more contrary to the glory of God, to the purity of the Church, and to the salvation of souls, than any conscientious dissent from ecclesiastical decisions, or separation from public worship, whilst accompanied with innocence of life. Why, then, does this burning zeal for God, for the Church, and for the salvation of souls— burning I say, literally, with fire and faggot—pass by those moral vices and wickednesses, without any chastisement, which are acknowledged by all men to be diametrically opposite to the profession of Christianity, and bend all its nerves either to the introducing of ceremonies, or to the establishment of opinions, which for the most part are about nice and intricate matters, that exceed the capacity of ordinary understandings? Which of the parties contending about these things is in the right, which of them is guilty of schism or heresy, whether those that domineer or those that suffer, will then at last be manifest when the causes of their separation comes to be judged of He, certainly, that follows Christ, embraces His doctrine, and bears His yoke, though he forsake both father and mother, separate from the public assemblies and ceremonies of his country, or whomsoever or whatsoever else he relinquishes, will not then be judged a heretic.

Now, though the divisions that are amongst sects should be allowed to be never so obstructive of the salvation of souls; yet, nevertheless, adultery, fornication, uncleanliness, lasciviousness, idolatry, and such-like things, cannot be denied to be works of the flesh, concerning which the apostle has expressly declared that "they who do them shall not inherit the kingdom of God." Whosoever, therefore, is sincerely solicitous about the kingdom of God and thinks it his duty to endeavour the enlargement of it amongst men, ought to apply himself with no less care and industry to the rooting out of these immoralities than to the extirpation of sects. But if anyone do otherwise, and whilst he is cruel and implacable towards those that differ from him in opinion, he be indulgent to such iniquities and immoralities as are unbecoming the name of a Christian, let such a one talk never so much of the Church, he plainly demonstrates by his actions that it is another kingdom he aims at and not the advancement of the kingdom of God.

That any man should think fit to cause another man—whose salvation he heartily desires—to expire in torments, and that even in an unconverted state, would, I confess, seem very strange to me, and I think, to any other also. But nobody, surely, will ever believe that such a carriage can proceed from charity, love, or goodwill. If anyone maintain that men ought to be compelled by fire and sword to profess certain doctrines, and conform to this or that exterior worship, without any regard had unto their morals; if anyone endeavour to convert those that are erroneous unto the faith, by forcing them to profess things that they do not believe and allowing them to practise things that the Gospel does not permit, it cannot be doubted indeed but such a one is desirous to have a numerous assembly joined in the same profession with himself; but that he principally intends by those means to compose a truly Christian Church is altogether incredible. It is not, therefore, to be wondered at if those who do not really contend for the advancement of the true religion, and of the Church of Christ, make use of arms that do not belong to the Christian warfare. If, like the Captain of our salvation, they sincerely desired the good of souls, they would tread in the steps and follow the perfect example of that Prince of Peace, who sent out His soldiers to the subduing of nations, and gathering them into His Church, not armed with the sword, or other instruments of force, but prepared with the Gospel of peace and with the exemplary holiness of their conversation. This was His method. Though if infidels were to be converted by force, if those that are either blind or obstinate were to be drawn off from their errors by armed soldiers, we know very well that it was much more easy for Him to do it with armies of heavenly legions than for any son of the Church, how potent soever, with all his dragoons.

The toleration of those that differ from others in matters of religion is so agreeable to the Gospel of Jesus Christ, and to the genuine reason of mankind, that it seems monstrous for men to be so blind as not to perceive the necessity and advantage of it in so clear a light. I will not here tax the pride and ambition of some, the passion and uncharitable zeal of others.

These are faults from which human affairs can perhaps scarce ever be perfectly freed; but yet such as nobody will bear the plain imputation of, without covering them with some specious colour; and so pretend to commendation, whilst they are carried away by their own irregular passions. But, however, that some may not colour their spirit of persecution and unchristian cruelty with a pretence of care of the public weal and observation of the laws; and that others, under pretence of religion, may not seek impunity for their libertinism and licentiousness; in a word, that none may impose either upon himself or others, by the pretences of loyalty and obedience to the prince, or of tenderness and sincerity in the worship of God; I esteem it above all things necessary to distinguish exactly the business of civil government from that of religion and to settle the just bounds that lie between the one and the other. If this be not done, there can be no end put to the controversies that will be always arising between those that have, or at least pretend to have, on the one side, a concernment for the interest of men's souls, and, on the other side, a care of the commonwealth. . . .

Now that the whole jurisdiction of the magistrate reaches only to . . . civil concernments, and that all civil power, right and dominion, is bounded and confined to the only care of promoting these things; and that it neither can nor ought in any manner to be extended to the salvation of souls, these following considerations seem unto me abundantly to demonstrate.

First, because the care of souls is not committed to the civil magistrate, any more than to other men. It is not committed unto him, I say, by God; because it appears not that God has ever given any such authority to one man over another as to compel anyone to his religion. Nor can any such power be vested in the magistrate by the consent of the people, because no man can so far abandon the care of his own salvation as blindly to leave to the choice of any other, whether prince or subject, to prescribe to him what faith or worship he shall embrace. For no man can, if he would, conform his faith to the dictates of another. All the life and power of true religion consist in the inward and full persuasion of the mind; and faith is not faith without believing. Whatever profession we make, to whatever outward worship we conform, if we are not fully satisfied in our own mind that the one is true and the other well pleasing unto God, such profession and such practice, far from being any furtherance, are indeed great obstacles to our salvation. For in this manner, instead of expiating other sins by the exercise of religion, I say, in offering thus unto God Almighty such a worship as we esteem to be displeasing unto Him, we add unto the number of our other sins those also of hypocrisy and contempt of His Divine Majesty.

In the second place, the care of souls cannot belong to the civil magistrate, because his power consists only in outward force; but true and saving religion consists in the inward persuasion of the mind, without which nothing can be acceptable to God. And such is the nature of the understanding, that it cannot be compelled to the belief of anything by outward force. Confiscation of estate, imprisonment, torments, nothing of that nature can have any such efficacy as to make men change the inward judgement that they have framed of things.

It may indeed be alleged that the magistrate may make use of arguments, and, thereby; draw the heterodox into the way of truth, and procure their salvation. I grant it; but this is common to him with other men. In teaching, instructing, and redressing the erroneous by reason, he may certainly do what becomes any good man to do. Magistracy does not oblige him to put off either humanity or Christianity; but it is one thing to persuade, another to command; one thing to press with arguments, another with penalties. This civil power alone has a right to do; to the other, goodwill is authority enough. Every man has commission to admonish, exhort, convince another of error, and, by reasoning, to draw him into truth; but to give laws, receive obedience, and compel with the sword, belongs to none but the magistrate. And, upon this ground, I affirm that the magistrate's power extends not to the establishing of any articles of faith, or forms of worship, by the force of his laws. For laws are of no force at all without penalties, and penalties in this case are absolutely impertinent, because they are not proper to convince the mind. Neither the profession of any articles of faith, nor the conformity to any outward form of worship (as has been already said), can be available to the salvation of souls, unless the truth of the one and the acceptableness of the other unto God be thoroughly believed by those that so profess and practise. But penalties are no way capable to produce such belief. It is only light and evidence that can work a change in men's opinions; which light can in no manner proceed from corporal sufferings, or any other outward penalties.

In the third place, the care of the salvation of men's souls cannot belong to the magistrate; because, though the rigour of laws and the force of penalties were capable to convince and change men's minds, yet would not that help at all to the salvation of their souls. For there being but one truth, one way to heaven, what hope is there that more men would be led into it if they had no rule but the religion of the court and were put under the necessity to quit the light of their own reason, and oppose the dictates of their own consciences, and blindly to resign themselves up to the will of their governors and to the religion which either ignorance, ambition, or superstition had chanced to establish in the countries where they were born? In the variety and contradiction of opinions in religion, wherein the princes of the world are as much divided as in their secular interests, the narrow way would be much straitened; one country alone would be in the right, and all the rest of the world put under an obligation of following their princes in the ways that lead to destruction; and that which heightens the absurdity, and very ill suits the notion of a Deity, men would owe their eternal happiness or misery to the places of their nativity.

These considerations, to omit many others that might have been urged to the same purpose, seem unto me sufficient to conclude that all the power of civil government relates only to men's civil interests, is confined to the care of the things of this world, and hath nothing to do with the world to come. . . .

. . . no private person has any right in any manner to prejudice another person in his civil enjoyments because he is of another church or religion. All the rights and franchises that belong to him as a man, or as a denizen, are inviolably to be preserved to him. These are not the business of religion. No violence nor injury is to be offered him, whether he be Christian or Pagan. Nay, we must not content ourselves with the narrow measures of bare justice; charity, bounty, and liberality must be added to it. This the Gospel enjoins, this reason directs, and this that natural fellowship we are born into requires of us. If any man err from the right way, it is his own misfortune, no injury to thee; nor therefore art thou to punish him in the things of this life because thou supposest he will be miserable in that which is to come.

What I say concerning the mutual toleration of private persons differing from one another in religion, I understand also of particular churches which stand, as it were, in the same relation to each other as private persons among themselves: nor has any one of them any manner of jurisdiction over any other; no, not even when the civil magistrate (as it sometimes happens) comes to be of this or the other communion. For the civil government can give no new right to the church, nor the church to the civil government. So that, whether the magistrate join himself to any church, or separate from it, the church remains always as it was before—a free and voluntary society. It neither requires the power of the sword by the magistrate's coming to it, nor does it lose the right of instruction and excommunication by his going from it. This is the fundamental and immutable right of a spontaneous society—that it has power to remove any of its members who transgress the rules of its institution; but it cannot, by the accession of any new members, acquire any right of jurisdiction over those that are not joined with it. And therefore peace, equity, and friendship are always mutually to be observed by particular churches, in the same manner as by private persons, without any pretence of superiority or jurisdiction over one another. . . .

Nobody . . . neither single persons nor churches, nay, nor even commonwealths, have any just title to invade the civil rights and worldly goods of each other upon pretence of religion. Those that are of another opinion would do well to consider with themselves how pernicious a seed of discord and war, how powerful a provocation to endless hatreds, rapines, and slaughters they thereby furnish unto mankind. No peace and security, no, not so much as common friendship, can ever be established or preserved amongst men so long as this opinion prevails, that dominion is founded in grace and that religion is to be propagated by force of arms. . . .

But this is not all. It is not enough that ecclesiastical men abstain from violence and rapine and all manner of persecution. He that pretends to be a successor of the apostles, and takes upon him the office of teaching, is obliged also to admonish his hearers of the duties of peace and goodwill towards all men, as well towards the erroneous as the orthodox; towards those that differ from them in faith and worship as well as towards those that agree with them therein. And he ought industriously to exhort all men, whether private persons or magistrates (if any such there be in his church), to charity, meekness, and toleration, and diligently endeavour to ally and temper all that heat and unreasonable averseness of mind which either any man's fiery zeal for his own sect or the craft of others has kindled against dissenters. I will not undertake to represent how happy and how great would be the fruit, both in Church and State, if the pulpits everywhere sounded with this doctrine of peace and toleration, lest I should seem to reflect too severely upon those men whose dignity I desire not to detract from, nor would have it diminished either by others or themselves. But this I say, that thus it ought to be. And if anyone that professes himself to be a minister of the Word of God, a preacher of the gospel of peace, teach otherwise, he either understands not or neglects the business of his calling and shall one day give account thereof unto the Prince of Peace. If Christians are to be admonished that they abstain from all manner of revenge, even after repeated provocations and multiplied injuries, how much more ought they who suffer nothing, who have had no harm done them, forbear violence and abstain from all manner of ill-usage towards those from whom they have received none! This caution and temper they ought certainly to use towards those. who mind only their own business and are solicitous for nothing but that (whatever men think of them) they may worship God in that manner which they are persuaded is acceptable to Him and in which they have the strongest hopes of eternal salvation. In private domestic affairs, in the management of estates, in the conservation of bodily health, every man may consider what suits his own convenience and follow what course he likes best. No man complains of the ill-management of his neighbour's affairs. No man is angry with another for an error committed in sowing his land or in marrying his daughter. Nobody corrects a spendthrift for consuming his substance in taverns. Let any man pull down, or build, or make whatsoever expenses he pleases, nobody murmurs, nobody controls him; he has his liberty. But if any man do not frequent the church, if he do not there conform his behaviour exactly to the accustomed ceremonies, or if he brings not his children to be initiated in the sacred mysteries of this or the other congregation, this immediately causes an uproar. The neighbourhood is filled with noise and clamour. Everyone is ready to be the avenger of so great a crime, and the zealots hardly have the patience to refrain from violence and rapine so long till the cause be heard and the poor man be, according to form, condemned to the loss of liberty, goods, or life. Oh, that our ecclesiastical orators of every sect would apply themselves with all the strength of arguments that they are able to the confounding of men's errors! But let them spare their persons. Let them not supply their want of reasons with the instruments of force, which belong to another jurisdiction and do ill become a Churchman's hands. Let them not call in the magistrate's authority to the aid of their eloquence or learning, lest perhaps, whilst they pretend only love for the truth, this their intemperate zeal, breathing nothing but fire and sword, betray their ambition and show that what they desire is temporal dominion. For it will be very difficult to persuade men of sense that he who with dry eyes and satisfaction of mind can deliver his brother to the executioner to be burnt alive, does sincerely and heartily concern himself to save that brother from the flames of hell in the world to come. . . .

Further, the magistrate ought not to forbid the preaching or professing of any speculative opinions in any Church because they have no manner of relation to the civil rights of the subjects. If a Roman Catholic believe that to be really the body of Christ which another man calls bread, he does no injury thereby to his neighbour. If a Jew do not believe the New Testament to be the Word of God, he does not thereby alter anything in men's civil rights. If a heathen doubt of both Testaments, he is not therefore to be punished as a pernicious citizen. The power of the magistrate and the estates of the people may be equally secure whether any man believe these things or no. I readily grant that these opinions are false and absurd. But the business of laws is not to provide for the truth of opinions, but for the safety and security of the commonwealth and of every particular man's goods and person. And so it ought to be. For the truth certainly would do well enough if she were once left to shift for herself. She seldom has received and, I fear, never will receive much assistance from the power of great men, to whom she is but rarely known and more rarely welcome. She is not taught by laws, nor has she any need of force to procure her entrance into the minds of men. Errors, indeed, prevail by the assistance of foreign and borrowed succours. But if Truth makes not her way into the understanding by her own light, she will be but the weaker for any borrowed force violence can add to her. . . .

These things being thus explained, it is easy to understand to what end the legislative power ought to be directed and by what measures regulated; and that is the temporal good and outward prosperity of the society; which is the sole reason of men's entering into society, and the only thing they seek and aim at in it. And it is also evident what liberty remains to men in reference to their eternal salvation, and that is that every one should do what he in his conscience is persuaded to be acceptable to the Almighty, on whose good pleasure and acceptance depends their eternal happiness. For obedience is due, in the first place, to God and, afterwards to the laws.

But some may ask: "What if the magistrate should enjoin anything by his authority that appears unlawful to the conscience of a private person?" I answer that, if government be faithfully administered and the counsels of the magistrates be indeed directed to the public good, this will seldom happen. But if, perhaps, it do so fall out, I say, that such a private person is to abstain from the action that he judges unlawful, and he is to undergo the punishment which it is not unlawful for him to bear. For the private judgement of any person concerning a law enacted in political matters, for the public good, does not take away the obligation of that law, nor deserve a dispensation. But if the law, indeed, be concerning things that lie not within the verge of the magistrate's authority (as, for example, that the people, or any party amongst them, should be compelled to embrace a strange religion, and join in the worship and ceremonies of another Church), men are not in these cases obliged by that law, against their consciences. For the political society is instituted for no other end, but only to secure every man's possession of the things of this life. The care of each man's soul and of the things of heaven, which neither does belong to the commonwealth nor can be subjected to it, is left entirely to every man's self. Thus the safeguard of men's lives and of the things that belong unto this life is the business of the commonwealth; and the preserving of those things unto their owners is the duty of the magistrate. And therefore the magistrate cannot take away these worldly things from this man or party and give them to that; nor change propriety amongst fellow subjects (no not even by a law), for a cause that has no relation to the end of civil government, I mean for their religion, which whether it be true or false does no prejudice to the worldly concerns of their fellow subjects, which are the things that only belong unto the care of the commonwealth. . . .

Appendix 5. Jefferson's Notes on Virginia, 1782

. . . The error seems not sufficiently eradicated, that the operations of the mind, as well as the acts of the body, are subject to the coercion of the laws. But our rulers can have no authority over such natural rights, only as we have submitted to them. The rights of conscience we never submitted, we could not submit. We are answerable for them to our God. The legitimate powers of government extend to such acts only as are injurious to others. But it does me no injury for my neighbor to say there are twenty gods, or no God. It neither picks my pocket nor breaks my leg. . . .

Reason and free inquiry are the only effectual agents against error. Give a loose to them, they will support the true religion by bringing every false one to their tribunal, to the test of their investigation. They are the natural enemies of error, and of error only. . . . Galileo was sent to the Inquisition for affirming that the earth was a sphere; the government had declared it to be as flat as a trencher, and Galileo was obliged to abjure his error. This error, however, at length prevailed, the earth became a globe, and Descartes declared it was whirled round its axis by a vortex. . . .

It is error alone which needs the support of government. Truth can stand by itself. Subject opinions to coercion: whom will you make your inquisitors? Fallible men; men governed by bad passions, by private as well as public reasons. And why subject it to coercion? To produce uniformity. But is uniformity of opinion desirable? No more than of face and stature. Introduce the bed of Procrustes then, as there is danger that the large men may beat the small, make us all of a size, by lopping the former and stretching the latter. Difference of opinion is advantageous in religion. The several sects perform the office of a *censor morum* over each other. Is uniformity attainable? Millions of innocent men, women, and children, since the introduction of Christianity, have been burnt, tortured, fined, imprisoned; yet we have not advanced one inch towards uniformity. What has been the effect of coercion? To make one half the world fools, and the other half hypocrites. To support roguery and error all over the earth. . . .

Appendix 6. James Madison's Memorial and Remonstrance against Religious Assessments, 1785

To the Honorable the General Assembly of the Commonwealth of Virginia

We the subscribers, citizens of the said Commonwealth, having taken into serious consideration, a Bill printed by order of the last Session of General Assembly, entitled "A Bill establishing a provision for Teachers of the Christian Religion," and conceiving that the same if finally armed with the sanctions of a law, will be a dangerous abuse of power, are bound as faithful members of a free State to remonstrate against it, and to declare the reasons by which we are determined. We remonstrate against the said Bill,

1. Because we hold it for a fundamental and undeniable truth, "that religion or the duty which we owe to our Creator and the manner of discharging it, can be directed only by reason and conviction, not by force or violence." The Religion then of every man must be left to the conviction and conscience of every man; and it is the right of every man to exercise it as these may dictate. This right is in its nature an unalienable right. It is unalienable, because the opinions of men, depending only on the evidence contemplated by their own minds cannot follow the dictates of other men: It is unalienable also, because what is here a right towards men, is a duty towards the Creator. It is the duty of every man to render to the Creator such homage and such only as he believes to be acceptable to him. This duty is precedent, both in order of time and in degree of obligation, to the claims of Civil Society. Before any man can be considered as a member of Civil Society, he must be considered as a subject of the Governour of the Universe: And if a member of Civil Society, do it with a saving of his allegiance to the Universal Sovereign. We maintain therefore that in matters of Religion, no man's right is abridged by the institution of Civil Society and that Religion is wholly exempt from its cognizance. True it is, that no other rule exists, by which any question which may divide a Society, can be ultimately determined, but the will of the majority; but it is also true that the majority may trespass on the rights of the minority.

2. Because Religion be exempt from the authority of the Society at large, still less can it be subject to that of the Legislative Body. The latter are but the creatures and vicegerents of the former. Their jurisdiction is

both derivative and limited: it is limited with regard to the co-ordinate departments, more necessarily is it limited with regard to the constituents. The preservation of a free Government requires not merely, that the metes and bounds which separate each department of power be invariably maintained; but more especially that neither of them be suffered to overleap the great Barrier which defends the rights of the people. The Rulers who are guilty of such an encroachment, exceed the commission from which they derive their authority, and are Tyrants. The People who submit to it are governed by laws made neither by themselves nor by an authority derived from them, and are slaves.

3. Because it is proper to take alarm at the first experiment on our liberties. We hold this prudent jealousy to be the first duty of Citizens, and one of the noblest characteristics of the late Revolution. The free men of America did not wait till usurped power had strengthened itself by exercise, and entangled the question in precedents. They saw all the consequences in the principle, and they avoided the consequences by denying the principle. We revere this lesson too much soon to forget it. Who does not see that the same authority which can establish Christianity, in exclusion of all other Religions, may establish with the same ease any particular sect of Christians, in exclusion of all other Sects? that the same authority which can force a citizen to contribute three pence only of his property for the support of any one establishment, may force him to conform to any other establishment in all cases whatsoever?

4. Because the Bill violates the equality which ought to be the basis of every law, and which is more indispensible, in proportion as the validity or expediency of any law is more liable to be impeached. If "all men are by nature equally free and independent," all men are to be considered as entering into Society on equal conditions; as relinquishing no more, and therefore retaining no less, one than another, of their natural rights. Above all are they to be considered as retaining an "equal title to the free exercise of Religion according to the dictates of Conscience." Whilst we assert for ourselves a freedom to embrace, to profess and to observe the Religion which we believe to be of divine origin, we cannot deny an equal freedom to those whose minds have not yet yielded to the evidence which has convinced us. If this freedom be abused, it is an offence against God, not against man: To God, therefore, not to man, must an account of it be rendered. As the Bill violates

equality by subjecting some to peculiar burdens, so it violates the same principle, by granting to others peculiar exemptions. Are the quakers and Menonists the only sects who think a compulsive support of their Religions unnecessary and unwarrantable? can their piety alone be entrusted with the care of public worship? Ought their Religions to be endowed above all others with extraordinary privileges by which proselytes may be enticed from all others? We think too favorably of the justice and good sense of these demoninations to believe that they either covet pre-eminences over their fellow citizens or that they will be seduced by them from the common opposition to the measure.

5. Because the Bill implies either that the Civil Magistrate is a competent Judge of Religious Truth; or that he may employ Religion as an engine of Civil policy. The first is an arrogant pretension falsified by the contradictory opinions of Rulers in all ages, and throughout the world: the second an unhallowed perversion of the means of salvation.

6. Because the establishment proposed by the Bill is not requisite for the support of the Christian Religion. To say that it is, is a contradiction to the Christian Religion itself, for every page of it disavows a dependence on the powers of this world: it is a contradiction to fact; for it is known that this Religion both existed and flourished, not only without the support of human laws, but in spite of every opposition from them, and not only during the period of miraculous aid, but long after it had been left to its own evidence and the ordinary care of Providence. Nay, it is a contradiction in terms; for a Religion not invented by human policy, must have pre-existed and been supported, before it was established by human policy. It is moreover to weaken in those who profess this Religion a pious confidence in its innate excellence and the patronage of its Author; and to foster in those who still reject it, a suspicion that its friends are too conscious of its fallacies to trust it to its own merits.

7. Because experience witnesseth that eccelsiastical establishments, instead of maintaining the purity and efficacy of Religion, have had a contrary operation. During almost fifteen centuries has the legal establishment of Christianity been on trial. What have been its fruits? More or less in all places, pride and indolence in the Clergy, ignorance and servility in the laity, in both, superstition, bigotry and persecution. Enquire of the Teachers of Christianity for the ages in which it appeared in its greatest lustre; those of every sect, point to the ages prior to its incorporation with Civil policy. Propose a restoration of this primitive State in which its

Teachers depended on the voluntary rewards of their flocks, many of them predict its downfall. On which Side ought their testimony to have greatest weight, when for or when against their interest?

8. Because the establishment in question is not necessary for the support of Civil Government. If it be urged as necessary for the support of Civil Government only as it is a means of supporting Religion, and it be not necessary for the latter purpose, it cannot be necessary for the former. If Religion be not within the cognizance of Civil Government how can its legal establishment be necessary to Civil Government? What influence in fact have ecclesiastical establishments had on Civil Society? In some instances they have been seen to erect a spiritual tyranny on the ruins of the Civil authority; in many instances they have been seen upholding the thrones of political tyranny: in no instance have they been seen the guardians of the liberties of the people. Rulers who wished to subvert the public liberty, may have found an established Clergy convenient auxiliaries. A just Government instituted to secure & perpetuate it needs them not. Such a Government will be best supported by protecting every Citizen in the enjoyment of his Religion with the same equal hand which protects his person and his property; by neither invading the equal rights of any Sect, nor suffering any Sect to invade those of another.

9. Because the proposed establishment is a departure from the generous policy, which, offering an Asylum to the persecuted and oppressed of every Nation and Religion, promised a lustre to our country, and an accession to the number of its citizens. What a melancholy mark is the Bill of sudden degeneracy? Instead of holding forth an Asylum to the persecuted, it is itself a signal of persecution. It degrades from the equal rank of Citizens all those whose opinions in Religion do not bend to those of the Legislative authority. Distant as it may be in its present form from the Inquisition, it differs from it only in degree. The one is the first step, the other the last in the career of intolerance. The maganimous sufferer under this cruel scourge in foreign Regions, must view the Bill as a Beacon on our Coast, warning him to seek some other haven, where liberty and philanthrophy in their due extent, may offer a more certain respose from his Troubles.

10. Because it will have a like tendency to banish our Citizens. The allurements presented by other situations are every day thinning their number. To superadd a fresh motive to emigration by revoking the liberty which they now enjoy, would be the same species of folly which has dishonoured and depopulated flourishing kingdoms.

11. Because it will destroy that moderation and harmony which the forbearance of our laws to intermeddle with Religion has produced among its several sects. Torrents of blood have been split in the old world, by vain attempts of the secular arm, to extinguish Religious disscord, by proscribing all difference in Religious opinion. Time has at length revealed the true remedy. Every relaxation of narrow and rigorous policy, wherever it has been tried, has been found to assuage the disease. The American Theatre has exhibited proofs that equal and compleat liberty, if it does not wholly eradicate it, sufficiently destroys its malignant influence on the health and prosperity of the State. If with the salutary effects of this system under our own eyes, we begin to contract the bounds of Religious freedom, we know no name that will too severely reproach our folly. At least let warning be taken at the first fruits of the threatened innovation. The very appearance of the Bill has transformed "that Christian forbearance, love and chairty," which of late mutually prevailed, into animosities and jeolousies, which may not soon be appeased. What mischiefs may not be dreaded, should this enemy to the public quiet be armed with the force of a law?

12. Because the policy of the Bill is adverse to the diffusion of the light of Christianity. The first wish of those who enjoy this precious gift ought to be that it may be imparted to the whole race of mankind. Compare the number of those who have as yet received it with the number still remaining under the dominion of false Religions; and how small is the former! Does the policy of the Bill tend to lessen the disproportion? No; it at once discourages those who are strangers to the light of revelation from coming into the Region of it; and countenances by example the nations who continue in darkness, in shutting out those who might convey it to them. Instead of Levelling as far as possible, every obstacle to the victorious progress of Truth, the Bill with an ignoble and unchristian timidity would circumscribe it with a wall of defence against the encroachments of error.

13. Because attempts to enforce by legal sanctions, acts obnoxious to go great a proportion of Citizens, tend to enervate the laws in general, and to slacken the bands of Society. If it be difficult to execute any law which is not generally deemed necessary or salutary, what must be the case, where it is deemed invalid and dangerous? And what may be the effect of so striking an example of impotency in the Government, on its general authority?

14. Because a measure of such singular magnitude and delicacy ought not to be imposed, without the clearest evidence that it is called for by a majority of citizens, and no satisfactory method is yet proposed by which the voice of the majority in this case may be determined, or its influence secured. The people of the respective counties are indeed requested to signify their opinion respecting the adoption of the Bill to the next Session of Assembly." But the representatives or of the Counties will be that of the people. Our hope is that neither of the former will, after due consideration, espouse the dangerous principle of the Bill. Should the event disappoint us, it will still leave us in full confidence, that a fair appeal to the latter will reverse the sentence against our liberties.

15. Because finally, "the equal right of every citizen to the free exercise of his Religion according to the dictates of conscience" is held by the same tenure with all our other rights. If we recur to its origin, it is equally the gift of nature; if we weigh its importance, it cannot be less dear to us; if we consult the "Declaration of those rights which pertain to the good people of Vriginia, as the basis and foundation of Government," it is enumerated with equal solemnity, or rather studied emphasis. Either the, we must say, that the Will of the Legislature is the only measure of their authority; and that in the plenitude of this authority, they may sweep away all our fundamental rights; or, that they are bound to leave this particular right untouched and sacred: Either we must say, that they may controul the freedom of the press, may abolish the Trial by Jury, may swallow up the Executive and Judiciary Powers of the State; nay that they may despoil us of our very right of suffrage, and erect themselves into an independent and hereditary Assembly or, we must say, that they have no authority to enact into the law the Bill under consideration. We the Subscribers say, that the General Assembly of this Commonwealth have no such authority: And that no effort may be omitted on our part against so dangerous an usurpation, we oppose to it, this remonstrance; earnestly praying, as we are in duty bound, that the Supreme Lawgiver of the Universe, by illuminating those to whom it is addressed, may on the one hand, turn their Councils from every act which would affront his holy prerogative, or violate the trust committed to them: and on the other, guide them into every measure which may be worthy of his [blessing, may re]dound to their own praise, and may establish more firmly the liberties, the prosperity and the happiness of the Commonweath.

Appendix 7. Virginia Act for Establishing Religious Freedom, 1786

I.   WHEREAS Almighty God hath created the mind free; that all attempts
     to influence it by temporal punishments or burthens, or by civil inca-
     pacitations, tend only to beget habits of hypocrisy and meanness, and
     are a departure from the plan of the Holy author of our religion, who
     being Lord both of body and mind, yet chose not to propagate it by co-
     ercions on either, as was in his Almighty power to do; that the impious
     presumption of legislators and rulers, civil as well as ecclesiastical, who
     being themselves but fallible and uninspired men, have assumed do-
     minion over the faith of others, setting up their own opinions and
     modes of thinking as the only true and infallible, and as such endeav-
     oring to impose them on others, hath established and maintained false
     religions over the greatest part of the world, and through all time; that
     to compel a man to furnish contributions of money for the propagation
     of opinions which he disbelieves, is sinful and tyrannical; that even the
     forcing him to support this or that teacher of his own religious persua-
     sion, is depriving him of the comfortable liberty of giving his contribu-
     tions to the particular pastor whose morals he would make his pattern,
     and whose powers he feels most persuasive to righteousness, and is
     withdrawing from the ministry those temporary rewards, which pro-
     ceeding from an approbation of their personal conduct, are an addi-
     tional incitement to earnest and unremitting labours for the instruction
     of mankind; that our civil rights have no dependence on our religious
     opinions, any more than our opinions in physics or geometry; that
     therefore the proscribing any citizen as unworthy to the public confi-
     dence by laying upon him an incapacity of being called to offices of
     trust and emolument, unless he profess or renounce this or that reli-
     gious opinion, is depriving him injuriously of those privileges and ad-
     vantages to which in common with his fellow-citizens he has a natural
     right, that it tends only to corrupt the principles of that religion it is
     meant to encourage, by bribing with a monopoly of worldly honours
     and emoluments, those who will externally profess and conform to it;
     that though indeed these are criminal who do not understand such
     temptation, yet neither are those innocent who lay the bait in their
     way; that to suffer the civil magistrate to intrude his powers into
     the field of opinion, and to restrain the profession or propagation of

principles on supposition of their ill tendency, is a dangerous fallacy, which at once destroys all religious liberty, because he being of course judge of that tendency will make his opinions the rule of judgment, and approve or condemn the sentiments of others only as they shall square with or differ from his own; that it is time enough for the rightful purposes of civil government, for its officers to intervene when principles break out into overt acts against peace and good order; and finally, that truth is great and will prevail if left to herself, that she is the proper and sufficient antagonist to error, and has nothing to fear from the conflict, unless by human interposition disarmed of her natural weapons, free argument and debate, errors ceasing to be dangerous when it is permitted freely to contradict them.

II. *Be it enacted by the General Assembly,* that no man shall be compelled to frequent or support any religious worship, place or ministry whatsoever, nor shall be enforced, restrained, molested, or burthened in his body or goods, nor shall otherwise suffer on account of his religious opinions or belief; but that all men shall be free to profess, and by argument to maintain, their opinion in matters of religion, and that the same shall in no wise diminish, enlarge or affect their civil capacities.

III. And though we all know that this assembly, elected by the people for the ordinary purposes of legislation only, have no power to restrain the acts of succeeding assemblies, constituted with powers equal to our own, and that therefore to declare this act to be irrevocable would be of no effect in law; yet as we are free to declare, and do declare, that the rights hereby asserted are of the natural rights of mankind, and that if any act shall hereafter be passed to repeal the present, or to narrow its operation, such act will be an infringement of natural right.

Appendix 8. Thomas Jefferson's Reply to the Danbury Baptist Association, 1802

MESSRS. NEHEMIAH DODGE, EPHRAIM ROBBINS, and STEPHEN S. NELSON, A Committee of the Danbury Baptist Association, in the State of Connecticut.

Washington, January 1, 1802

GENTLEMEN, - The affectionate sentiments of esteem and approbation which you are so good as to express towards me, on behalf of the Danbury Baptist Association, give me the highest satisfaction. My duties dictate a faithful and zealous pursuit of the interests of my constituents, and in proportion as they are persuaded of my fidelity to those duties, the discharge of them becomes more and more pleasing.

Believing with you that religion is a matter which lies solely between man and his God, that he owes account to none other for his faith or his worship, that the legislative powers of government reach actions only, and not opinions, I contemplate with sovereign reverence that act of the whole American people which declared that their legislature should "make no law respecting an establishment of religion, or prohibiting the free exercise thereof," thus building a wall of separation between Church and State. Adhering to this expression of the supreme will of the nation in behalf of the rights of conscience, I shall see with sincere satisfaction the progress of those sentiments which tend to restore to man all his natural rights, convinced he has no natural right in opposition to his social duties.

I reciprocate your kind prayers for the protection and blessing of the common Father and Creator of man, and tender you for yourselves and your religious association, assurances of my high respect and esteem.

Appendix 9. Engel v Vitale
370 U.S. 421 (1962)

MR. JUSTICE BLACK delivered the opinion of the Court.

The respondent Board of Education of Union Free School District No. 9, New Hyde Park, New York, acting in its official capacity under state law, directed the School District's principal to cause the following prayer to be said aloud by each class in the presence of a teacher at the beginning of each school day:

> Almighty God, we acknowledge our dependence upon Thee, and we beg Thy blessings upon us, our parents, our teachers and our Country."

This daily procedure was adopted on the recommendation of the State Board of Regents, a governmental agency created by the State Constitution to which the New York Legislature has granted broad supervisory, executive, and legislative powers over the State's public school system. These state officials composed the prayer which they recommended and published as a part of their "Statement on Moral and Spiritual Training in the Schools," saying: "We believe that this Statement will be subscribed to by all men and women of good will, and we call upon all of them to aid in giving life to our program."

Shortly after the practice of reciting the Regents' prayer was adopted by the School District, the parents of ten pupils brought this action in a New York State Court insisting that use of this official prayer in the public schools was contrary to the beliefs, religions, or religious practices of both themselves and their children. Among other things, these parents challenged the constitutionality of both the state law authorizing the School District to direct the use of prayer in public schools and the School District's regulation ordering the recitation of this particular prayer on the ground that these actions of official governmental agencies violate that part of the First Amendment of the Federal Constitution which commands that "Congress shall make no law respecting an establishment of religion"—a command which was "made applicable to the State of New York by the Fourteenth Amendment of the said Constitution." The New York Court of Appeals, over the dissents of Judges Dye and Fuld, sustained an order of the lower state courts which had upheld the power of New York to use the Regents' prayer as a part of the daily procedures of its public schools so long as the schools did not compel any pupil to join in the prayer over his or his parents' objection. We granted certiorari to review this important decision involving rights protected by the First and Fourteenth Amendments.

We think that by using its public school system to encourage recitation of the Regents' prayer, the State of New York has adopted a practice wholly inconsistent with the Establishment Clause. There can, of course, be no doubt that New York's program of daily classroom invocation of God's blessings as prescribed in the Regents' prayer is a religious activity. It is a solemn avowal of divine faith and supplication for the blessings of the Almighty. The nature of such a prayer has always been religious, none of the respondents has denied this and the trial court expressly so found:

> The religious nature of prayer was recognized by Jefferson and has been concurred in by theological writers, the United States Supreme Court and State courts and administrative officials, including New York's Commissioner of Education. . . . .

By the time of the adoption of the Constitution, our history shows that there was a widespread awareness among many Americans of the dangers of a union of Church and State. These people knew, some of them from bitter personal experience, that one of the greatest dangers to the freedom of the individual to worship in his own way lay in the Government's placing its official stamp of approval upon one particular kind of prayer or one particular form of religious services. They knew the anguish, hardship and bitter strife that could come when zealous religious groups struggled with one another to obtain the Government's stamp of approval from each King, Queen, or Protector that came to temporary power. The Constitution was intended to avert a part of this danger by leaving the government of this country in the hands of the people rather than in the hands of any monarch. But this safeguard was not enough. Our Founders were no more willing to let the content of their prayers and their privilege of praying whenever they pleased be influenced by the ballot box than they were to let these vital matters of personal conscience depend upon the succession of monarchs. The First Amendment was added to the Constitution to stand as a guarantee that neither the power nor the prestige of the Federal Government would be used to control, support or influence the kinds of prayer the American people can say that the people's religious must not be subjected to the pressures of government for change each time a new political administration is elected to office. Under that Amendment's prohibition against governmental establishment of religion, as reinforced by the provisions of the Fourteenth Amendment, government in this country, be it state or federal, is without power to prescribe by law any particular form of prayer which is to be used as an official prayer in carrying on any program of governmentally sponsored religious activity.

There can be no doubt that New York's state prayer program officially establishes the religious beliefs embodied in the Regents' prayer. The respondents' argument to the contrary, which is largely based upon the contention that the Regents' prayer is "non-denominational" and the fact that the program, as modified and approved by state courts, does not require all pupils to recite the prayer but permits those who wish to do so to remain silent or be excused from the room, ignores the essential nature of the program's constitutional defects. Neither the fact that the prayer may be denominationally neutral nor the fact that its observance on the part of the students is voluntary can serve to free it from the limitations of the Establishment Clause, as it might from the Free Exercise Clause, of the First Amendment, both of which are operative against the States by virtue of the Fourteenth Amendment. Although these two clauses may in certain instances overlap, they forbid two quite different kinds of governmental encroachment upon religious freedom. The Establishment Clause, unlike the Free Exercise Clause, does not depend upon any showing of direct governmental compulsion and is violated by the enactment of laws which establish an official religion whether those laws operate directly to coerce nonobserving individuals or not. This is not to say, of course, that laws officially prescribing a particular form of religious worship do not involve coercion of such individuals. When the power, prestige and financial support of government is placed behind a particular religious belief, the indirect coercive pressure upon religious minorities to conform to the prevailing officially approved religion is plain. But the purposes underlying the Establishment Clause go much further than that. Its first and most immediate purpose rested on the belief that a union of government and religion tends to destroy government and to degrade religion. The history of governmentally established religion, both in England and in this country, showed that whenever government had allied itself with one particular form of religion, the inevitable result had been that it had incurred the hatred, disrespect and even contempt of those who held contrary beliefs. That same history showed that many people had lost their respect for any religion that had relied upon the support of government to spread its faith. The Establishment Clause thus stands as an expression of principle on the part of the Founders of our Constitution that religion is too personal, too sacred, too holy, to permit its "unhallowed perversion" by a civil magistrate. Another purpose of the Establishment Clause rested upon an awareness of the historical fact that governmentally established religions and religious persecutions go hand in hand. The Founders knew that only a few years after the Book of Common Prayer became the only accepted form of religious services in the established Church of England, an Act of Uniformity was passed to compel all Englishmen to attend those services and to make it a criminal offense to conduct or attend religious gatherings of any other kind—a law which was consistently flouted by dissenting religious groups in England and which contributed to widespread persecutions of people like John Bunyan who persisted in holding "unlawful [religious] meetings . . . to the great disturbance and distraction of the good subjects of this kingdom. . . ." And they knew that similar persecutions had received the sanction of law in several of the colonies in this country soon after the establishment of official religions in those colonies. It was in large part to get completely away from this sort of systematic religious persecution that the Founders brought into being our Nation, our Constitution, and our Bill of Rights with its prohibition against any governmental establishment of religion. The New York laws officially prescribing the Regents' prayer are inconsistent both with the purposes of the Establishment Clause and with the Establishment Clause itself.

It has been argued that to apply the Constitution in such a way as to prohibit state laws respecting an establishment of religious services in public schools is to indicate a hostility toward religion or toward prayer. Nothing, of course, could be more wrong. The history of man is inseparable from the history of religion. And perhaps it is not too much to say that since the beginning of that history many people have devoutly believed that "More things are wrought by prayer than this world dreams of." It was doubtless largely due to men who believed this that there grew up a sentiment that caused men to leave the cross-currents of officially established state religions and religious persecution in Europe and come to this country filled with the hope that they could find a place in which they could pray when they pleased to the God of their faith in the language they chose. And there were men of this same faith in the power of prayer who led the fight for adoption of our Constitution and also for our Bill of Rights with the very guarantees of religious freedom that forbid the sort of governmental activity which New York has attempted here. These men knew that the First Amendment, which tried to put an end to governmental control of religion and of prayer, was not written to destroy either. They knew rather that it was written to quiet well-justified fears which nearly all of them felt arising out of an awareness that governments of the past had shackled men's tongues to make them speak only the religious thoughts that government wanted them to speak and to pray only to the God that government wanted them to pray to. It is neither sacrilegious nor antireligious to say that each separate government in this country should stay out of the business of writing or sanctioning official prayers and leave that purely religious function to the people themselves and to those the people choose to look to for religious guidance.

It is true that New York's establishment of its Regents' prayer as an officially approved religious doctrine of that State does not amount to a total establishment of one particular religious sect to the exclusion of all others—that, indeed, the governmental endorsement of that prayer seems relatively insignificant when compared to the governmental encroachments upon religion which were commonplace 200 years ago. To those who may subscribe to the view that because the Regents' official prayer is so brief and general there can be no danger to religious freedom in its governmental establishment, however, it may be appropriate to say in the words of James Madison, the author of the First Amendment:

> it is proper to take alarm at the first experiment on our liberties. . . . Who does not see that the same authority which can establish Christianity, in exclusion of all other Religions, may establish with the same ease any particular sect of Christians, in exclusion of all other Sects? That the same authority which can force a citizen to contribute three pence only of his property for the support of any one establishment, may force him to conform to any other establishment in all cases whatsoever?

The judgment of the Court of Appeals of New York is reversed and the cause remanded for further proceedings not inconsistent with this opinion.

MR. JUSTICE STEWART, dissenting.

The Court today decides that in permitting this brief nondenominational prayer the school board has violated the Constitution of the United States. I think this decision is wrong. The Court does not hold, nor could it, that New York has interfered with the free exercise of anybody's religion. For the state courts have made clear that those who object to reciting the prayer must be entirely free of any compulsion to do so, including any "embarrassments and pressures." But the Court says that in permitting school children to say this simple prayer, the New York authorities have established "an official religion."

With all respect, I think the Court has misapplied a great constitutional principle. I cannot see how an "official religion" is established by letting those who want to say a prayer say it. On the contrary, I think that to deny the wish of these school children to join in reciting this prayer is to deny them the opportunity of sharing in the spiritual heritage of our Nation. . . .

What is relevant to the issue here is not the history of an established church in sixteenth century England or in eighteenth century America, but the history of the religious traditions of our people, reflected in countless practices of the institutions and officials of our government. At the opening of each day's Session of this Court we stand, while one of our officials invokes the protection of God. Since the days of John Marshall our Crier has said, "God save the United States and this Honorable Court." Both the Senate and the House of Representatives open their daily Sessions with prayer. Each of our Presidents, from George Washington to John F. Kennedy, has upon assuming his Office asked the protection and help of God.

The Court today says that the state and federal governments are without constitutional power to prescribe any particular form of words to be recited by any group of the American people on any subject touching religion. One of the stanzas of "The Star-Spangled Banner," made our National Anthem by Act of Congress in 1931, contains these verses:

> Blest with victory and peace, may the heav'n rescued land
> Praise the Pow'r that hath made and preserved us a nation!
> Then conquer we must, when our cause it is just, And this be our motto 'In God is our Trust.'

In 1954 Congress added a phrase to the Pledge of Allegiance to the Flag so that it now contains the words "one Nation under God, indivisible, with liberty and justice for all." In 1952 Congress enacted legislation calling upon the President each year to proclaim a National Day of Prayer. Since 1865 the words "IN GOD WE TRUST" have been impressed on our coins.

Countless similar examples could be listed, but there is no need to belabor the obvious. It was all summed up by this Court just ten years ago in a single sentence: "We are a religious people whose institutions presuppose a Supreme Being." Zorach v. Clauson.

I do not believe that this Court, or the Congress, or the President has by the actions and practices I have mentioned established an "official religion" in violation of the Constitution. And I do not believe the State of New York has done so in this case. What each has done has been to recognize and to follow the deeply entrenched and highly cherished spiritual traditions of our Nation—traditions which come down to us from those who almost two hundred years ago avowed their "firm Reliance on the Protection of divine Providence" when they proclaimed the freedom and independence of this brave new world.

I dissent.

Appendix 10. Lemon v Kurtzman
403 U.S. 602 (1971)

MR. CHIEF JUSTICE BURGER delivered the opinion of the Court.

These two appeals raise questions as to Pennsylvania and Rhode Island statutes providing state aid to church-related elementary and secondary schools. Both statutes are challenged as violative of the Establishment and Free Exercise Clauses of the First Amendment and the Due Process Clause of the Fourteenth Amendment.

Pennsylvania has adopted a statutory program that provides financial support to nonpublic elementary and secondary schools by way of reimbursement for the cost of teachers' salaries, textbooks, and instructional materials in specified secular subjects. Rhode Island has adopted a statute under which the State pays directly to teachers in nonpublic elementary schools a supplement of 15% of their annual salary. Under each statute state aid has been given to church-related educational institutions. We hold that both statutes are unconstitutional.

The Rhode Island Salary Supplement Act was enacted in 1969. It rests on the legislative finding that the quality of education available in nonpublic elementary schools has been jeopardized by the rapidly rising salaries needed to attract competent and dedicated teachers. The Act authorizes state officials to supplement the salaries of teachers of secular subjects in nonpublic elementary schools by paying directly to a teacher an amount not in excess of 15% of his current annual salary. As supplemented, however, a nonpublic school teacher's salary cannot exceed the maximum paid to teachers in the State's public schools, and the recipient must be certified by the state board of education in substantially the same manner as public school teachers.

In order to be eligible for the Rhode Island salary supplement, the recipient must teach in a nonpublic school at which the average per-pupil expenditure on secular education is less than the average in the State's public schools during a specified period. Appellant State Commissioner of Education also requires eligible schools to submit financial data. If this information indicates a per-pupil expenditure in excess of the statutory limitation, the records of the school in question must be examined in order to assess how much of the expenditure is attributable to secular education and how much to religious activity.

The Act also requires that teachers eligible for salary supplements must teach only those subjects that are offered in the State's public schools. They must use "only teaching materials which are used in the public schools." Finally, any teacher applying for a salary supplement must first agree in writing "not to teach a course in religion for so long as or during such time as he or she receives any salary supplements" under the Act.

Appellees are citizens and taxpayers of Rhode Island. They brought this suit to have the Rhode Island Salary Supplement Act declared unconstitutional and its operation enjoined on the ground that it violates the Establishment and Free Exercise Clauses of the First Amendment. Appellants are state officials charged with administration of the Act, teachers eligible for salary supplements under the Act, and parents of children in church-related elementary schools whose teachers would receive state salary assistance.

A three-judge federal court was convened pursuant to 28 U.S.C. §§ 2281, 2284. It found that Rhode Island's nonpublic elementary schools accommodated approximately 25% of the State's pupils. About 95% of these pupils attended schools affiliated with the Roman Catholic church. To date some 250 teachers have applied for benefits under the Act. All of them are employed by Roman Catholic schools.

The court held a hearing at which extensive evidence was introduced concerning the nature of the secular instruction offered in the Roman Catholic schools whose teachers would be eligible for salary assistance under the Act. Although the court found that concern for religious values does not necessarily affect the content of secular subjects, it also found that the parochial school system was "an integral part of the religious mission of the Catholic Church."

The District Court concluded that the Act violated the Establishment Clause, holding that it fostered "excessive entanglement" between government and religion. In addition two judges thought that the Act had the impermissible effect of giving "significant aid to a religious enterprise." We affirm.

Pennsylvania has adopted a program that has some but not all of the features of the Rhode Island program. The Pennsylvania Nonpublic Elementary and Secondary Education Act was passed in 1968 in response to a crisis that the Pennsylvania Legislature found existed in the State's nonpublic schools due to rapidly rising costs. The statute affirmatively reflects the legislative conclusion that the State's educational goals could appropriately be fulfilled by government support of "those purely secular educational objectives achieved through nonpublic education. . . ."

The statute authorizes appellee state Superintendent of Public Instruction to "purchase" specified "secular educational services" from nonpublic schools. Under the "contracts" authorized by the statute, the State directly reimburses nonpublic schools solely for their actual expenditures for teachers' salaries, textbooks, and instructional materials. A school seeking reimbursement must maintain prescribed accounting procedures that identify the "separate" cost of the "secular educational service." These accounts are subject to state audit. The funds for this program were originally derived from a new tax on horse and harness racing, but the Act is now financed by a portion of the state tax on cigarettes.

There are several significant statutory restrictions on state aid. Reimbursement is limited to courses "presented in the curricula of the public schools." It is further limited "solely" to courses in the following "secular" subjects: mathematics, modern foreign languages, physical science, and physical education. Textbooks and instructional materials included in the program must be approved by the state Superintendent of Public Instruction. Finally, the statute prohibits reimbursement for any course that contains "any subject matter expressing religious teaching, or the morals or forms of worship of any sect."

The Act went into effect on July 1, 1968, and the first reimbursement payments to schools were made on September 2, 1969. It appears that some $5 million has been expended annually under the Act. The State has now entered into contracts with some 1,181 nonpublic elementary and secondary schools with a student population of some 535,215 pupils— more than 20% of the total number of students in the State. More than 96% of these pupils attend church-related schools, and most of these schools are affiliated with the Roman Catholic church.

Appellants brought this action in the District Court to challenge the constitutionality of the Pennsylvania statute. The organizational plaintiffs-appellants are associations of persons resident in Pennsylvania declaring belief in the separation of church and state; individual plaintiffs-appellants are citizens and taxpayers of Pennsylvania. Appellant Lemon, in addition to being a citizen and a taxpayer, is a parent of a child attending public school in Pennsylvania. Lemon also alleges that he purchased a ticket at a race track and thus had paid the specific tax that supports the expenditures under the Act. Appellees are state officials who have the responsibility for administering the Act. In addition seven church-related schools are defendants-appellees.

A three-judge federal court . . . held that the Act violated neither the Establishment nor the Free Exercise Clause, Chief Judge Hastie dissenting. We reverse. . . .

The language of the Religion Clauses of the First Amendment is at best opaque, particularly when compared with other portions of the Amendment. Its authors did not simply prohibit the establishment of a state church or a state religion, an area history shows they regarded as very important and fraught with great dangers. Instead they commanded that there should be "no law *respecting* an establishment of religion." A law may be one "respecting" the forbidden objective while falling short of its total realization. A law "respecting" the proscribed result, that is, the establishment of religion, is not always easily identifiable as one violative of the Clause. A given law might not *establish* a state religion but nevertheless be one "respecting" that end in the sense of being a step that could lead to such establishment and hence offend the First Amendment.

In the absence of precisely stated constitutional prohibitions, we must draw lines with reference to the three main evils against which the Establishment Clause was intended to afford protection: "sponsorship, financial support, and active involvement of the sovereign in religious activity." *Walz v. Tax Commission.*

Every analysis in this area must begin with consideration of the cumulative criteria developed by the Court over many years. Three such tests may be gleaned from our cases. First, the statute must have a secular legislative purpose; second, its principal or primary effect must be one that neither advances nor inhibits religion; finally, the statute must not foster "an excessive government entanglement with religion."

Inquiry into the legislative purposes of the Pennsylvania and Rhode Island statutes affords no basis for a conclusion that the legislative intent was to advance religion. On the contrary, the statutes themselves clearly state that they are intended to enhance the quality of the secular education in all schools covered by the compulsory attendance laws. There is no reason to believe the legislatures meant anything else. A State always has a legitimate concern for maintaining minimum standards in all schools it allows to operate. . . . The two legislatures, however, have also recognized that church-related elementary and secondary schools have a significant religious mission and that a substantial portion of their activities is religiously oriented. They have therefore sought to create statutory restrictions designed to guarantee the separation between secular and religious educational functions and to ensure that State financial aid supports only the former. All these provisions are precautions taken in candid recognition that these programs approached, even if they did not intrude upon, the forbidden areas under the Religion Clauses. We need not decide whether these legislative precautions restrict the principal or primary effect of the programs to the point where they do not offend the Religion Clauses, for we conclude that the cumulative impact of the entire relationship arising under the statutes in each State involves excessive entanglement between government and religion. . . .

Our prior holdings do not call for total separation between church and state; total separation is not possible in an absolute sense. Some relationship between government and religious organizations is inevitable. . . . Fire inspections, building and zoning regulations, and state requirements under compulsory school-attendance laws are examples of necessary and permissible contacts. Indeed, under the statutory exemption before us in *Walz*, the State had a continuing burden to ascertain that the exempt property was in fact being used for religious worship. Judicial caveats against entanglement must recognize that the line of separation, far from being a "wall," is a blurred, indistinct, and variable barrier depending on all the circumstances of a particular relationship. . . .

In order to determine whether the government entanglement with religion is excessive, we must examine the character and purposes of the institutions that are benefited, the nature of the aid that the State provides, and the resulting relationship between the government and the religious authority.

(A) RHODE ISLAND PROGRAM

. . . the church schools involved in the program are located close to parish churches. This understandably permits convenient access for religious exercises since instruction in faith and morals is part of the total educational process. The school buildings contain identifying religious symbols such as crosses on the exterior and crucifixes, and religious paintings and statues either in the classrooms or hallways. Although only approximately 30 minutes a day are devoted to direct religious instruction, there are religiously oriented extracurricular activities. Approximately two-thirds of the teachers in these schools are nuns of various religious orders. Their dedicated efforts provide an atmosphere in which religious instruction and religious vocations are natural and proper parts of life in such schools. Indeed, as the District Court found, the role of teaching nuns in enhancing the religious atmosphere has led the parochial school authorities to attempt to maintain a one-to-one ratio between nuns and lay teachers in all schools rather than to permit some to be staffed almost entirely by lay teachers. . . .

The various characteristics of the schools make them "a powerful vehicle for transmitting the Catholic faith to the next generation." This process of inculcating religious doctrine is, of course, enhanced by the impressionable age of the pupils, in primary schools particularly. In short, parochial schools involve substantial religious activity and purpose. . . .

We cannot ignore the danger that a teacher under religious control and discipline poses to the separation of the religious from the purely secular aspects of pre-college education. The conflict of functions inheres in the situation. . . .

We do not assume, however, that parochial school teachers will be unsuccessful in their attempts to segregate their religious beliefs from their secular educational responsibilities. But the potential for impermissible fostering of religion is present. The Rhode Island Legislature has not, and could not, provide state aid on the basis of a mere assumption that secular teachers under religious discipline can avoid conflicts. The State must be certain, given the Religion Clauses, that subsidized teachers do not inculcate religion—indeed the State here has undertaken to do so. To ensure that no trespass occurs, the State has therefore carefully conditioned its aid with pervasive restrictions. An eligible recipient must teach only those courses that are offered in the public schools and use only those texts and materials that are found in the public schools. In addition the teacher must not engage in teaching any course in religion.

A comprehensive, discriminating, and continuing state surveillance will inevitably be required to ensure that these restrictions are obeyed and the First Amendment otherwise respected. Unlike a book, a teacher cannot be inspected once so as to determine the extent and intent of his or her personal beliefs and subjective acceptance of the limitations imposed by the First Amendment. These prophylactic contacts will involve excessive and enduring entanglement between state and church.

There is another area of entanglement in the Rhode Island program that gives concern. The statute excludes teachers employed by nonpublic schools whose average per-pupil expenditures on secular education equal or exceed the comparable figures for public schools. In the event that the total expenditures of an otherwise eligible school exceed this norm, the program requires the government to examine the school's records in order to determine how much of the total expenditures is attributable to secular education and how much to religious activity. This kind of state inspection and evaluation of the religious content of a religious organization is fraught with the sort of entanglement that the Constitution forbids. It is a relationship pregnant with dangers of excessive government direction of church schools and hence of churches. The Court noted "the hazards of government supporting churches" in *Walz* v. *Tax Commission* and we cannot ignore here the danger that pervasive modern governmental power will ultimately intrude on religion and thus conflict with the Religion Clauses.

(B) PENNSYLVANIA PROGRAM

The Pennsylvania statute also provides state aid to church-related schools for teachers' salaries. The complaint describes an educational system that is very similar to the one existing in Rhode Island. . . .

The Pennsylvania statute, moreover, has the further defect of providing state financial aid directly to the church-related school. This factor distinguishes both *Everson* and *Allen,* for in both those cases the Court was careful to point out that state aid was provided to the student and his parents—not to the church-related school. In *Walz* . . . the Court warned of the danger of direct payments to religious organizations.

A broader base of entanglement of yet a different character is presented by the divisive political potential of these state programs. In a community where such a large number of pupils are served by church-related schools, it can be assumed that state assistance will entail considerable political activity. Partisans of parochial schools, understandably concerned with rising costs and sincerely dedicated to both the religious and secular educational missions of their schools, will inevitably champion this cause and promote political action to achieve their goals. Those who oppose state aid, whether for constitutional, religious, or fiscal reasons, will inevitably respond and employ all of the usual political campaign techniques to prevail. Candidates will be forced to declare and voters to choose. It would be unrealistic to ignore the fact that many people confronted with issues of this kind will find their votes aligned with their faith. . . . The potential divisiveness of such conflict is a threat to the normal political process. . . . The history of many countries attests to the hazards of religion's intruding into the political arena or of political power intruding into the legitimate and free exercise of religious belief. . . . In *Walz* we dealt with a status under state tax laws for the benefit of all religious groups. Here we are confronted with successive and very likely permanent annual appropriations that benefit relatively few religious groups. Political fragmentation and divisiveness on religious lines are thus likely to be intensified. . . .

. . . nothing we have said can be construed to disparate the role of church-related elementary schools and secondary schools in our national life. There contribution has been and is enormous. Nor do we ignore their economic plight in a period of rising costs and expanding need. Taxpayers generally have been spared vast sums by the maintenance of these educational institututions by religious organizations, by the gifts of faithful adherents.

The merit and benefit of these schools, however, are not the issue before us in these cases. The sole question is whether state aid to these schools can be squared with the Religion Clauses. Under our system the choice has been made that government is to be entirely excluded from the area of religious instruction and churches excluded from the affairs of government. The Constitution decrees that religion must be a private matter for the individual, the family, and the institutions of private choice, and that while some involvement and entanglement are inevitable, lines must be drawn. . . .

The judgment of the Rhode Island District Court . . . is affirmed. The judgment of the Pennsylvania District Court . . . is reversed, and the case is remanded for further proceedings consistent with this opinion.

Appendix 11. Wisconsin v Yoder
406 U.S. 205 (1972)

Mr. JUSTICE BURGER delivered the opinion of the Court.

. . . Respondents Jonas Yoder and Wallace Miller are members of the Old Order Amish religion, and respondent Adin Yutzy is a member of the Conservative Amish Mennonite Church. They and their families are residents of Green County, Wisconsin. Wisconsin's compulsory school-attendance law required them to cause their children to attend public or private school until reaching age 16 but the respondents declined to send their children, ages 14 and 15, to public school after they completed the eighth grade. The children were not enrolled in any private school, or within any recognized exception to the compulsory-attendance law, and they are conceded to be subject to the Wisconsin statute.

On complaint of the school district administrator for the public schools, respondents were charged, tried, and convicted of violating the compulsory-attendance law in Green County Court and were fined the sum of $5 each. Respondents defended on the ground that the application of the compulsory-attendance law violated their rights under the First and Fourteenth Amendments. The trial testimony showed that respondents believed, in accordance with the tenets of Old Order Amish communities generally, that their children's attendance at high school, public or private, was contrary to the Amish religion and way of life. They believed that by sending their children to high school, they would not only expose themselves to the danger of the censure of the church community, but, as found by the county court, also endanger their own salvation and that of their children. The State stipulated that respondents' religious beliefs were sincere.

In support of their position, respondents presented as expert witnesses scholars on religion and education whose testimony is uncontradicted. They expressed their opinions on the relationship of the Amish belief concerning school attendance to the more general tenets of their religion, and described the impact that compulsory high school attendance could have on the continued survival of Amish communities as they exist in the United States today. The history of the Amish sect was given in some detail, beginning with the Swiss Anabaptists of the 16th century who rejected institutionalized churches and sought to return to the early, simple, Christian life de-emphasizing material success, rejecting the competitive spirit, and seeking to insulate themselves from the modern world. As a result of their common heritage, Old Order Amish communities today are characterized by a fundamental belief that salvation requires life in a church community separate and apart from the world and worldly influence. This concept of life aloof from the world and its values is central to their faith.

A related feature of Old Order Amish communities is their devotion to a life in harmony with nature and the soil, as exemplified by the simple life of the early Christian era that continued in America during much of our early national life. Amish beliefs require members of the community to make their living by farming or closely related activities. Broadly speaking, the Old Order Amish religion pervades and determines the entire mode of life of its adherents.

Amish objection to formal education beyond the eighth grade is firmly grounded in these central religious concepts. They object to the high school, and higher education generally, because the values they teach are in marked variance with Amish values and the Amish way of life; they view secondary school education as an impermissible exposure of their children to a "worldly" influence in conflict with their beliefs. The high school tends to emphasize intellectual and scientific accomplishments, self-distinction, competitiveness, worldly success, and social life with other students. Amish society emphasizes informal learning-through-doing; a life of "goodness," rather than a life of intellect; wisdom, rather than technical knowledge; community welfare, rather than competition; and separation from, rather than integration with, contemporary worldly society.

Formal high school education beyond the eighth grade is contrary to Amish beliefs, not only because it places Amish children in an environment hostile to Amish beliefs with increasing emphasis on competition in class work and sports and with pressure to conform to the styles, manners, and ways of the peer group, but also because it takes them away from their community, physically and emotionally, during the crucial and formative adolescent period of life. During this period, the children must acquire Amish attitudes favoring manual work and self-reliance and the specific skills needed to perform the adult role of an Amish farmer or housewife. Once a child has learned basic reading, writing, and elementary mathematics, these traits, skills, and attitudes admittedly fall within the category of those best learned through example and "doing" rather than in a classroom. And, at this time in life, the Amish child must also grow in his faith and his relationship to the Amish community if he is to be prepared to accept the heavy obligations imposed by adult baptism. In short, high school attendance with teachers who are not of the Amish faith—and may even be hostile to it—interposes a serious barrier to the integration of the Amish child into the Amish religious community. Dr. John Hostetler, one of the experts on Amish society, testified that the modern high school is not equipped, in curriculum or social environment, to impart the values promoted by Amish society.

The Amish do not object to elementary education through the first eight grades as a general proposition because they agree that their children must have basic skills in the "three R's" in order to read the Bible, to be good farmers and citizens, and to be able to deal with non-Amish people when necessary in the course of daily affairs. They view such a basic education as acceptable because it does not significantly expose their children to worldly values or interfere with their development in the Amish community during the crucial adolescent period. While Amish accept compulsory elementary education generally, wherever possible they have established their own elementary schools in many respects like the small local schools of the past. In the Amish belief higher learning tends to develop values they reject as influences that alienate man from God.

On the basis of such considerations, Dr. Hostetler testified that compulsory high school attendance could not only result in great psychological harm to Amish children, because of the conflicts it would produce, but would also, in his opinion, ultimately result in the destruction of the Old Order Amish church community as it exists in the United States today. The testimony of Dr. Donald A. Erickson, an expert witness on education, also showed that the Amish succeed in preparing their high school age children to be productive members of the Amish community. He described their system of learning through doing the skills directly relevant to their adult roles in the Amish community as "ideal" and perhaps superior to ordinary high school education. The evidence also showed that the Amish have an excellent record as law-abiding and generally self-sufficient members of society. . . .

There is no doubt as to the power of a State, having a high responsibility for education of its citizens, to impose reasonable regulations for the control and duration of basic education. . . . Providing public schools ranks at the very apex of the function of a State. Yet even this paramount responsibility was, in *Pierce v. Society of Sisters,* made to yield to the right of parents to provide an equivalent education in a privately operated system. There the Court held that Oregon's statute compelling attendance in a public school from age eight to age 16 unreasonably interfered with the interest of parents in directing the rearing of their offspring, including their education in church-operated schools. As that case suggests, the values of parental direction of the religious upbringing and education of their children in their early and formative years have a high place in our society. . . . Thus, a State's interest in universal education, however highly we rank it, is not totally free from a balancing process when it impinges on fundamental rights and interests, such as those specifically protected by the Free Exercise Clause of the First Amendment, and the traditional interest of parents with respect to the religious upbringing of their children so long as they "prepare [them] for additional obligations."

It follows that in order for Wisconsin to compel school attendance beyond the eighth grade against a claim that such attendance interferes with the practice of a legitimate religious belief, it must appear either that the State does not deny the free exercise of religious belief by its requirement, or that there is a state interest of sufficient magnitude to override the interest claiming protection under the Free Exercise Clause. . . .

The essence of all that has been said and written on the subject is that only those interests of the highest order and those not otherwise served can overbalance legitimate claims to the free exercise of religion. We can accept it as settled, therefore, that, however strong the State's interest in universal compulsory education, it is by no means absolute to the exclusion or subordination of all other interests.

We come then to the quality of the claims of the respondents concerning the alleged encroachment of Wisconsin's compulsory school-attendance statute on their rights and the rights of their children to the free exercise of the religious beliefs they and their forebears have adhered to for almost three centuries. In evaluating those claims we must be careful to determine whether the Amish religious faith and their mode of life are, as they claim, inseparable and interdependent. A way of life, however virtuous and admirable, may not be interposed as a barrier to reasonable state regulation of education if it is based on purely secular considerations; to have the protection of the Religion Clauses, the claims must be rooted in religious belief. Although a determination of what is a "religious" belief or practice entitled to constitutional protection may present a most delicate question, the very concept of ordered liberty precludes allowing every person to make his own standards on matters of conduct in which society as a whole has important interests. Thus, if the Amish asserted their claims because of their subjective evaluation and rejection of the contemporary secular values accepted by the majority, much as Thoreau rejected the social values of his time and isolated himself at Walden Pond, their claims would not rest on a religious basis. Thoreau's choice was philosophical and personal rather than religious, and such belief does not rise to the demands of the Religion Clauses.

Giving no weight to such secular considerations, however, we see that the record in this case abundantly supports the claim that the traditional way of life of the Amish is not merely a matter of personal preference, but one of deep religious conviction, shared by an organized group, and intimately related to daily living. . . . As the record strongly shows, the values and programs of the modern secondary school are in sharp conflict with the fundamental mode of life mandated by the Amish religion. . . . The conclusion is inescapable that secondary schooling, by exposing Amish children to worldly influences in terms of attitudes, goals, and values contrary to beliefs, and by substantially interfering with the religious development of the Amish child and his integration into the way of life of the Amish faith community at the crucial adolescent stage of development, contravenes the basic religious tenets and practice of the Amish faith, both as to the parent and the child.

The impact of the compulsory-attendance law on respondents' practice of the Amish religion is not only severe, but inescapable, for the Wisconsin law affirmatively compels them, under threat of criminal sanction, to perform acts undeniably at odds with fundamental tenets of their religious beliefs. . . . As the record shows, compulsory school attendance to age 16 for Amish children carries with it a very real threat of undermining the Amish community and religious practice as they exist today; they must either abandon belief and be assimilated into society at large, or be forced to migrate to some other and more tolerant region.

In sum, the unchallenged testimony of acknowledged experts in education and religious history, almost 300 years of consistent practice, and strong evidence of a sustained faith pervading and regulating respondents' entire mode of life support the claim that enforcement of the State's requirement of compulsory formal education after the eighth grade would gravely endanger if not destroy the free exercise of respondents' religious beliefs.

Neither the findings of the trial court nor the Amish claims as to the nature of their faith are challenged in this Court by the State of Wisconsin. Its position is that the State's interest in universal compulsory formal secondary education to age 16 is so great that it is paramount to the undisputed claims of respondents that their mode of preparing their youth for Amish life, after the traditional elementary education, is an essential part of their religious belief and practice. . . .

Nor can this case be disposed of on the grounds that Wisconsin's requirement for school attendance to age 16 applies uniformly to all citizens of the State and does not, on its face, discriminate against religions or a particular religion, or that it is motivated by legitimate secular concerns. A regulation neutral on its face may, in its application, nonetheless offend the constitutional requirement for governmental neutrality if it unduly burdens the free exercise of religion.

The State advances two primary arguments in support of its system of compulsory education. It notes, as Thomas Jefferson pointed out early in our history, that some degree of education is necessary to prepare citizens to participate effectively and intelligently in our open political system if we are to preserve freedom and independence. Further, education prepares individuals to be self-reliant and self-sufficient participants in society. We accept these propositions.

However, the evidence adduced by the Amish in this case is persuasively to the effect that an additional one or two years of formal high school for Amish children in place of their long-established program of informal vocational education would do little to serve those interests. Respondents' experts testified at trial, without challenge, that the value of all education must be assessed in terms of its capacity to prepare the child for life. It is one thing to say that compulsory education for a year or two beyond the eighth grade may be necessary when its goal is the preparation of the child for life in modern society as the majority live, but it is quite another if the goal of education be viewed as the preparation of the child for life in the separated agrarian community that is the keystone of the Amish faith.

The State attacks respondents' position as one fostering "ignorance" from which the child must be protected by the State. No one can question the State's duty to protect children from ignorance but this argument does not square with the facts disclosed in the record. Whatever their idiosyncrasies as seen by the majority, this record strongly shows that the Amish community has been a highly successful social unit within our society, even if apart from the conventional "mainstream." Its members are productive and very law-abiding members of society; they reject public welfare in any of its usual modern forms.

The State, however, supports its interest in providing an additional one or two years of compulsory high school education to Amish children because of the possibility that some such children will choose to leave the

Amish community, and that if this occurs they will be ill-equipped for life. The State argues that if Amish children leave their church they should not be in the position of making their way in the world without the education available in the one or two additional years the State requires. However, on this record, that argument is highly speculative. There is no specific evidence of the loss of Amish adherents by attrition, nor is there any showing that upon leaving the Amish community Amish children, with their practical agricultural training and habits of industry and self-reliance, would become burdens on society because of educational short-comings. . . .

Finally, the State, on authority of *Prince* v. *Massachusetts*, argues that a decision exempting Amish children from the State's requirement fails to recognize the substantive right of the Amish child to a secondary education, and fails to give due regard to the power of the State as *parens patriae* to extend the benefit of secondary education to children regardless of the wishes of their parents. . . .

This case, of course, is not one in which any harm to the physical or mental health of the child or to the public safety, peace, order, or welfare has been demonstrated or may be properly inferred. The record is to the contrary, and any reliance on that theory would find no support in the evidence.

Contrary to the suggestion of the dissenting opinion of MR. JUSTICE DOUGLAS, our holding today in no degree depends on the assertion of the religious interest of the child as contrasted with that of the parents. It is the parents who are subject to prosecution here for failing to cause their children to attend school, and it is their right of free exercise, not that of their children, that must determine Wisconsin's power to impose criminal penalties on the parent. The dissent argues that a child who expresses a desire to attend public high school in conflict with the wishes of his parents should not be prevented from doing so. There is no reason for the Court to consider that point since it is not an issue in the case. The children are not parties to this litigation. The State has at no point tried this case on the theory that respondents were preventing their children from attending school against their expressed desires, and indeed the record is to the contrary. The State's position from the outset has been that it is empowered to apply its compulsory-attendance law to Amish parents in the same manner as to other parents—that is, without regard to the wishes of the child. That is the claim we reject today.

Our holding in no way determines the proper resolution of possible competing interests of parents, children, and the State in an appropriate state court proceeding in which the power of the State is asserted on the theory that Amish parents are preventing their minor children from attending high school despite their expressed desires to the contrary. . . .

MR. JUSTICE DOUGLAS, dissenting in part.

I agree with the Court that the religious scruples of the Amish are opposed to the education of their children beyond the grade schools, yet I disagree with the Court's conclusion that the matter is within the dispensation of parents alone. The Court's analysis assumes that the only interests at stake in the case are those of the Amish parents on the one hand, and those of the State on the other. The difficulty with this approach is that, despite the Court's claim, the parents are seeking to vindicate not only their own free exercise claims, but also those of their high-school-age children. . . .

Recent cases, however, have clearly held that the children themselves have constitutionally protectible interests. These children are "persons" within the meaning of the Bill of Rights. We have so held over and over again. . . .

On this important and vital matter of education, I think the children should be entitled to be heard. While the parents, absent dissent, normally speak for the entire family, the education of the child is a matter on which the child will often have decided views. He may want to be a pianist or an astronaut or an oceanographer. To do so he will have to break from the Amish tradition.

It is the future of the student, not the future of the parents, that is imperiled by today's decision. If a parent keeps his child out of school beyond the grade school, then the child will be forever barred from entry into the new and amazing world of diversity that we have today. The child may decide that that is the preferred course, or he may rebel. It is the student's judgment, not his parents,' that is essential if we are to give full meaning to what we have said about the Bill of Rights and of the right of students to be masters of their own destiny. If he is harnessed to the Amish way of life by those in authority over him and if his education is truncated, his entire life may be stunted and deformed. The child, therefore, should be given an opportunity to be heard before the State gives the exemption which we honor today.

The views of the two children in question were not canvassed by the Wisconsin courts. The matter should be explicitly reserved so that new hearings can be held on remand of the case.

Appendix 12. Marsh v Chambers
463 U.S. 783 (1983)

CHIEF JUSTICE BURGER delivered the opinion of the Court.

The question presented is whether the Nebraska Legislature's practice of opening each legislative day with a prayer by a chaplain paid by the State violates the Establishment Clause of the First Amendment.

The Nebraska Legislature begins each of its sessions with a prayer offered by a chaplain who is chosen biennially by the Executive Board of the Legislative Council and paid out of public funds. Robert E. Palmer, a Presbyterian minister, has served as chaplain since 1965 at a salary of $319.75 per month for each month the legislature is in session.

Ernest Chambers is a member of the Nebraska Legislature and a taxpayer of Nebraska. Claiming that the Nebraska Legislature's chaplaincy practice violates the Establishment Clause of the First Amendment, he brought this action . . . seeking to enjoin enforcement of the practice. . . . The District Court held that the Establishment Clause was not breached by the prayers, but was violated by paying the chaplain from public funds. It therefore enjoined the legislature from using public funds to pay the chaplain; it declined to enjoin the policy of beginning sessions with prayers. Cross-appeals were taken.

The Court of Appeals for the Eighth Circuit . . . refused to treat respondent's challenges as separable issues as the District Court had done. Instead, the Court of Appeals assessed the practice as a whole because "[parsing] out [the] elements" would lead to "an incongruous result."

Applying the three-part test of *Lemon* v. *Kurtzman* . . . the court held that the chaplaincy practice violated all three elements of the test: the purpose and primary effect of selecting the same minister for 16 years and publishing his prayers was to promote a particular religious expression; use of state money for compensation and publication led to entanglement. . . . Accordingly, the Court of Appeals modified the District Court's injunction and prohibited the State from engaging in any aspect of its established chaplaincy practice.

We granted certiorari limited to the challenge to the practice of opening sessions with prayers by a state-employed clergyman, and we reverse.

The opening of sessions of legislative and other deliberative public bodies with prayer is deeply embedded in the history and tradition of this country. From colonial times through the founding of the Republic and

ever since, the practice of legislative prayer has coexisted with the principles of disestablishment and religious freedom. In the very courtrooms in
which the United States District Judge and later three Circuit Judges heard
and decided this case, the proceedings opened with an announcement that
concluded, "God save the United States and this Honorable Court." The
same invocation occurs at all sessions of this Court.

The tradition in many of the Colonies was, of course, linked to an established church, but the Continental Congress, beginning in 1774, adopted the
traditional procedure of opening its sessions with a prayer offered by a paid
chaplain. . . . Although prayers were not offered during the Constitutional
Convention, the First Congress, as one of its early items of business, adopted
the policy of selecting a chaplain to open each session with prayer. . . .

On September 25, 1789, three days after Congress authorized the appointment of paid chaplains, final agreement was reached on the language
of the Bill of Rights. . . . Clearly the men who wrote the First Amendment
Religion Clauses did not view paid legislative chaplains and opening
prayers as a violation of that Amendment, for the practice of opening sessions with prayer has continued without interruption ever since that early
session of Congress. It has also been followed consistently in most of the
states, including Nebraska, where the institution of opening legislative sessions with prayer was adopted even before the State attained statehood.

Standing alone, historical patterns cannot justify contemporary violations of constitutional guarantees, but there is far more here than simply
historical patterns. In this context, historical evidence sheds light not only
on what the draftsmen intended the Establishment Clause to mean, but
also on how they thought that Clause applied to the practice authorized by
the First Congress—their actions reveal their intent. . . .

It can hardly be thought that in the same week Members of the First
Congress voted to appoint and to pay a chaplain for each House and also
voted to approve the draft of the First Amendment for submission to the
states, they intended the Establishment Clause of the Amendment to forbid
what they had just declared acceptable. In applying the First Amendment
to the states through the Fourteenth Amendment, *Cantwell v. Connecticut*, it
would be incongruous to interpret that Clause as imposing more stringent
First Amendment limits on the states than the draftsmen imposed on the
Federal Government.

This unique history leads us to accept the interpretation of the First
Amendment draftsmen who saw no real threat to the Establishment
Clause arising from a practice of prayer similar to that now challenged. We

conclude that legislative prayer presents no more potential for establishment than the provision of school transportation . . . beneficial grants for higher education, or tax exemptions for religious organizations. . . .

Respondent . . . argues that we should not rely too heavily on "the advice of the Founding Fathers" because the messages of history often tend to be ambiguous and not relevant to a society far more heterogeneous than that of the Framers. Respondent also points out that John Jay and John Rutledge opposed the motion to begin the first session of the Continental Congress with prayer.

We do not agree that evidence of opposition to a measure weakens the force of the historical argument; indeed it infuses it with power by demonstrating that the subject was considered carefully and the action not taken thoughtlessly, by force of long tradition and without regard to the problems posed by a pluralistic society. Jay and Rutledge specifically grounded their objection on the fact that the delegates to the Congress "were so divided in religious sentiments . . . that [they] could not join in the same act of worship." Their objection was met by Samuel Adams, who stated that "he was no bigot, and could hear a prayer from a gentleman of piety and virtue, who was at the same time a friend to his country."

This interchange emphasizes that the delegates did not consider opening prayers as a proselytizing activity or as symbolically placing the government's official seal of approval on one religious view. Rather, the Founding Fathers looked at invocations as "conduct whose . . . effect . . . [harmonized] with the tenets of some or all religions." . . . The Establishment Clause does not always bar a state from regulating conduct simply because it "harmonizes with religious canons." . . . Here, the individual claiming injury by the practice is an adult, presumably not readily susceptible to "religious indoctrination." . . .

In light of the unambiguous and unbroken history of more than 200 years, there can be no doubt that the practice of opening legislative sessions with prayer has become part of the fabric of our society. To invoke Divine guidance on a public body entrusted with making the laws is not, in these circumstances, an "establishment" of religion or a step toward establishment; it is simply a tolerable acknowledgment of beliefs widely held among the people of this country. As Justice Douglas observed, "[we] are a religious people whose institutions presuppose a Supreme Being." *Zorach v. Clauson.*

We turn then to the question of whether any features of the Nebraska practice violate the Establishment Clause. Beyond the bare fact that a prayer is offered, three points have been made: first, that a clergyman of only one denomination—Presbyterian—has been selected for 16 years; second, that the chaplain is paid at public expense; and third, that the prayers are in the Judeo-Christian tradition. Weighed against the historical background, these factors do not serve to invalidate Nebraska's practice.

The Court of Appeals was concerned that Palmer's long tenure has the effect of giving preference to his religious views. We cannot, any more than Members of the Congresses of this century, perceive any suggestion that choosing a clergyman of one denomination advances the beliefs of a particular church. To the contrary, the evidence indicates that Palmer was reappointed because his performance and personal qualities were acceptable to the body appointing him. Palmer was not the only clergyman heard by the legislature; guest chaplains have officiated at the request of various legislators and as substitutes during Palmer's absences. Absent proof that the chaplain's reappointment stemmed from an impermissible motive, we conclude that his long tenure does not in itself conflict with the Establishment Clause.

Nor is the compensation of the chaplain from public funds a reason to invalidate the Nebraska Legislature's chaplaincy; remuneration is grounded in historic practice initiated, as we noted earlier, by the same Congress that drafted the Establishment Clause of the First Amendment. The Continental Congress paid its chaplain, as did some of the states. . . . Currently, many state legislatures and the United States Congress provide compensation for their chaplains. . . . The content of the prayer is not of concern to judges where, as here, there is no indication that the prayer opportunity has been exploited to proselytize or advance any one, or to disparage any other, faith or belief. That being so, it is not for us to embark on a sensitive evaluation or to parse the content of a particular prayer.

We do not doubt the sincerity of those, who like respondent, believe that to have prayer in this context risks the beginning of the establishment the Founding Fathers feared. But this concern is not well founded, for as Justice Goldberg aptly observed in his concurring opinion in *Abington*:

> It is of course true that great consequences can grow from small beginnings, but the measure of constitutional adjudication is the ability and willingness to distinguish between real threat and mere shadow.

The unbroken practice for two centuries in the National Congress and for more than a century in Nebraska and in many other states gives abundant assurance that there is no real threat "while this Court sits."

The judgment of the Court of Appeals is Reversed.

JUSTICE BRENNAN, with whom JUSTICE MARSHALL joins, dissenting.

The Court today has written a narrow and, on the whole, careful opinion. In effect, the Court holds that officially sponsored legislative prayer, primarily on account of its "unique history" . . . is generally exempted from the First Amendment's prohibition against "an establishment of religion." The Court's opinion is consistent with dictum in at least one of our prior decisions, and its limited rationale should pose little threat to the overall fate of the Establishment Clause. Moreover, disagreement with the Court requires that I confront the fact that some 20 years ago, in a concurring opinion in one of the cases striking down official prayer and ceremonial Bible reading in the public schools, I came very close to endorsing essentially the result reached by the Court today. Nevertheless, after much reflection, I have come to the conclusion that I was wrong then and that the Court is wrong today. I now believe that the practice of official invocational prayer, as it exists in Nebraska and most other state legislatures, is unconstitutional. It is contrary to the doctrine as well the underlying purposes of the Establishment Clause, and it is not saved either by its history or by any of the other considerations suggested in the Court's opinion. I respectfully dissent.

The Court makes no pretense of subjecting Nebraska's practice of legislative prayer to any of the formal "tests" that have traditionally structured our inquiry under the Establishment Clause. That it fails to do so is, in a sense, a good thing, for it simply confirms that the Court is carving out an exception to the Establishment Clause rather than reshaping Establishment Clause doctrine to accommodate legislative prayer. For my purposes, however, I must begin by demonstrating what should be obvious: that, if the Court were to judge legislative prayer through the unsentimental eye of our settled doctrine, it would have to strike it down as a clear violation of the Establishment Clause.

The most commonly cited formulation of prevailing Establishment Clause doctrine is found in *Lemon v. Kurtzman:*

> Every analysis in this area must begin with consideration of the cumulative criteria developed by the Court over many years. Three such tests may be gleaned from our cases. First, the statute [at issue] must have a secular legislative purpose; second, its principal or primary effect must be one that neither advances nor inhibits; finally, the statute must not foster "an excessive government entanglement with religion."

That the "purpose" of legislative prayer is pre-eminently religious rather than secular seems to me to be self-evident. "To invoke Divine guidance on a public body entrusted with making the laws," is nothing but a religious act. Moreover, whatever secular functions legislative prayer might play— formally opening the legislative session, getting the members of the body to quiet down, and imbuing them with a sense of seriousness and high purpose—could so plainly be performed in a purely nonreligious fashion that to claim a secular purpose for the prayer is an insult to the perfectly honorable individuals who instituted and continue the practice.

The "primary effect" of legislative prayer is also clearly religious. As we said in the context of officially sponsored prayers in the public schools, "prescribing a particular form of religious worship," even if the individuals involved have the choice not to participate, places "indirect coercive pressure upon religious minorities to conform to the prevailing officially approved religion. . . ." *Engel v. Vitale.* More importantly, invocations in Nebraska's legislative halls explicitly link religious belief and observance to the power and prestige of the State. "[The] mere appearance of a joint exercise of legislative authority by Church and State provides a significant symbolic benefit to religion in the minds of some by reason of the power conferred."

The Court argues that legislators are adults, "presumably not readily susceptible to . . . peer pressure." . . . Quite apart from the debatable constitutional significance of this argument, I am now most uncertain as to whether it is even factually correct: Legislators, by virtue of their instinct for political survival, are often loath to assert in public religious views that their constituents might perceive as hostile or nonconforming. . . .

Finally, there can be no doubt that the practice of legislative prayer leads to excessive "entanglement" between the State and religion. *Lemon* pointed out that "entanglement" can take two forms: First, a state statute or program might involve the state impermissibly in monitoring and overseeing religious affairs. In the case of legislative prayer, the process of choosing a "suitable" chaplain, whether on a permanent or rotating basis, and insuring that the chaplain limits himself or herself to "suitable" prayers, involves precisely the sort of supervision that agencies of government should if at all possible avoid.

Second, excessive "entanglement" might arise out of "the divisive political potential" of a state statute or program. . . . In this case, this second aspect of entanglement is also clear. The controversy between Senator Chambers and his colleagues, which had reached the stage of difficulty and rancor long before this lawsuit was brought, has split the Nebraska Legislature precisely on issues of religion and religious conformity. The record in this case also reports a series of instances, involving legislators other than Senator Chambers, in which invocations by Reverend Palmer and others led to controversy along religious lines. . . . And in general, the history of legislative prayer has been far more eventful—and divisive—than a hasty reading of the Court's opinion might indicate.

In sum, I have no doubt that, if any group of law students were asked to apply the principles of *Lemon* to the question of legislative prayer, they would nearly unanimously find the practice to be unconstitutional.

The path of formal doctrine, however, can only imperfectly capture the nature and importance of the issues at stake in this case. A more adequate analysis must therefore take into account the underlying function of the Establishment Clause, and the forces that have shaped its doctrine.

Most of the provisions of the Bill of Rights, even if they are not generally enforceable in the absence of state action, nevertheless arise out of moral intuitions applicable to individuals as well as governments. The Establishment Clause, however, is quite different. It is, to its core, nothing less and nothing more than a statement about the proper role of *government* in the society that we have shaped for ourselves in this land.

The Establishment Clause embodies a judgment, born of a long and turbulent history, that, in our society, religion "must be a private matter for the individual, the family, and the institutions of private choice. . . ."

The principles of "separation" and "neutrality" implicit in the Establishment Clause serve many purposes. Four of these are particularly relevant here.

The first, which is most closely related to the more general conceptions of liberty found in the remainder of the First Amendment, is to guarantee the individual right to conscience. The right to conscience, in the religious sphere, is not only implicated when the government engages in direct or indirect coercion. It is also implicated when the government requires individuals to support the practices of a faith with which they do not agree.

The second purpose of separation and neutrality is to keep the state from interfering in the essential autonomy of religious life, either by taking upon itself the decision of religious issues, or by unduly involving itself in the supervision of religious institutions or officials.

The third purpose of separation and neutrality is to prevent the trivialization and degradation of religion by too close an attachment to the organs of government. The Establishment Clause "stands as an expression of principle on the part of the Founders of our Constitution that religion is too personal, too sacred, too holy, to permit its 'unhallowed perversion' by a civil magistrate." . . .

Finally, the principles of separation and neutrality help assure that essentially religious issues, precisely because of their importance and sensitivity, not become the occasion for battle in the political arena. . . . With regard to most issues, the government may be influenced by partisan argument and may act as a partisan itself. In each case, there will be winners and losers in the political battle, and the losers' most common recourse is the right to dissent and the right to fight the battle again another day. With regard to matters that are essentially religious, however, the Establishment Clause seeks that there should be no political battles, and that no American should at any point feel alienated from his government because that government has declared or acted upon some "official" or "authorized" point of view on a matter of religion.

The imperatives of separation and neutrality are not limited to the relationship of government to religious institutions or denominations, but extend as well to the relationship of government to religious beliefs and practices. In *Torcaso v. Watkins,* for example, we struck down a state provision requiring a religious oath as a qualification to hold office, not only because it violated principles of free exercise of religion, but also because it violated the principles of nonestablishment of religion. And, of course, in the pair of cases that hang over this one like a reproachful set of parents, we held that official prayer and prescribed Bible reading in the public schools represent a serious encroachment on the Establishment Clause. As we said in *Engel,* "[it] is neither sacrilegious nor antireligious to say that each separate government in this country should stay out of the business of writing or sanctioning official prayers and leave that purely religious function to the people themselves and to those the people choose to look to for religious guidance."

Nor should it be thought that this view of the Establishment Clause is a recent concoction of an overreaching judiciary. Even before the First Amendment was written, the Framers of the Constitution broke with the practice of the Articles of Confederation and many state constitutions, and did not invoke the name of God in the document. This "omission of a reference to the Deity was not inadvertent; nor did it remain unnoticed." Moreover, Thomas Jefferson and Andrew Jackson, during their respective terms as President, both refused on Establishment Clause grounds to declare national days of thanksgiving or fasting. And James Madison, writing subsequent to his own Presidency on essentially the very issue we face today, stated:

> Is the appointment of Chaplains to the two Houses of Congress consistent with the Constitution, and with the pure principle of religious freedom? In strictness, the answer on both points must be in the negative. . . .

Legislative prayer clearly violates the principles of neutrality and separation that are embedded within the Establishment Clause. . . . It intrudes on the right to conscience by forcing some legislators either to participate in a "prayer opportunity," with which they are in basic disagreement, or to make their disagreement a matter of public comment by declining to participate. It forces all residents of the State to support a religious exercise that may be contrary to their own beliefs. It requires the State to commit itself on fundamental theological issues. It has the potential for degrading religion by allowing a religious call to worship to be intermeshed with a secular call to order. And it injects religion into the political sphere by creating the potential that each and every selection of a chaplain, or consideration of a particular prayer, or even reconsideration of the practice itself, will provoke a political battle along religious lines and ultimately alienate some religiously identified group of citizens.

One response to the foregoing account, of course, is that "neutrality" and "separation" do not exhaust the full meaning of the Establishment Clause as it has developed in our cases. It is indeed true that there are certain tensions inherent in the First Amendment itself, or inherent in the role of religion and religious belief in any free society, that have shaped the doctrine of the Establishment Clause, and required us to deviate from an absolute adherence to separation and neutrality. Nevertheless, these considerations, although very important, are also quite specific, and where none of them is present, the Establishment Clause gives us no warrant simply to look the other way and treat an unconstitutional practice as if it were constitutional. . . .

A number of our cases have recognized that religious institutions and religious practices may, in certain contexts, receive the benefit of government programs and policies generally available, on the basis of some secular criterion, to a wide class of similarly situated nonreligious beneficiaries, and the precise cataloging of those contexts is not necessarily an easy task. I need not tarry long here, however, because the provision for a daily official invocation by a nonmember officer of a legislative body could by no stretch of the imagination appear anywhere in that catalog.

Conversely, our cases have recognized that religion can encompass a broad, if not total, spectrum of concerns, overlapping considerably with the range of secular concerns, and that not every governmental act which coincides with or conflicts with a particular religious belief is for that reason an establishment of religion. See e.g. *McGowan* . . . (Sunday Laws); . . . *Harris* . . . (abortion restrictions). The Court seems to suggest at one point that the practice of legislative prayer may be excused on this ground, but I cannot really believe that it takes this position seriously. The practice of legislative prayer is nothing like the statutes we considered in *McGowan* . . . and *Harris;* prayer is not merely "conduct whose . . . effect . . . [harmonizes] with the tenets of some or all religions"; prayer is fundamentally and necessarily religious.

We have also recognized that government cannot, without adopting a decidedly *anti*-religious point of view, be forbidden to recognize the religious beliefs and practices of the American people as an aspect of our history and culture. Certainly, bona fide classes in comparative religion can be offered in the public schools. And certainly, the text of Abraham Lincoln's Second Inaugural Address which is inscribed on a wall of the Lincoln Memorial need not be purged of its profound theological content. The practice of offering invocations at legislative sessions cannot, however, simply be dismissed as "a tolerable *acknowledgment of beliefs* widely held among the people of this country." . . . Reverend Palmer and other members of the clergy who offer invocations at legislative sessions are not museum pieces put on display once a day for the edification of the legislature. Rather, they are engaged by the legislature to lead it—as a body—in an act of religious worship. If upholding the practice requires denial of this fact, I suspect that many supporters of legislative prayer would feel that they had been handed a pyrrhic victory.

Our cases have recognized that the purposes of the Establishment Clause can sometimes conflict. For example, in *Walz* . . . we upheld tax exemptions for religious institutions in part because subjecting those institutions to taxation might foster serious administrative entanglement. Here, however, no such tension exists; the State can vindicate *all* the purposes of the Establishment Clause by abolishing legislative prayer.

Finally, our cases recognize that, in one important respect, the Constitution is *not* neutral on the subject of religion: Under the Free Exercise Clause, religiously motivated claims of conscience may give rise to constitutional rights that other strongly held beliefs do not. Moreover, even when the government is not compelled to do so by the Free Exercise

Clause, it may to some extent act to facilitate the opportunities of individuals to practice their religion. . . . This is not, however, a case in which a State is accommodating individual religious interests. We are not faced here with the right of the legislature to allow its members to offer prayers during the course of general legislative debate. We are certainly not faced with the right of legislators to form voluntary groups for prayer or worship. We are not even faced with the right of the State to employ members of the clergy to minister to the private religious needs of individual legislators. Rather, we are faced here with the regularized practice of conducting official prayers, on behalf of the entire legislature, as part of the order of business constituting the formal opening of every single session of the legislative term. If this is free exercise, the Establishment Clause has no meaning whatsoever. . . .

I sympathize with the Court's reluctance to strike down a practice so prevalent and so ingrained as legislative prayer. I am, however, unconvinced by the Court's arguments, and cannot shake my conviction that legislative prayer violates both the letter and the spirit of the Establishment Clause.

The Court's main argument for carving out an exception sustaining legislative prayer is historical. The Court cannot—and does not—purport to find a pattern of "undeviating acceptance." . . . I agree that historical practice is "of considerable import in the interpretation of abstract constitutional language." . . . This is a case, however, in which—absent the Court's invocation of history—there would be no question that the practice at issue was unconstitutional. And despite the surface appeal of the Court's argument, there are at least three reasons why specific historical practice should not in this case override that clear constitutional imperative.

First, it is significant that the Court's historical argument does not rely on the legislative history of the Establishment Clause itself. Indeed, that formal history is profoundly unilluminating on this and most other subjects. Rather, the Court assumes that the Framers of the Establishment Clause would not have themselves authorized a practice that they thought violated the guarantees contained in the Clause. This assumption, however, is questionable. Legislators, influenced by the passions and exigencies of the moment, the pressure of constituents and colleagues, and the press of business, do not always pass sober constitutional judgment on every piece of legislation they enact, and this must be assumed to be as true of the Members of the First Congress as any other. Indeed, the fact that James Madison, who voted for the bill authorizing the payment of the first congressional chaplains later expressed the view that the practice was unconstitutional is instructive on precisely this point. Madison's later views may not have represented so much a change of *mind* as a change of *role*, from a Member of Congress engaged in the hurly-burly of legislative activity to a detached observer engaged in unpressured reflection. Since the latter role is precisely the one with which this Court is charged, I am not at all sure that Madison's later writings should be any less influential in our deliberations than his earlier vote.

Second, the Court's analysis treats the First Amendment simply as an Act of Congress, as to whose meaning the intent of Congress is the single touchstone. Both the Constitution and its Amendments, however, became supreme law only by virtue of their ratification by the States, and the understanding of the States should be as relevant to our analysis as the understanding of Congress. . . . This observation is especially compelling in considering the meaning of the Bill of Rights. The first 10 Amendments were not enacted because the Members of the First Congress came up with a bright idea one morning; rather, their enactment was forced upon Congress by a number of the States as a condition for their ratification of the original Constitution. To treat any practice authorized by the First Congress as presumptively consistent with the Bill of Rights is therefore somewhat akin to treating any action of a party to a contract as presumptively consistent with the terms of the contract. The latter proposition, if it were accepted, would of course resolve many of the heretofore perplexing issues in contract law.

Finally, and most importantly, the argument tendered by the Court is misguided because the Constitution is not a static document whose meaning on every detail is fixed for all time by the life experience of the Framers. We have recognized in a wide variety of constitutional contexts that the practices that were in place at the time any particular guarantee was enacted into the Constitution do not necessarily fix forever the meaning of that guarantee. To be truly faithful to the Framers, "our use of the history of their time must limit itself to broad purposes, not specific practices."

The inherent adaptability of the Constitution and its amendments is particularly important with respect to the Establishment Clause. "[Our] religious composition makes us a vastly more diverse people than were our forefathers. . . . In the face of such profound changes, practices which may have been objectionable to no one in the time of Jefferson and Madison may today be highly offensive to many persons, the deeply devout and the nonbelievers alike." . . . The Members of the First Congress should be treated, not as sacred figures whose every action must be emulated, but as the authors of a document meant to last for the ages. Indeed, a proper respect for the Framers themselves forbids us to give so static and lifeless a meaning to their work. To my mind, the Court's focus here on a narrow piece of history is, in a fundamental sense, a betrayal of the lessons of history.

Of course, the Court does not rely entirely on the practice of the First Congress in order to validate legislative prayer. There is another theme which, although implicit, also pervades the Court's opinion. It is exemplified by the Court's comparison of legislative prayer with the formulaic recitation of "God save the United States and this Honorable Court." It is also exemplified by the Court's apparent conclusion that legislative prayer is, at worst, a "'mere shadow'" on the Establishment Clause rather than a "'real threat'" to it. Simply put, the Court seems to regard legislative prayer as at most a *de minimis* violation, somehow unworthy of our attention. I frankly do not know what should be the proper disposition of features of our public life such as "God save the United States and this Honorable Court," "In God We Trust," "One Nation Under God," and the like. I might well adhere to the view expressed in *Schempp* that such mottos are consistent with the Establishment Clause, not because their import is *de minimis,* but because they have lost any true religious significance. Legislative invocations, however, are very different. . . . I agree with the Court that the federal judiciary should not sit as a board of censors on individual prayers, but to my mind the better way of avoiding that task is by striking down all official legislative invocations. . . . *Any* practice of legislative prayer, even if it might look "nonsectarian" to nine Justices of the Supreme Court, will inevitably and continuously involve the State in one or another religious debate. Prayer is serious business—serious theological business—and it is not a mere "acknowledgment of beliefs widely held among the people of this country" for the State to immerse itself in that business. . . . In this case, we are faced with potential religious objections to an activity at the very center of religious life, and it is simply beyond the competence of government, and inconsistent with our conceptions of liberty, for the State to take upon itself the role of ecclesiastical arbiter.

The argument is made occasionally that a strict separation of religion and state robs the Nation of its spiritual identity. I believe quite the contrary. It may be true that individuals cannot be "neutral" on the question of religion. But the judgment of the Establishment Clause is that neutrality by the organs of *government* on questions of religion is both possible and imperative. . . . If the Court had struck down legislative prayer today, it would likely have stimulated a furious reaction. But it would also, I am convinced, have invigorated both the "spirit of religion" and the "spirit of freedom."

I respectfully dissent.

JUSTICE STEVENS, dissenting.

In a democratically elected legislature, the religious beliefs of the chaplain tend to reflect the faith of the majority of the lawmakers' constituents. Prayers may be said by a Catholic priest in the Massachusetts Legislature and by a Presbyterian minister in the Nebraska Legislature, but I would not expect to find a Jehovah's Witness or a disciple of Mary Baker Eddy or the Reverend Moon serving as the official chaplain in any state legislature. Regardless of the motivation of the majority that exercises the power to appoint the chaplain, it seems plain to me that the designation of a member of one religious faith to serve as the sole official chaplain of a state legislature for a period of 16 years constitutes the preference of one faith over another in violation of the Establishment Clause of the First Amendment. . . .

The Court declines to "embark on a sensitive evaluation or to parse the content of a particular prayer." Perhaps it does so because it would be unable to explain away the clearly sectarian content of some of the prayers given by Nebraska's chaplain. Or perhaps the Court is unwilling to acknowledge that the tenure of the chaplain must inevitably be conditioned on the acceptability of that content to the silent majority.

I would affirm the judgment of the Court of Appeals.

Appendix 13. Lynch v Donnelly
465 U.S. 668 (1984)

CHIEF JUSTICE BURGER delivered the opinion of the Court.

We granted certiorari to decide whether the Establishment Clause of the First Amendment prohibits a municipality from including a creche, or Nativity scene, in its annual Christmas display.

Each year, in cooperation with the downtown retail merchants' association, the city of Pawtucket, R.I., erects a Christmas display as part of its observance of the Christmas holiday season. . . . The District Court found that, by including the creche in the Christmas display, the city has "tried to endorse and promulgate religious beliefs." . . . The city was permanently enjoined from including the creche in the display. . . . A divided panel of the Court of Appeals for the First Circuit affirmed. We granted certiorari, and we reverse.

This Court has explained that the purpose of the Establishment and Free Exercise Clauses of the First Amendment is

> to prevent, as far as possible, the intrusion of either [the church or the state] into the precincts of the other. *Lemon v. Kurtzman.*

At the same time, however, the Court has recognized that

> total separation is not possible in an absolute sense. Some relationship between government and religious organizations is inevitable. *Ibid.*

In every Establishment Clause case, we must reconcile the inescapable tension between the objective of preventing unnecessary intrusion of either the church or the state upon the other, and the reality that, as the Court has so often noted, total separation of the two is not possible.

The Court has sometimes described the Religion Clauses as erecting a "wall" between church and state. . . . The concept of a "wall" of separation is a useful figure of speech probably deriving from views of Thomas Jefferson. The metaphor has served as a reminder that the Establishment Clause forbids an established church or anything approaching it. But the metaphor itself is not a wholly accurate description of the practical aspects of the relationship that in fact exists between church and state.

No significant segment of our society and no institution within it can exist in a vacuum or in total or absolute isolation from all the other parts, much less from government. "It has never been thought either possible or desirable to enforce a regime of total separation." . . . Nor does the Constitution require complete separation of church and state; it affirmatively mandates accommodation, not merely tolerance, of all religions, and forbids hostility toward any. . . . Anything less would require the "callous indifference" we have said was never intended by the Establishment Clause. Indeed, we have observed, such hostility would bring us into "war with our national tradition as embodied in the First Amendment's guaranty of the free exercise of religion."

The Court's interpretation of the Establishment Clause has comported with what history reveals was the contemporaneous understanding of its guarantees. . . . There is an unbroken history of official acknowledgment by all three branches of government of the role of religion in American life from at least 1789. Our history is replete with official references to the value and invocation of Divine guidance in deliberations and pronouncements of the Founding Fathers and contemporary leaders. . . .

This history may help explain why the Court consistently has declined to take a rigid, absolutist view of the Establishment Clause. . . .

Rather than mechanically invalidating all governmental conduct or statutes that confer benefits or give special recognition to religion in general or to one faith—as an absolutist approach would dictate—the Court has scrutinized challenged legislation or official conduct to determine whether, in reality, it establishes a religion or religious faith, or tends to do so.

In each case, the inquiry calls for line-drawing; no fixed, per se rule can be framed. The Establishment Clause like the Due Process Clauses is not a precise, detailed provision in a legal code capable of ready application. The purpose of the Establishment Clause "was to state an objective, not to write a statute." . . .

The District Court plainly erred by focusing almost exclusively on the creche. When viewed in the proper context of the Christmas Holiday season, it is apparent that, on this record, there is insufficient evidence to establish that the inclusion of the creche is a purposeful or surreptitious effort to express some kind of subtle governmental advocacy of a particular religious message. In a pluralistic society a variety of motives and purposes are implicated. . . . . The display is sponsored by the city to celebrate the Holiday and to depict the origins of that Holiday. These are legitimate secular purposes.

The dissent asserts some observers may perceive that the city has aligned itself with the Christian faith by including a Christian symbol in its display and that this serves to advance religion. We can assume, arguendo, that the display advances religion in a sense; but our precedents plainly contemplate that on occasion some advancement of religion will result from governmental action. . . . Here, whatever benefit there is to one faith or religion or to all religions, is indirect, remote, and incidental; display of the creche is no more an advancement or endorsement of religion than the Congressional and Executive recognition of the origins of the Holiday itself as "Christ's Mass," or the exhibition of literally hundreds of religious paintings in governmentally supported museums. . . .

Of course the creche is identified with one religious faith but no more so than the examples we have set out from prior cases in which we found no conflict with the Establishment Clause. . . . To forbid the use of this one passive symbol—the crèche—at the very time people are taking note of the season with Christmas hymns and carols in public schools and other public places, and while the Congress and legislatures open sessions with prayers by paid chaplains, would be a stilted overreaction contrary to our history and to our holdings. . . . Any notion that these symbols pose a real danger of establishment of a state church is farfetched indeed.

We hold that, notwithstanding the religious significance of the creche, the city of Pawtucket has not violated the Establishment Clause of the First Amendment. Accordingly, the judgment of the Court of Appeals is reversed.

JUSTICE O'CONNOR, concurring.

I concur in the opinion of the Court. I write separately to suggest a clarification of our Establishment Clause doctrine. The suggested approach leads to the same result in this case as that taken by the Court, and the Court's opinion, as I read it, is consistent with my analysis.

Our prior cases have used the three-part test articulated in *Lemon v. Kurtzman.* . . . It has never been entirely clear, however, how the three parts of the test relate to the principles enshrined in the Establishment Clause. Focusing on institutional entanglement and on endorsement or disapproval of religion clarifies the Lemon test as an analytical device.

In this case, as even the District Court found, there is no institutional entanglement. Nevertheless, the respondents contend that the political divisiveness caused by Pawtucket's display of its creche violates the excessive-entanglement prong of the Lemon test. . . . In my view, political divisiveness along religious lines should not be an independent test of constitutionality. . . . Political divisiveness is admittedly an evil addressed by the Establishment Clause. Its existence may be evidence that institutional entanglement is excessive or that a government practice is perceived as an endorsement of religion. But the constitutional inquiry should focus ultimately on the character of the government activity that might cause such divisiveness, not on the divisiveness itself.

The central issue in this case is whether Pawtucket has endorsed Christianity by its display of the creche. . . .

The purpose prong of the Lemon test asks whether government's actual purpose is to endorse or disapprove of religion. The effect prong asks whether, irrespective of government's actual purpose, the practice under review in fact conveys a message of endorsement or disapproval. . . . The proper inquiry under the purpose prong of Lemon, I submit, is whether the government intends to convey a message of endorsement or disapproval of religion. . . .

Applying that formulation to this case, I would find that Pawtucket did not intend to convey any message of endorsement of Christianity or disapproval or nonChristian religions. . . . The display celebrates a public holiday, and no one contends that declaration of that holiday is understood to be an endorsement of religion. The holiday itself has very secular components and traditions. . . .

Every government practice must be judged in its unique circumstances to determine whether it constitutes an endorsement or disapproval of religion. . . . Giving the challenged practice the careful scrutiny it deserves, I cannot say that the particular creche display at issue in this case was intended to endorse or had the effect of endorsing Christianity. I agree with the Court that the judgment below must be reversed.

JUSTICE BRENNAN, with whom JUSTICE MARSHALL, JUSTICE BLACK-MUN, and JUSTICE STEVENS join, dissenting.

. . . the Court reaches an essentially narrow result which turns largely upon the particular holiday context in which the city of Pawtucket's nativity scene appeared. The Court's decision implicitly leaves open questions concerning the constitutionality of the public display on public property of a creche standing alone, or the public display of other distinctively religious symbols such as a cross. Despite the narrow contours of the Court's opinion, our precedents in my view compel the holding that Pawtucket's inclusion of a life-sized display depicting the biblical description of the birth of Christ as part of its annual Christmas celebration is unconstitutional. Nothing in the history of such practices or the setting in which the city's creche is presented obscures or diminishes the plain fact that Pawtucket's action amounts to an impermissible governmental endorsement of a particular faith. . . .

. . . I am persuaded that the city's inclusion of the creche in its Christmas display simply does not reflect a "clearly secular . . . purpose." . . . In the present case, the city claims that its purposes were exclusively secular. Pawtucket sought, according to this view, only to participate in the celebration of a national holiday and to attract people to the downtown area in order to promote pre-Christmas retail sales and to help engender the spirit of goodwill and neighborliness commonly associated with the Christmas season.

Despite these assertions, two compelling aspects of this case indicate that our generally prudent "reluctance to attribute unconstitutional motives" to a governmental body . . . should be overcome. First . . . all of Pawtucket's "valid secular objectives can be readily accomplished by other means." Plainly, the city's interest in celebrating the holiday and in promoting both retail sales and goodwill are fully served by the elaborate display of Santa Claus, reindeer, and wishing wells that are already a part of Pawtucket's annual Christmas display. More importantly, the nativity scene, unlike every other element of the Hodgson Park display, reflects a sectarian exclusivity that the avowed purposes of celebrating the holiday season and promoting retail commerce simply do not encompass. To be found constitutional, Pawtucket's seasonal celebration must at least be nondenominational and not serve to promote religion. The inclusion of a distinctively religious element like the creche, however, demonstrates that a narrower sectarian purpose lay behind the decision to include a nativity scene. . . .

The Court, by focusing on the holiday "context" in which the nativity scene appeared, seeks to explain away the clear religious import of the creche. . . . But it blinks reality to claim, as the Court does, that by including such a distinctively religious object as the creche in its Christmas display. . . .

Moreover, the city has done nothing to disclaim government approval of the religious significance of the creche. . . .

Finally, and most importantly, even in the context of Pawtucket's seasonal celebration, the creche retains a specifically Christian religious meaning. . . .

The Court also attempts to justify the creche by entertaining a beguilingly simple, yet faulty syllogism. The Court begins by noting that government may recognize Christmas Day as a public holiday; the Court then asserts that the creche is nothing more than a traditional element of Christmas celebrations. . . . The vice of this dangerously superficial argument is that it overlooks the fact that the Christmas holiday in our national culture contains both secular and sectarian elements. To say that government may recognize the holiday's traditional, secular elements of gift-giving, public festivities, and community spirit, does not mean that government may indiscriminately embrace the distinctively sectarian aspects of the holiday. . . . Unlike such secular figures as Santa Claus, reindeer, and carolers, a nativity scene represents far more than a mere "traditional" symbol of Christmas. . . . To suggest, as the Court does that such a symbol is merely "traditional" and therefore no different from Santa's house or reindeer is not only offensive to those for whom the creche has profound significance, but insulting to those who insist for religious or personal reasons that the story of Christ is in no sense a part of "history" nor an unavoidable element of our national "heritage." . . .

. . . the Court takes a long step backwards to the days when Justice Brewer could arrogantly declare for the Court that "this is a Christian nation." . . . Those days, I had thought, were forever put behind us by the Court's decision in *Engel v. Vitale*, in which we rejected a similar argument advanced by the State of New York that its Regent's Prayer was simply an acceptable part of our "spiritual heritage."

The American historical experience concerning the public celebration of Christmas, if carefully examined, provides no support for the Court's decision. . . . The Court's complete failure to offer any explanation of its assertion is perhaps understandable, however, because the historical record points in precisely the opposite direction. Two features of this history are worth noting. First, at the time of the adoption of the Constitution and the Bill of Rights, there was no settled pattern of celebrating Christmas, either as a purely religious holiday or as a public event. Second, the historical evidence, such as it is, offers no uniform pattern of widespread acceptance of the holiday and indeed suggests that the development of Christmas as a public holiday is a comparatively recent phenomenon. . . . To the Puritans, the celebration of Christmas represented a "Popish" practice lacking any foundation in Scripture. . . .

. . . the city's action should be recognized for what it is: a coercive, though perhaps small, step toward establishing the sectarian preferences of the majority at the expense of the minority, accomplished by placing public facilities and funds in support of the religious symbolism and theological tidings that the creche conveys. As Justice Frankfurter, writing in *McGowan v. Maryland,* observed, the Establishment Clause "withdr[aws] from the sphere of legitimate legislative concern and competence a specific, but comprehensive, area of human conduct: man's belief or disbelief in the verity of some transcendental idea and man's expression in action of that belief or disbelief." That the Constitution sets this realm of thought and feeling apart from the pressures and antagonisms of government is one of its supreme achievements. Regrettably, the Court today tarnishes that achievement.

I dissent.

Appendix 14. Wallace v Jaffree
472 U.S. 38 (1985)

JUSTICE STEVENS delivered the opinion of the Court.

Appellee Ishmael Jaffree is a resident of Mobile County, Alabama. On May 28, 1982, he filed a complaint on behalf of three of his minor children; two of them were second-grade students and the third was then in kindergarten. The complaint named members of the Mobile County School Board, various school officials, and the minor plaintiffs' three teachers as defendants. The complaint alleged that the appellees brought the action "seeking principally a declaratory judgment and an injunction restraining the Defendants and each of them from maintaining or allowing the maintenance of regular religious prayer services or other forms of religious observances in the Mobile County Public Schools in violation of the First Amendment as made applicable to states by the Fourteenth Amendment to the United States Constitution." The complaint further alleged that two of the children had been subjected to various acts of religious indoctrination "from the beginning of the school year in September, 1981"; that the defendant teachers had "on a daily basis" led their classes in saying certain prayers in unison; that the minor children were exposed to ostracism from their peer group class members if they did not participate; and that Ishmael Jaffree had repeatedly but unsuccessfully requested that the devotional services be stopped.

On August 2, 1982, the District Court held an evidentiary hearing on appellees' motion for a preliminary injunction. At that hearing, State Senator Donald G. Holmes testified that he was the "prime sponsor" of the bill that was enacted in 1981 as § 16-1-20.1. He explained that the bill was an "effort to return voluntary prayer to our public schools . . . it is a beginning and a step in the right direction." Apart from the purpose to return voluntary prayer to public school, Senator Holmes unequivocally testified that he had "no other purpose in mind." A week after the hearing, the District Court entered a preliminary injunction.

In November 1982, the District Court held a 4-day trial on the merits. . . . The District Court concluded that "the establishment clause of the first amendment to the United States Constitution does not prohibit the state from establishing a religion."

The Court of Appeals . . . not surprisingly . . . reversed . . . [and] held that the teachers' religious activities violated the Establishment Clause of the First Amendment.

. . . Just as the right to speak and the right to refrain from speaking are complementary components of a broader concept of individual freedom of mind, so also the individual's freedom to choose his own creed is the counterpart of his right to refrain from accepting the creed established by the majority. At one time it was thought that this right merely proscribed the preference of one Christian sect over another, but would not require equal respect for the conscience of the infidel, the atheist, or the adherent of a non-Christian faith such as Islam or Judaism. But when the underlying principle has been examined in the crucible of litigation, the Court has unambiguously concluded that the individual freedom of conscience protected by the First Amendment embraces the right to select any religious faith or none at all. . . .

In applying the purpose test, it is appropriate to ask "whether government's actual purpose is to endorse or disapprove of religion." In this case, the answer to that question is dispositive. For the record not only provides us with an unambiguous affirmative answer, but it also reveals that the enactment of § 16-1-20.1 was not motivated by any clearly secular purpose—indeed, the statute had *no* secular purpose.

The legislative intent to return prayer to the public schools is, of course, quite different from merely protecting every student's right to engage in voluntary prayer during an appropriate moment of silence during the schoolday. The 1978 statute already protected that right, containing nothing that prevented any student from engaging in voluntary prayer during a silent minute of meditation. Appellants have not identified any secular purpose that was not fully served by § 16-1-20 before the enactment of § 16-1-20.1. . . . We must, therefore, conclude that the Alabama Legislature intended to change existing law. . . . The addition of "or voluntary prayer" indicates that the State intended to characterize prayer as a favored practice. Such an endorsement is not consistent with the established principle that the government must pursue a course of complete neutrality toward religion.

The importance of that principle does not permit us to treat this as an inconsequential case involving nothing more than a few words of symbolic speech on behalf of the political majority. . . . Keeping in mind, as we must, "both the fundamental place held by the Establishment Clause in our constitutional scheme and the myriad, subtle ways in which Establishment

Clause values can be eroded" we conclude that § 16-1-20.1 violates the First Amendment.

The judgment of the Court of Appeals is affirmed.

JUSTICE REHNQUIST, dissenting.

Thirty-eight years ago this Court, in *Everson v. Board of Education* summarized its exegesis of Establishment Clause doctrine thus:

> In the words of Jefferson, the clause against establishment of religion by law was intended to erect "a wall of separation between church and State." *Reynolds v. United States.*

This language from *Reynolds,* a case involving the Free Exercise Clause of the First Amendment rather than the Establishment Clause, quoted from Thomas Jefferson's letter to the Danbury Baptist Association the phrase "I contemplate with sovereign reverence that act of the whole American people which declared that their legislature should 'make no law respecting an establishment of religion, or prohibiting the free exercise thereof,' thus building a wall of separation between church and State."

It is impossible to build sound constitutional doctrine upon a mistaken understanding of constitutional history, but unfortunately the Establishment Clause has been expressly freighted with Jefferson's misleading metaphor for nearly 40 years. Thomas Jefferson was of course in France at the time the constitutional Amendments known as the Bill of Rights were passed by Congress and ratified by the States. His letter to the Danbury Baptist Association was a short note of courtesy, written 14 years after the Amendments were passed by Congress. He would seem to any detached observer as a less than ideal source of contemporary history as to the meaning of the Religion Clauses of the First Amendment.

Jefferson's fellow Virginian, James Madison, with whom he was joined in the battle for the enactment of the Virginia Statute of Religious Liberty of 1786, did play as large a part as anyone in the drafting of the Bill of Rights. He had two advantages over Jefferson in this regard: he was present in the United States, and he was a leading Member of the First Congress. But when we turn to the record of the proceedings in the First Congress leading up to the adoption of the Establishment Clause of the Constitution, including Madison's significant contributions thereto, we see a far different picture of its purpose than the highly simplified "wall of separation between church and State." . . .

On the basis of the record of these proceedings in the House of Representatives, James Madison was undoubtedly the most important architect among the Members of the House of the Amendments which became the Bill of Rights, but it was James Madison speaking as an advocate of sensible legislative compromise, not as an advocate of incorporating the Virginia Statute of Religious Liberty into the United States Constitution. . . .

It seems indisputable from . . . glimpses of Madison's thinking, as reflected by actions on the floor of the House in 1789, that he saw the Amendment as designed to prohibit the establishment of a national religion, and perhaps to prevent discrimination among sects. He did not see it as requiring neutrality on the part of government between religion and irreligion. Thus the Court's opinion in *Everson*—while correct in bracketing Madison and Jefferson together in their exertions in their home State leading to the enactment of the Virginia Statute of Religious Liberty—is totally incorrect in suggesting that Madison carried these views onto the floor of the United States House of Representatives when he proposed the language which would ultimately become the Bill of Rights. . . .

None of the other Members of Congress who spoke during the August 15th debate expressed the slightest indication that they thought the language before them from the Select Committee, or the evil to be aimed at, would require that the Government be absolutely neutral as between religion and irreligion. The evil to be aimed at, so far as those who spoke were concerned, appears to have been the establishment of a national church, and perhaps the preference of one religious sect over another; but it was definitely not concerned about whether the Government might aid all religions evenhandedly. . . .

The actions of the First Congress, which reenacted the Northwest Ordinance for the governance of the Northwest Territory in 1789, confirm the view that Congress did not mean that the Government should be neutral between religion and irreligion. . . . The Northwest Ordinance reenacted the Northwest Ordinance of 1787 and provided that "[religion], morality, and knowledge, being necessary to good government and the happiness of mankind, schools and the means of education shall forever be encouraged." Land grants for schools in the Northwest Territory were not limited to public schools. It was not until 1845 that Congress limited land grants in the new States and Territories to nonsectarian schools. . . .

On the day after the House of Representatives voted to adopt the form of the First Amendment Religion Clauses which was ultimately proposed and ratified, Representative Elias Boudinot proposed a resolution asking President George Washington to issue a Thanksgiving Day proclamation. . . .

George Washington, John Adams, and James Madison all issued Thanksgiving Proclamations; Thomas Jefferson did not. . . . There is simply no historical foundation for the proposition that the Framers intended to build the "wall of separation" that was constitutionalized in *Everson*.

Notwithstanding the absence of a historical basis for this theory of rigid separation, the wall idea might well have served as a useful albeit misguided analytical concept, had it led this Court to unified and principled results in Establishment Clause cases. The opposite, unfortunately, has been true; in the 38 years since *Everson* our Establishment Clause cases have been neither principled nor unified. Our recent opinions, many of them hopelessly divided pluralities, have with embarrassing candor conceded that the "wall of separation" is merely a "blurred, indistinct, and variable barrier," which "is not wholly accurate" and can only be "dimly perceived."

Whether due to its lack of historical support or its practical unworkability, the *Everson* "wall" has proved all but useless as a guide to sound constitutional adjudication. It illustrates only too well the wisdom of Benjamin Cardozo's observation that "[metaphors] in law are to be narrowly watched, for starting as devices to liberate thought, they end often by enslaving it."

But the greatest injury of the "wall" notion is its mischievous diversion of judges from the actual intentions of the drafters of the Bill of Rights. . . . The "wall of separation between church and State" is a metaphor based on bad history, a metaphor which has proved useless as a guide to judging. It should be frankly and explicitly abandoned.

The Court strikes down the Alabama statute because the State wished to "characterize prayer as a favored practice." It would come as much of a shock to those who drafted the Bill of Rights as it will to a large number of thoughtful Americans today to learn that the Constitution, as construed by the majority, prohibits the Alabama Legislature from "endorsing" prayer. George Washington himself, at the request of the very Congress which passed the Bill of Rights, proclaimed a day of "public thanksgiving and prayer, to be observed by acknowledging with grateful hearts the many and signal favors of Almighty God." History must judge whether it was the Father of his Country in 1789, or a majority of the Court today, which has strayed from the meaning of the Establishment Clause.

The State surely has a secular interest in regulating the manner in which public schools are conducted. Nothing in the Establishment Clause of the First Amendment, properly understood, prohibits any such generalized "endorsement" of prayer. I would therefore reverse the judgment of the Court of Appeals.

Appendix 15. Lee v Weisman
505 U.S. 577 (1992)

JUSTICE KENNEDY delivered the opinion of the Court.

School principals in the public school system of the city of Providence, Rhode Island, are permitted to invite members of the clergy to offer invocation and benediction prayers as part of the formal graduation ceremonies for middle schools and for high schools. The question before us is whether including clerical members who offer prayers as part of the official school graduation ceremony is consistent with the Religion Clauses of the First Amendment, provisions the Fourteenth Amendment makes applicable with full force to the States and their school districts. . . .

It has been the custom of Providence school officials to provide invited clergy with a pamphlet entitled "Guidelines for Civic Occasions," prepared by the National Conference of Christians and Jews. The Guidelines recommend that public prayers at nonsectarian civic ceremonies be composed with "inclusiveness and sensitivity," though they acknowledge that "prayer of any kind may be inappropriate on some civic occasions." . . .

These dominant facts mark and control the confines of our decision: State officials direct the performance of a formal religious exercise at promotional and graduation ceremonies for secondary schools. Even for those students who object to the religious exercise, their attendance and participation in the state-sponsored religious activity are in a fair and real sense obligatory, though the school district does not require attendance as a condition for receipt of the diploma. . . .

The principle that government may accommodate the free exercise of religion does not supersede the fundamental limitations imposed by the Establishment Clause. It is beyond dispute that, at a minimum, the Constitution guarantees that government may not coerce anyone to support or participate in religion or its exercise, or otherwise act in a way which "establishes a [state] religion or religious faith, or tends to do so." The State's involvement in the school prayers challenged today violates these central principles.

That involvement is as troubling as it is undenied. A school official, the principal, decided that an invocation and a benediction should be given; this is a choice attributable to the State, and from a constitutional perspective it is as if a state statute decreed that the prayers must occur. The principal chose the religious participant, here a rabbi, and that choice is also attributable to the State. The reason for the choice of a rabbi is not disclosed by the record, but the potential for divisiveness over the choice of a particular member of the clergy to conduct the ceremony is apparent.

Divisiveness, of course, can attend any state decision respecting religions, and neither its existence nor its potential necessarily invalidates the State's attempts to accommodate religion in all cases. The potential for divisiveness is of particular relevance here though, because it centers around an overt religious exercise in a secondary school environment where, as we discuss below, subtle coercive pressures exist and where the student had no real alternative which would have allowed her to avoid the fact or appearance of participation.

The State's role did not end with the decision to include a prayer and with the choice of a clergyman. Principal Lee provided Rabbi Gutterman with a copy of the "Guidelines for Civic Occasions," and advised him that his prayers should be nonsectarian. Through these means the principal directed and controlled the content of the prayers. . . .

Petitioners argue, and we find nothing in the case to refute it, that the directions for the content of the prayers were a good-faith attempt by the school to ensure that the sectarianism which is so often the flashpoint for religious animosity be removed from the graduation ceremony. The concern is understandable, as a prayer which uses ideas or images identified with a particular religion may foster a different sort of sectarian rivalry than an invocation or benediction in terms more neutral. The school's explanation, however, does not resolve the dilemma caused by its participation. The question is not the good faith of the school in attempting to make the prayer acceptable to most persons, but the legitimacy of its undertaking that enterprise at all when the object is to produce a prayer to be used in a formal religious exercise which students, for all practical purposes, are obliged to attend.

We are asked to recognize the existence of a practice of nonsectarian prayer, prayer within the embrace of what is known as the Judeo-Christian tradition, prayer which is more acceptable than one which, for example, makes explicit references to the God of Israel, or to Jesus Christ, or to a patron saint. There may be some support, as an empirical observation, to the statement of the Court of Appeals for the Sixth Circuit, picked up by Judge Campbell's dissent in the Court of Appeals in this case, that there has emerged in this country a civic religion, one which is tolerated when sectarian exercises are not. . . . If common ground can be defined which permits once conflicting faiths to express the shared conviction that there is an ethic and a morality which transcend human invention, the sense of community and purpose sought by all decent societies might be advanced. But though the First Amendment does not allow the government to stifle prayers which aspire to these ends, neither does it permit the government to undertake that task for itself.

The First Amendment's Religion Clauses mean that religious beliefs and religious expression are too precious to be either proscribed or prescribed by the State. The design of the Constitution is that preservation and transmission of religious beliefs and worship is a responsibility and a choice committed to the private sphere, which itself is promised freedom to pursue that mission. It must not be forgotten then, that while concern must be given to define the protection granted to an objector or a dissenting nonbeliever, these same Clauses exist to protect religion from government interference. James Madison, the principal author of the Bill of Rights, did not rest his opposition to a religious establishment on the sole ground of its effect on the minority. A principal ground for his view was: "Experience witnesseth that ecclesiastical establishments, instead of maintaining the purity and efficacy of Religion, have had a contrary operation. . . ."

These concerns have particular application in the case of school officials, whose effort to monitor prayer will be perceived by the students as inducing a participation they might otherwise reject. Though the efforts of the school officials in this case to find common ground appear to have been a good-faith attempt to recognize the common aspects of religions and not the divisive ones, our precedents do not permit school officials to assist in composing prayers as an incident to a formal exercise for their students. And these same precedents caution us to measure the idea of a civic religion against the central meaning of the Religion Clauses of the First Amendment, which is that all creeds must be tolerated and none favored. The suggestion that government may establish an official or civic religion as a means of avoiding the establishment of a religion with more specific creeds strikes us as a contradiction that cannot be accepted. . . .

The lessons of the First Amendment are as urgent in the modern world as in the 18th century when it was written. One timeless lesson is that if citizens are subjected to state-sponsored religious exercises, the State disavows its own duty to guard and respect that sphere of inviolable conscience and belief which is the mark of a free people. To compromise that principle today would be to deny our own tradition and forfeit our standing to urge others to secure the protections of that tradition for themselves.

As we have observed before, there are heightened concerns with protecting freedom of conscience from subtle coercive pressure in the elementary and secondary public schools. . . . What to most believers may seem
nothing more than a reasonable request that the nonbeliever respect their
religious practices, in a school context may appear to the nonbeliever or
dissenter to be an attempt to employ the machinery of the State to enforce
a religious orthodoxy.

We need not look beyond the circumstances of this case to see the phenomenon at work. The undeniable fact is that the school district's supervision and control of a high school graduation ceremony places public
pressure, as well as peer pressure, on attending students to stand as a
group or, at least, maintain respectful silence during the invocation and
benediction. This pressure, though subtle and indirect, can be as real as any
overt compulsion. . . .

There was a stipulation in the District Court that attendance at graduation and promotional ceremonies is voluntary. . . . Petitioners and the
United States, as *amicus,* made this a center point of the case, arguing that
the option of not attending the graduation excuses any inducement or coercion in the ceremony itself. The argument lacks all persuasion. Law
reaches past formalism. And to say a teenage student has a real choice not
to attend her high school graduation is formalistic in the extreme. . . .
Everyone knows that in our society and in our culture high school graduation is one of life's most significant occasions. A school rule which excuses
attendance is beside the point. Attendance may not be required by official
decree, yet it is apparent that a student is not free to absent herself from
the graduation exercise in any real sense of the term "voluntary," for absence would require forfeiture of those intangible benefits which have motivated the student through youth and all her high school years.
Graduation is a time for family and those closest to the student to celebrate
success and express mutual wishes of gratitude and respect, all to the end
of impressing upon the young person the role that it is his or her right and
duty to assume in the community and all of its diverse parts. . . .

Inherent differences between the public school system and a session of
a state legislature distinguish this case from *Marsh v. Chambers.* The considerations we have raised in objection to the invocation and benediction
are in many respects similar to the arguments we considered in *Marsh.*
But there are also obvious differences. The atmosphere at the opening of
a session of a state legislature where adults are free to enter and leave
with little comment and for any number of reasons cannot compare with

the constraining potential of the one school event most important for the student to attend. The influence and force of a formal exercise in a school graduation are far greater than the prayer exercise we condoned in *Marsh*. . . .

Our jurisprudence in this area is of necessity one of line-drawing, of determining at what point a dissenter's rights of religious freedom are infringed by the State. . . .

Our society would be less than true to its heritage if it lacked abiding concern for the values of its young people, and we acknowledge the profound belief of adherents to many faiths that there must be a place in the student's life for precepts of a morality higher even than the law we today enforce. We express no hostility to those aspirations, nor would our oath permit us to do so. A relentless and all-pervasive attempt to exclude religion from every aspect of public life could itself become inconsistent with the Constitution. . . . We recognize that, at graduation time and throughout the course of the educational process, there will be instances when religious values, religious practices, and religious persons will have some interaction with the public schools and their students. . . . But these matters, often questions of accommodation of religion, are not before us. The sole question presented is whether a religious exercise may be conducted at a graduation ceremony in circumstances where, as we have found, young graduates who object are induced to conform. No holding by this Court suggests that a school can persuade or compel a student to participate in a religious exercise. That is being done here, and it is forbidden by the Establishment Clause of the First Amendment.

For the reasons we have stated, the judgment of the Court of Appeals is Affirmed.

JUSTICE SOUTER, with whom JUSTICE STEVENS and JUSTICE O'CONNOR join, concurring.

I join the whole of the Court's opinion, and fully agree that prayers at public school graduation ceremonies indirectly coerce religious observance. I write separately nonetheless on two issues of Establishment Clause analysis that underlie my independent resolution of this case: whether the Clause applies to governmental practices that do not favor one religion or denomination over others, and whether state coercion of religious conformity, over and above state endorsement of religious exercise or belief, is a necessary element of an Establishment Clause violation.

Forty-five years ago, this Court announced a basic principle of constitutional law from which it has not strayed: the Establishment Clause forbids not only state practices that "aid one religion . . . or prefer one religion over another," but also those that "aid all religions." Today we reaffirm that principle, holding that the Establishment Clause forbids state-sponsored prayers in public school settings no matter how nondenominational the prayers may be. In barring the State from sponsoring generically theistic prayers where it could not sponsor sectarian ones, we hold true to a line of precedent from which there is no adequate historical case to depart.

Since *Everson*, we have consistently held the Clause applicable no less to governmental acts favoring religion generally than to acts favoring one religion over others. . . . Such is the settled law. . . .

Some have challenged this precedent by reading the Establishment Clause to permit "nonpreferential" state promotion of religion. The challengers argue that, as originally understood by the Framers, "the Establishment Clause did not require government neutrality between religion and irreligion nor did it prohibit the Federal Government from providing nondiscriminatory aid to religion." . . . While a case has been made for this position, it is not so convincing as to warrant reconsideration of our settled law; indeed, I find in the history of the Clause's textual development a more powerful argument supporting the Court's jurisprudence following *Everson*. . . .

While these considerations are, for me, sufficient to reject the nonpreferentialist position, one further concern animates my judgment. In many contexts, including this one, non-preferentialism requires some distinction between "sectarian" religious practices and those that would be, by some measure, ecumenical enough to pass Establishment Clause muster. Simply by requiring the enquiry, nonpreferentialists invite the courts to engage in comparative theology. I can hardly imagine a subject less amenable to the competence of the federal judiciary, or more deliberately to be avoided where possible.

This case is nicely in point. Since the nonpreferentiality of a prayer must be judged by its text, JUSTICE BLACKMUN pertinently observes that Rabbi Gutterman drew his exhortation "'to do justly, to love mercy, to walk humbly'" straight from the King James version of Micah, ch. 6, v. 8. At some undefinable point, the similarities between a state-sponsored prayer and the sacred text of a specific religion would so closely identify the former with the latter that even a nonpreferentialist would have to concede a breach of the Establishment Clause. And even if Micah's thought is sufficiently generic for most believers, it still embodies a straightforwardly theistic premise, and so does the rabbi's prayer. Many Americans who consider themselves religious are not theistic; some, like several of the Framers, are deists who would question Rabbi Gutterman's plea for divine advancement of the country's political and moral good. Thus, a nonpreferentialist who would condemn subjecting public school graduates to, say, the Anglican liturgy would still need to explain why the government's preference for theistic over nontheistic religion is constitutional.

Nor does it solve the problem to say that the State should promote a "diversity" of religious views; that position would necessarily compel the government and, inevitably, the courts to make wholly inappropriate judgments about the number of religions the State should sponsor and the relative frequency with which it should sponsor each. In fact, the prospect would be even worse than that. As Madison observed in criticizing religious Presidential proclamations, the practice of sponsoring religious messages tends, over time, "to narrow the recommendation to the standard of the predominant sect." . . . We have not changed much since the days of Madison, and the judiciary should not willingly enter the political arena to battle the centripetal force leading from religious pluralism to official preference for the faith with the most votes.

Petitioners rest most of their argument on a theory that, whether or not the Establishment Clause permits extensive nonsectarian support for religion, it does not forbid the state to sponsor affirmations of religious belief that coerce neither support for religion nor participation in religious observance. I appreciate the force of some of the arguments supporting a "coercion" analysis of the Clause. . . . But we could not adopt that reading without abandoning our settled law, a course that, in my view, the text of the Clause would not readily permit. Nor does the extratextual evidence of original meaning stand so unequivocally at odds with the textual premise inherent in existing precedent that we should fundamentally reconsider our course.

Over the years, this Court has declared the invalidity of many noncoercive state laws and practices conveying a message of religious endorsement. For example . . . we forbade the prominent display of a nativity scene on public property; without contesting the dissent's observation that the creche coerced no one into accepting or supporting whatever message it proclaimed, five Members of the Court found its display unconstitutional as a state endorsement of Christianity . . . we struck down a state law requiring a moment of silence in public classrooms not because the statute coerced students to participate in prayer (for it did not), but because the manner of its enactment "conveyed a message of state approval of prayer activities in the public schools." . . .

In *Epperson v. Arkansas* we invalidated a state law that barred the teaching of Darwin's theory of evolution because, even though the statute obviously did not coerce anyone to support religion or participate in any religious practice, it was enacted for a singularly religious purpose. . . .

Our precedents may not always have drawn perfectly straight lines. They simply cannot, however, support the position that a showing of coercion is necessary to a successful Establishment Clause claim. . . .

While petitioners insist that the prohibition extends only to the "coercive" features and incidents of establishment, they cannot easily square that claim with the constitutional text. The First Amendment forbids not just laws "respecting an establishment of religion," but also those "prohibiting the free exercise thereof." Yet laws that coerce nonadherents to "support or participate in any religion or its exercise" . . . would virtually by definition violate their right to religious free exercise. . . .

That government must remain neutral in matters of religion does not foreclose it from ever taking religion into account. The State may "accommodate" the free exercise of religion by relieving people from generally applicable rules that interfere with their religious callings. . . . Such accommodation does not necessarily signify an official endorsement of religious observance over disbelief. . . . In everyday life, we routinely accommodate religious beliefs that we do not share. A Christian inviting an Orthodox Jew to lunch might take pains to choose a kosher restaurant; an atheist in a hurry might yield the right of way to an Amish man steering a horse-drawn carriage. In so acting, we express respect for, but not endorsement of, the fundamental values of others. We act without expressing a position on the theological merit of those values or of religious belief in general, and no one perceives us to have taken such a position.

The government may act likewise. Most religions encourage devotional practices that are at once crucial to the lives of believers and idiosyncratic in the eyes of nonadherents. By definition, secular rules of general application are drawn from the nonadherent's vantage and, consequently, fail to take such practices into account. Yet when enforcement of such rules cuts across religious sensibilities, as it often does, it puts those affected to the choice of taking sides between God and government. In such circumstances, accommodating religion reveals nothing beyond a recognition that general rules can unnecessarily offend the religious conscience when they offend the conscience of secular society not at all. Thus, in freeing the Native American Church from federal laws forbidding peyote use . . . the government conveys no endorsement of peyote rituals, the Church, or religion as such; it simply respects the centrality of peyote to the lives of certain Americans. . . .

Whatever else may define the scope of accommodation permissible under the Establishment Clause, one requirement is clear: accommodation must lift a discernible burden on the free exercise of religion. . . . Concern for the position of religious individuals in the modern regulatory State cannot justify official solicitude for a religious practice unburdened by general rules; such gratuitous largesse would effectively favor religion over disbelief. By these lights one easily sees that, in sponsoring the graduation prayers at issue here, the State has crossed the line from permissible accommodation to unconstitutional establishment.

Religious students cannot complain that omitting prayers from their graduation ceremony would, in any realistic sense, "burden" their spiritual callings. To be sure, many of them invest this rite of passage with spiritual significance, but they may express their religious feelings about it before and after the ceremony. They may even organize a privately sponsored baccalaureate if they desire the company of like-minded students. Because they accordingly have no need for the machinery of the State to affirm their beliefs, the government's sponsorship of prayer at the graduation ceremony is most reasonably understood as an official endorsement of religion and, in this instance, of theistic religion. . . .

Petitioners would deflect this conclusion by arguing that graduation prayers are no different from Presidential religious proclamations and similar official "acknowledgments" of religion in public life. But religious invocations in Thanksgiving Day addresses and the like, rarely noticed, ignored without effort, conveyed over an impersonal medium, and directed at no one in particular, inhabit a pallid zone worlds apart from official prayers delivered to a captive audience of public school students and their families. . . . But that logic permits no winking at the practice in question here. When public school officials, armed with the State's authority, convey an endorsement of religion to their students, they strike near the core of the Establishment Clause. However "ceremonial" their messages may be, they are flatly unconstitutional.

JUSTICE SCALIA, with whom THE CHIEF JUSTICE, JUSTICE WHITE, and JUSTICE THOMAS join, dissenting.

. . . In holding that the Establishment Clause prohibits invocations and benedictions at public school graduation ceremonies, the Court—with nary a mention that it is doing so—lays waste a tradition that is as old as public school graduation ceremonies themselves, and that is a component of an even more longstanding American tradition of nonsectarian prayer to God at public celebrations generally. As its instrument of destruction, the bulldozer of its social engineering, the Court invents a boundless, and boundlessly manipulable, test of psychological coercion. . . .

The Court presumably would separate graduation invocations and benedictions from other instances of public "preservation and transmission of religious beliefs" on the ground that they involve "psychological coercion." I find it a sufficient embarrassment that our Establishment Clause jurisprudence regarding holiday displays . . . has come to "require scrutiny more commonly associated with interior decorators than with the judiciary." But interior decorating is a rock-hard science compared to psychology practiced by amateurs. A few citations of "research in psychology" that have no particular bearing upon the precise issue here, cannot disguise the fact that the Court has gone beyond the realm where judges know what they are doing. The Court's argument that state officials have "coerced" students to take part in the invocation and benediction at graduation ceremonies is, not to put too fine a point on it, incoherent. . . .

The Court declares that students' "attendance and participation in the [invocation and benediction] are in a fair and real sense obligatory." But what exactly is this "fair and real sense"? According to the Court, students at graduation who want "to avoid the fact or appearance of participation," in the invocation and benediction are *psychologically* obligated by "public pressure, as well as peer pressure, . . . to stand as a group or, at least, maintain respectful silence" during those prayers. This assertion—*the very linchpin of the Court's opinion*—is almost as intriguing for what it does not say as for what it says. It does not say, for example, that students are psychologically coerced to bow their heads, place their hands in a Durer-like prayer position, pay attention to the prayers, utter "Amen," or in fact pray. (Perhaps further intensive psychological research remains to be done on these matters.) It claims only that students are psychologically coerced "to stand . . . *or*, at least, maintain respectful silence."

. . . The Court's notion that a student who simply *sits* in "respectful silence" during the invocation and benediction (when all others are standing) has somehow joined—or would somehow be perceived as having joined—in the prayers is nothing short of ludicrous. We indeed live in a vulgar age. But surely "our social conventions," have not coarsened to the point that anyone who does not stand on his chair and shout obscenities can reasonably be deemed to have assented to everything said in his presence. Since the Court does not dispute that students exposed to prayer at graduation ceremonies retain (despite "subtle coercive pressures,") the free will to sit, there is absolutely no basis for the Court's decision. . . .

The opinion manifests that the Court itself has not given careful consideration to its test of psychological coercion. For if it had, how could it observe, with no hint of concern or disapproval, that students stood for the Pledge of Allegiance, which immediately preceded Rabbi Gutterman's invocation? . . . Since the Pledge of Allegiance has been revised since *Barnette* to include the phrase "under God," recital of the Pledge would appear to raise the same Establishment Clause issue as the invocation and benediction. If students were psychologically coerced to remain standing during the invocation, they must also have been psychologically coerced, moments before, to stand for (and thereby, in the Court's view, take part in or appear to take part in) the Pledge. Must the Pledge therefore be barred from the public schools (both from graduation ceremonies and from the classroom)? In *Barnette* we held that a public school student could not be compelled to *recite* the Pledge; we did not even hint that she could not be compelled to observe respectful silence—indeed, even to *stand* in respectful silence—when those who wished to recite it did so. Logically, that ought to be the next project for the Court's bulldozer. . . .

. . . Many graduating seniors, of course, are old enough to vote. Why, then, does the Court treat them as though they were first-graders? Will we soon have a jurisprudence that distinguishes between mature and immature adults?

The deeper flaw in the Court's opinion does not lie in its wrong answer to the question whether there was state-induced "peer-pressure" coercion; it lies, rather, in the Court's making violation of the Establishment Clause hinge on such a precious question. The coercion that was a hallmark of historical establishments of religion was coercion of religious orthodoxy and of financial support *by force of law and threat of penalty.* Typically, attendance at the state church was required; only clergy of the official church could lawfully perform sacraments; and dissenters, if tolerated, faced an array of civil disabilities. . . . Thus, for example, in the Colony of Virginia, where the Church of England had been established, ministers were required by law to conform to the doctrine and rites of the Church of England; and all persons were required to attend church and observe the Sabbath, were tithed for the public support of Anglican ministers, and were taxed for the costs of building and repairing churches. . . .

. . . while I have no quarrel with the Court's general proposition that the Establishment Clause "guarantees that government may not coerce anyone to support or participate in religion or its exercise," I see no warrant for expanding the concept of coercion beyond acts backed by threat of penalty— a brand of coercion that, happily, is readily discernible to those of us who have made a career of reading the disciples of Blackstone rather than of Freud. The Framers were indeed opposed to coercion of religious worship by the National Government; but, as their own sponsorship of nonsectarian prayer in public events demonstrates, they understood that "speech is not coercive; the listener may do as he likes." . . . The Court today demonstrates the irrelevance of *Lemon* by essentially ignoring it, and the interment of that case may be the one happy byproduct of the Court's otherwise lamentable decision. Unfortunately, however, the Court has replaced *Lemon* with its psycho-coercion test, which suffers the double disability of having no roots whatever in our people's historic practice, and being as infinitely expandable as the reasons for psychotherapy itself. . . .

I must add one final observation: The Founders of our Republic knew the fearsome potential of sectarian religious belief to generate civil dissension and civil strife. And they also knew that nothing, absolutely nothing, is so inclined to foster among religious believers of various faiths a toleration—no, an affection—for one another than voluntarily joining in prayer together, to the God whom they all worship and seek. Needless to say, no one should be compelled to do that, but it is a shame to deprive our public culture of the opportunity, and indeed the encouragement, for people to do it voluntarily. The Baptist or Catholic who heard and joined in the simple and inspiring prayers of Rabbi Gutterman on this official and patriotic occasion was inoculated from religious bigotry and prejudice in a manner that cannot be replicated. To deprive our society of that important unifying mechanism, in order to spare the nonbeliever what seems to me the minimal inconvenience of standing or even sitting in respectful nonparticipation, is as senseless in policy as it is unsupported in law.

For the foregoing reasons, I dissent.

Notes

Chapter 1. Historical Background

1. See appendix 1.
2. See appendix 8.
3. See, for example, *The General Laws and Liberties of the Massachusetts Bay Colony,* appendix 2.
4. See appendix 6.
5. See appendix 7.
6. See appendix 5.
7. See appendix 3.
8. John Semonche, *Religion and Constitutional Government in the United States* (Carrboro, N.C.: Signal Books, 1986), 22–23.
9. See appendix 4.
10. According to Semonche, *Religion and Constitutional Government,* 20, the phrase "free exercise thereof" first appeared in Maryland's "Act Concerning Religion" of 1649, whose "tolerance," as we noted earlier, was limited to Christians.
11. John T. Noonan Jr. and Edward McGlynn Gaffney Jr., *Religious Freedom,* 2d ed. (New York: Foundation Press, 2001), 639.
12. Elizabeth Fleet, ed., *Madison's 'Detached Memoranda,'* 3 William and Mary Quarterly 554 (1946).
13. Letter to Edward Livingston, 10 July 1822, in Adrienne Koch, ed., *The American Enlightenment: The Shaping of the American Experiment and a Free Society* (New York: G. Braziller, 1965), 465–66.
14. Leonard Levy, *The Establishment Clause* (New York: Macmillan, 1986), 64.
15. Carl Van Doren, *Benjamin Franklin* (New York: Viking Press, 1938), 777–78.
16. Anson Phelps Stokes, *Church and State in the United States* (New York: Harpers, 1950), 495.
17. Hunter Miller, ed., *Treaties and other International Acts of the United States of America* (Washington D.C.: U.S. Government Printing Office, 1931), 365.

18. Thomas J. Curry, *The First Freedoms: Church and State in America to the Passage of the First Amendment* (New York: Oxford University Press, 1986), 162.
19. Howard 127, 189–99 (1844).
20. US 457, 465–70 (1892).
21. David J. Brewer, *The United States: A Christian Nation* (Philadelphia: John C. Winston, 1959), 11–12.
22. US 605, 620 (1931).
23. 330 US 1 (1947).

Chapter 2. Understanding the First Amendment

1. Derek Davis, *Original Intent* (Buffalo, N.Y.: Prometheus Books, 1991), 45.
2. *Plessy v Ferguson*, 163 US 537 (1896).
3. *Brown v Board of Education*, 347 US 483 (1954).
4. Address at Hyde Park, N.Y., *Recorder*, 8 November 1989.
5. *Missouri v Holland*, 252 US 416, 433 (1920).
6. US 38, 91–114 (1985). See also appendix 14.
7. Robert Cord, *Separation of Church and State: Historical Fact and Current Fiction* (New York: Lambeth Press, 1982).
8. Leonard Levy, *The Establishment Clause* (New York: Macmillan, 1986).
9. Douglas Laycock, *"Non-Preferential" Aid to Religion: A False Claim about Original Intent*, 27 William and Mary Law Review 873 (1986).
10. Cord, *Separation of Church and State*, xiv. See also Philip Hamburger, *Separation of Church and State* (Cambridge, Mass.: Harvard University Press, 2002) for essentially this same argument.
11. Cord, *Separation of Church and State*, 15.
12. Ibid., 30–39.
13. Ibid., 122.
14. U.S 1, 18 (1947).
15. Cord, *Separation of Church and State*, 122–24.
16. Levy, *Establishment Clause*, 60 62.
17. Ibid., 81–84.
18. Laycock, *"Non-Preferential" Aid*, 877–81.
19. Paul J. Weber, ed., *Equal Separation* (New York: Greenwood Press, 1990), 4.
20. *Zorach v Clausen*, 343 US 306 (1952).

21. Ibid.
22. Weber, *Equal Separation*, 5.
23. Laurence Tribe, *American Constitutional Law*, 3d ed. (Mineola, N.Y.: Foundation Press, 1988), 1189.
24. 397 US 664 (1970).
25. John Hart Ely, *Democracy and Distrust* (Cambridge, Mass.: Harvard University Press, 1980), 51.
26. *Palko v Connecticut*, 302 US 319 (1937).
27. Phillip Bobbitt, *Constitutional Interpretation* (New York: Blackwell, 1991).
28. Alexander Bickel, *The Least Dangerous Branch* (New Haven, Conn.: Yale University Press, 1962).
29. Michael Perry, *The Constitution, the Courts, and Human Rights* (New Haven, Conn.: Yale University Press, 1982).
30. *Bush v Gore*, 531 US 98 (2000).
31. John Semonche, *Religion and Constitutional Government in the United States* (Carrboro, N.C.: Signal Books, 1986), 35.
32. Akhil Reed Amar, *Bill of Rights* (New Haven, Conn.: Yale University Press, 1998).
33. 268 US 652 (1925).
34. Ely, *Democracy and Distrust*, 30.
35. Amar, *Bill of Rights*
36. 299 US 353 (1937).
37. *Cantwell v Connecticut*, 310 US 296 (1940).
38. *Buckley v Valeo*, 424 US 1, 291 (1976).

Chapter 3. Religious Expression in Public Places

1. *Lynch v Donnelly*, 464 US 668 (1984). See appendix, 13.
2. *Allegheny County v ACLU*, 492 US 573 (1989).
3. Peter Irons, *Brennan v. Rehnquist: The Battle for the Constitution* (New York: Alfred A. Knopf, 1994), 136.
4. *ACLU v City of Pittsburgh*, 492 US 573 (1989).
5. *Ellis v City of La Mesa*, 990 F2d 1518 (9th Cir 1993).
6. *Paulson v City of San Diego*, 262 F3d 885 (9th Cir 2001).
7. *Paulson v City of San Diego*, 294 F3d 1124 (9th Cir 2002). Denied review by the U.S. Supreme Court on 21 April 2002, Order No. 02-1093.
8. *Carpenter v City and County of San Francisco*, 93 F3d 627 (9th Cir 1996).
9. Bob Egelko, "Top Court Backs S.F.'s Cross Sale," *San Francisco Chronicle*, 29 April 2003.

10. *Friedman v Board of County Commissioners of Bernalillo,* 781 F2d 777 (10th Cir 1985).

11. *City of Edmond v Wayne Robinson,* 689 F3d 1226 (10th Cir 1995).

12. *Hewitt v Joyner,* 940 F2d 1561 (9th Cir 1991).

13. *Doe v Small,* 964 F2d 611 (7th Cir 1992).

14. *ACLU v Capitol Square Review Board,* 243 F3d 289 (6th Cir 2001).

15. *Lemon v Kurtzman,* 403 US 602 (1971). See appendix 10.

16. *Stone v Graham,* 449 US 39 (1980).

17. *Anderson v Salt Lake City Corp.,* 475 F2d 19 (10th Cir 1973); *Books v Elkhart,* 235 F2d 292 (7th Cir 2000); *Adland v Russ* (6th Cir Oct. 9, 2002).

18. Linda Greenhouse, "Justices to Take Up Interstate Water Fight," *New York Times,* 29 April 2003.

19. *Elkhart v Books,* 532 US 1058 (2001).

20. *Indiana Civil Liberties Union v O'Bannon,* 259 F3d 766 (7th Cir 2001).

21. Rick Braggs, "Judge Faces Deadline on Religious Display,"*New York Times,* 13 February 1997.

22. *Glassroth v Moore,* 2003 U.S. App. Lexis 13412 (11th Cir 2003).

23. *Capitol Square Review Board v Pinette,* 575 US 753 (1995).

24. Leonard W. Levy, *The Establishment Clause* (New York: Macmillan, 1986), 98.

25. Ibid., 99–100.

26. *Marsh v Chambers,* 463 US 783 (1983). See appendix 12.

27. *McGowan v Maryland,* 366 US 420 (1961).

28. *Cammack v* Waihee, 932 F2d 765 (9th Cir 1991).

29. *Granzeier v Middleton,* 173 F2d 568 (6th Cir 1999).

30. *Bridenbaugh v O'Bannon,* 185 F3d 796 (7th Cir 1999).

31. *Koenick v Felton,* 190 F3d 259 (4th Cir 1999).

32. *Newdow v U. S. Congress,* 292 F3d 597 (9th Cir 2002).

33. The Senate resolution, adopted 99-0 after a lengthy preamble, reaffirmed the laws of 1954 and 1956, and ordered it to be so noted in the U.S. Code. The House of Representatives passed a shorter resolution, 416-3, and sent the Senate resolution to committee, where it languished over the summer before being passed with slight modifications, by a 401-5 vote in October 2002. The Senate agreed to those changes and the bill was signed by the president in November.

34. *U.S. v Ballard,* 322 US 78 (1944).

35. *Ballard v U.S.,* 329 US 187 (1946).

Chapter 4. Religious Expression in Public Schools

1. 370 US 421 (1962). See appendix 9.
2. *Abington Township School District v Schempp*, 374 U S 203 (1963).
3. *Wallace v Jaffree*, 472 US 38, 91–114 (1985). See also appendix 14.
4. *May v Cooperman*, 780 F2d 240 (3d Cir 1985).
5. 862 F2d 824 (11th Cir 1989).
6. *Jones v Clear Creek Independent School District*, 930 F2d 416 (5th Cir 1991).
7. 505 US 77 (1992). See appendix 15.
8. *Jones v Clear Creek Independent School District*, 977 F2d 963 (5th Cir 1992).
9. 508 US 967 (1993).
10. Catherine C. Manegold, "Senate Decides It's Time to Let Students Meditate," *New York Times*, 5 February 1994.
11. "School Prayer Anxieties," *New York Times*, 13 July 1995.
12. Steven A. Holmes, "Federal Guide for Religions in U.S. Schools," *New York Times*, 26 August 1995.
13. *Harris v Joint School District*, 41 F3d 447 (9th Cir 1994).
14. *Harris v Joint School District*, 62 F3d 1233 (1995).
15. *Missoulian*, 18 November 1994, 1.
16. David G. Savage, "Court Refuses to Reconsider School Prayer," *San Francisco Chronicle*, 5 November 1996.
17. *Ingebretsen v Jackson Public School District*, 88 F3d 274 (5th Cir 1996).
18. *Moore v Ingebretsen*, 519 US 965 (1996).
19. 530 US 290 (2000).
20. Kevin Sack, "In South, Prayer is a Form of Protest," *New York Times*, 8 November 1997.
21. C. Bryson Hull, "Prayer of Protest is Barely Heard at Texas School's Opening Game," *San Francisco Examiner*, 2 September 2000.
22. *Chandler v James*, 180 F3d 1254 (11th Cir 1999).
23. *Chandler v Siegelman*, 533 US 916 (2001).
24. *Chandler v Siegelman*, 230 F3d 1313 (11th Cir 2000).
25. *Adler v Duval County School Board*, 206 F3d 1070 (2000).
26. *Adler v Duval County School Board*, 531 US 801 (2000).
27. *Adler v Duval County School Board*, 250 F3d 1330 (2001).
28. *Adler v Duval County School Board*, 534 US 1065 (2001).
29. *Minersville School District v Gobitis*, 310 US 586 (1940).
30. *West Virginia State Board of Education v Barnette*, 319 US 624 (1943).

31. Justice Breyer's views were expressed in his James Madison Lecture at New York University on 22 October 2001, published at 77 New York University Law Review 245 (2002).
32. *Hague v CIO*, 307 US 496 (1939).
33. *Perry Educational Association v Perry Local Educators' Association*, 460 US 37 (1983).
34. *Lamb's Chapel v Center Moriches School District*, 508 US 383 (1993).
35. *Widmar v Vincent*, 454 US 263 (1981).
36. *Board of Education, Westside Community Schools v Mergens*, 496 US 226 (1990).
37. *Good News Club v Milford Central School*, 21 FSupp2d 147 (NDNY 1998).
38. *Good News Club v Milford Central School*, 202 F3d 502 (2000).
39. *Good News/Good News Sports Club v School District of Ladue*, 28 F3d 1501 (8th Cir 1994).
40. *Good News Club v Milford Central School*, 533 US 98 (2001).
41. *McCollum v Board of Education*, 333 US 203 (1948).
42. *Zorach v Clausen*, 343 US 306 (1952).
43. John T. Scopes and James Presley, *Center of the Storm: Memoirs of John T. Scopes* (New York: Holt, Rinehart, and Winston, 1967).
44. Samuel Walker, *In Defense of American Liberties: A History of the ACLU* (New York: Oxford University Press, 1990), 73.
45. *Epperson v State of Arkansas*, 393 US 97 (1968)
46. Ibid.
47. *McLean v Arkansas Board of Education*, 529 FSupp 1255 (ED Ark 1982).
48. *Edwards v Aguillard*, 482 US 578 (1987).
49. Francis X. Clines, "In Ohio School Hearing a New Theory Will Seek a Place Alongside Evolution," *New York Times*, 11 February 2002.
50. *O'Connor v Hendrick*, 184 NY 421, 77 NE 612 (1906).
51. *Zellers v Huff*, 55 NM 501, 236 P2d 949 (1951).
52. *Cooper v Eugene School District No. 4J*, 301 Or 358, 272 P2d 298 (1986).
53. 480 US 942 (1987).
54. *Hysong v Gallitzer School District*, 164 Pa 629, 30 A 482 (1894).
55. *Commonwealth v Herr*, 229 Pa 132, 78 A 68 (1910).
56. *United States v Board of Education of Philadelphia*, 911 F3d 882 (3d Cir 1990).
57. *Metzl v Leininger*, 57 F3d 618 (7th Cir 1995).
58. *Board of Education, Island Trees Union Free School District v Pico*, 457 US 853 (1982).
59. *Mozert v Hawkins County Public Schools*, 827 F2d 1058 (6th Cir 1987).

60. *Jaffree v Board of School Commissioners of Mobile County,* 554 FSupp 1104, 1128 (SD Ala 1983).
61. *Smith v Board of Commissioners,* 655 FSupp 399 (SD Ala 1987).
62. *Smith v Board of Commissioners,* 827 F2d 684 (11th Cir 1987).
63. *Grove v Mead School District,* 753 F2d 376 (8th Cir 1985).
64. 474 US 826 (1986).
65. The commonly quoted phrase, "Eternal vigilance is the price of liberty," has been credited to a speech given in 1852 to the Massachusetts Anti-Slavery Society by Wendell Phillips, but is said to have been the paraphrasing of an earlier "Speech Upon the Right of Election" by the Irish orator John Philpot Curran in 1790. Bergen Evans, *The Dictionary of Quotations* (New York: Delacorte Press, 1968) and *Bartlett's Familiar Quotations,* 13th ed. (Boston: Little, Brown and Company, 1955). The phrase has also sometimes been attributed to Thomas Jefferson.

Chapter 5. Public Funding of Religious Schools

1. Leonard Levy, *The Establishment Clause* (New York: Macmillan, 1986), 128.
2. John T. Noonan Jr. and Edward McGlynn Gaffney Jr., *Religious Freedom* (New York: Foundation Press, 2001), 740. The quotation from Dean Choper is, as noted, from his book on *Securing Religious Liberty* (Chicago: University of Chicago Press, 1995), 16.
3. Noonan and Gaffney, *Religious Freedom,* 215.
4. Ibid.
5. John T. Noonan Jr., *The Lustre of our Country: The American Experience of Religious Freedom* (Berkeley, Calif.: University of California Press, 1998), 107–8, quoting Angelique de Tocqueville, the younger sister of Alexis, writing an unpublished account of her travels in America in 1835, which was translated by Judge Noonan.
6. Ibid. The case referred to was *Worcester v Georgia,* 31 US (6 Pet) 515 (1832).
7. Noonan and Gaffney, *Religious Freedom, 215.*
8. *Chrisman v Sisters of St. Joseph of Peace,* 506 F2d 308 (9th Cir 1974).
9. *Cochran v Board of Education,* 281 US 370 (1930).
10. 392 US 236 (1968).
11. *Lemon v Kurtzman,* 403 US 602 (1971). See appendix 10

12. *Levitt v Committee for Public Education and Religious Liberty,* 413 US 472 (1973).
13. *Committee for Public Education and Religious Liberty v Nyquist,* 413 US 756 (1973).
14. *Meek v Pettinger,* 421 US 349 (1975).
15. *Wolman v Walter,* 433 US 229 (1977).
16. *Committee for Public Education and Religious Liberty v Regan,* 444 US 646 (1980).
17. *Mueller v Allen,* 463 US 388 (1983).
18. *Grand Rapids School District v Ball,* 473 US 373 (1985).
19. *Aguilar v Felton,* 473 US 402 (1985).
20. *Zobrest v Catalina Foothills School District,* 521 US 203 (1993).
21. *Agostini v Felton,* 521 US 203.
22. *Mitchell v Helms,* 530 US 793 (2000).
23. I was myself a beneficiary of this program, attending graduate school at a private school, Northwestern University, which had originally been founded as a Methodist institution, though it ceased to be closely affiliated with that church well before the time I attended.
24. *Tilton v Richardson,* 432 US 672 (1971).
25. *Hunt v McNair,* 413 US 734 (1973).
26. *Roemer v Board of Public Works of Maryland,* 426 US 736 (1976).
27. *Witters v Washington Department of Services for the Blind,* 474 US 481 (1986).
28. *McCrary v Runyon,* 515 F2d 1082 (1975).
29. 427 US 160 (1976).
30. *Bob Jones University v United States,* 461 US 574 (1983).
31. *Rosenberger v University of Virginia,* 515 US 574 (1995).
32. *Jackson v Benson,* 218 Wis2d 835, 578 NW2d 602 (1998).
33. *Simmons-Harris v Goff,* 1997 Ohio App Lexis 1766.
34. *Simmons-Harris v Goff,* 86 Ohio St 3d 1, 711 NE2d 203 (1999).
35. *Simmons-Harris v Zelman,* 234 F3d 945 (6th Cir 2000).
36. Jodi Wilgoren, "School Vouchers Are Ruled Unconstitutional in Florida," *New York Times,* 15 March 2000.
37. *Bush v Holmes,* 767 So2d 668 (2000).
38. *Holmes v Bush,* 2001 Fla Lexis 952.
39. 521 US 203 (1997).
40. 530 US 793 (2000).
41. *Zelman v Simmons-Harris,* 536 US 639 (2002).

Chapter 6. Historical Issues of Religious Expression versus Competing Social Interests

1. John T. Noonan Jr., *The Lustre of our Country: The American Experience of Religious Freedom* (Berkeley, Calif.: University of California Press, 1998), 84.
2. 397 US 664 (1970).
3. *Brushaber v Union Pacific Railroad*, 240 US 1 (1916).
4. *United States v Lee*, 455 US 252 (1982).
5. *Texas Monthly, Inc. v Bullock*, 489 US 1 (1989).
6. *Jimmy Swaggart Ministries v California State Board of Equalization*, 493 US 378 (1990).
7. 98 US 145 (1879).
8. John T. Noonan Jr. and Edward McGlynn Gaffney Jr., *Religious Freedom* (New York: Foundation Press, 2001), 289.
9. *Virginia Statute Establishing Religious Freedom* (1779).
10. *Reynolds v United States*, 98 US 145 (1878).
11. Noonan and Gaffney, *Religious Freedom*, 396.
12. *Arver v United States*, 245 US 366 (1918).
13. *United States v Seeger*, 380 US 163 (1965).
14. *Gillette v United States, Negre v Larsen*, 401 US 437 (1971).
15. Noonan and Gaffney, *Religious Freedom*, 409.
16. *United States v Schwimmer*, 279 US 644 (1929).
17. *United States v Macintosh*, 283 US 605 (1931).
18. *Girouard v United States*, 328 US 61 (1946).
19. Tribe, *American Constitutional Law*, 1189.
20. *Employment Division, Department of Human Resources of Oregon v Smith*, 494 US 872 (1990).
21. *City of Boerne v Flores*, 512 US 507 (1997).
22. Pam Belluck, "Many States Ceding Regulation to Church Groups," *New York Times*, 27 July 2001.
23. Ibid.
24. Noonan and Gaffney, *Religious Freedom*, 537.
25. *Church of Lukumi Babalu Aye v City of Hialeah*, 508 US 520 (1993).
26. 531 US 98 (2000).
27. Linda Greenhouse, "Another Kink of Bitter Split," *New York Times*, 14 December 2000.
28. Linda Greenhouse, "Election Case a Test and a Trauma for Justices," *New York Times*, 20 February 2001.

29. Ibid.

30. Ibid.

Chapter 7. Current Issues of Religious Expression versus Competing Social Interests

1. *Prince v Massachusetts,* 321 US 158 (1944).

2. 406 US 205 (1972). See appendix 11.

3. *Jacobson v Massachusetts,* 197 US 511 (1905).

4. *Commonwealth v Twitchell,* 416 Mass 114, 617 NE2d 609 (1993).

5. *State v McKown,* 475 NW2d 63 (Minn 1991).

6. 502 US 1036 (1992).

7. *Lundman v McKown,* 530 NW2d 807 (1995).

8. *McKown v Lundman,* 516 US 1099 (1996).

9. *In re E.G.,* 133 Ill2d 98, 549 NE2d 322 (1989).

10. *In re Hughes,* New Jersey Superior Court, 1992.

11. *Werth v Taylor,* Michigan Court of Appeals, 1991.

12. *State v Hershberger* I, 444 NW2d 282 (1989).

13. *Minnesota v Hershberger,* 495 US 901 (1990).

14. *State v Hershberger* II, 462 N.W2d 393 (1990).

15. Larry Fruhling, "As a Matter of Conscience, Amish Fight Law Governing Their Privies," *Chicago Tribune,* 18 November 1995.

16. Michael DeCouroy Hinds, "Amish Man v. Law: Centuries Collide," *New York Times,* 23 January 1990.

17. John T. Noonan Jr. and Edward McGlynn Gaffney Jr., *Religious Freedom* (New York: Foundation Press, 2001), 434.

18. *Sherbert v Verner,* 374 US 398 (1963).

19. *Thomas v Review Board of Indiana Employment Security Division,* 450 US 707 (1981).

20. *Trans World Airlines v Hardison,* 432 US 63 (1977).

21. *Corporation of Presiding Bishop, Church of Latter-Day Saints v Amos,* 483 US 327 (1987).

22. *Bowen v Kendrick,* 487 US 589 (1988).

23. Laurie Goodstein, "Many Churches Slow to Accept Government Monies to Help Poor," *New York Times,* 17 October 2000.

24. Laurie Goodstein, "Bush's Call to Church Groups to Get Untraditional Replies," *New York Times,* 20 February 2001.

25. Ibid.

26. Laurie Goodstein, "Eager States Have Been Steering Religious Charities Toward Aid," *New York Times,* 21 July 2001.

27. Iver Peterson, "Aid and Religion Mix at Publicly Funded Church Charities," *New York Times,* 5 July 2001.

28. *Valley Forge Christian College v Americans United for Separation of Church and State,* 454 US 464 (1982).

29. David Gonzalez, "U.S. Cautions Group on Mixing Religion and Salvador Quake Aid," *New York Times,* 5 March 2001.

30. David Gonzalez, "U.S. Aids Conversion-Minded Quake Relief in El Salvador," *New York Times,* 8 March 2001.

31. Elizabeth Becker, "Aid on Track to Religious Charities," *New York Times,* 14 March 2001.

32. Laurie Goodstein, "A Clerical, and Racial, Gap over Federal Help," *New York Times,* 24 March 2001.

33. Ibid.

34. *Corporation of Presiding Bishop, Church of Latter-Day Saints v Amos,* 483 US 327 (1987).

35. Elizabeth Becker, "Bush Plan Would Revive Bill to Aid Charities," *New York Times,* 8 November 2001.

36. Elizabeth Bumiller, "Accord Reached on Charity Aid Bill after Bush Gives in on Hiring," *New York Times,* 8 February 2002.

37. Ibid.

Chapter 8. Religious Expression and Political Life

1. *We Hold These Truths: Reflections on the American Experience* (New York: Sheed and Ward, 1960).

2. *Church, State, and Freedom* (Boston: Beacon Press, 1967).

3. "Prayer and the Civil Religion," *New York Times,* 24 December 1996.

4. *Papal Sin: Structures of Deceit* (New York: Doubleday, 2000).

5. *Torcasco v Watkins,* 367 US 488 (1961).

6. *McDaniel v Paty,* 435 US 618 (1978).

7. *Kirkley v Maryland,* 381 FSupp 323 (1974).

8. *Why Churches Should Pay No Taxes* (New York: Harper and Row, 1977), 86.

9. John T. Noonan Jr., *The Lustre of our Country: The American Experience of Religious Freedom* (Berkeley, Calif.: University of California Press, 1998), 259–60.

10. *Griswold v Connecticut,* 381 US 479.

11. *Eisenstadt v Baird*, 405 US 438 (1972).
12. 410 US 113 (1973).
13. *McRae v Califano*, 491 FSupp 634 (E.D.N.Y. 1980).
14. *Harris v McRae*, 448 US 297 (1980).
15. Franklyn S. Haiman, *"Speech Acts" and the First Amendment* (Carbondale, Ill.: Southern Illinois University Press, 1993), 85.
16. Ann Swicker Kerr, "Fighting Fundamentalism with Education," *Washington Post National Weekly Edition*, 4–10 February 2002.
17. "County of the Scopes Trial is Told to Halt Bible Classes in Schools," *New York Times*, 9 February 2002.
18. Ibid.
19. Laurie Goodstein, "Churches on Right Seek Right to Back Candidates," *New York Times*, 3 February 2002.
20. Diana Jean Schemo, "Revival of School Prayer Has Limited Success," *New York Times*, 23 October 2001.
21. John W. Fountain, "Prayer Warriors Fight Church-State Division," *New York Times*, 18 November 2001.
22. Dahleen Glanton, "Ten Commandments Become Weapon in Church-State Battle," *Chicago Tribune*, 15 December 2001.

Index of Cases

General Index